SLOW

COOK

MODERN

SLOW
COOK
MODERN

200 Recipes for the
Way We Eat Today

LIANA KRISSOFF

PHOTOGRAPHY BY
RINNE ALLEN

ABRAMS, NEW YORK

CONTENTS

INTRODUCTION

Dear reader, I don't know what your life is like, but I do know that if you work during the day you're probably not all that interested in slow cooker recipes that require less than eight hours of cooking time or some sort of intermediate attention during the cooking process. You're probably not going to need a bunch of slow cooker recipes for shellfish, or desserts, or side dishes, either.

What you need, I'm guessing, are recipes for slow cooker main dishes that can cook completely unattended for at least as long as the typical workday, that are delicious and family-pleasing but also interesting and varied. And you probably wouldn't mind some easy, streamlined accompaniments and suggestions for rounding out each meal. You probably want dinners to come home to.

If this is an accurate representation of your needs and desires, you've opened the right book.

All the main dishes here can be put in the slow cooker in the morning, left unattended for at least eight hours, and finished up in the evening (or just served without further ado). The very simple side dishes and accompaniments—breads and grains, vegetables, salads, toppings, and sauces—can either be made in the morning and stashed in the fridge or be thrown together in the evening just before serving. Some of them are so simple that they really don't need a recipe at all, while others are just a little more involved.

I've tried to match slow cooker main dishes with accompaniments in such a way that the timing makes sense: If you're doing a fair amount of prep on one of them, whether in the morning or evening, ideally you won't have to do too much work on the other at the same time; if you have to puree a sauce in the slow cooker or do some other finishing task in the evening, a side is either already waiting or roasting quietly on its own in the oven. In short, you'll never have all the burners going, literally or figuratively.

As you flip through these recipes, you'll note that some dishes will need a bit of attention just before serving. Please don't feel discouraged because you know how exhausted you will be by the time you get back to your kitchen. Here's a mental trick I've learned over the years that's really helped me cook better, more complete and interesting meals on a reasonably frequent basis: It's easier to motivate yourself to finish up meal preparations if you have a plan, and especially if that plan is already in motion when you walk in the door. There will be food—a lot of food, a finished meal or an almost-finished meal—waiting for you in the slow cooker, and all you have to do is *this* and *this*...and look, the bowl and immersion blender you need to do that are out and ready, the brown rice to accompany the slow cooker dish has been parboiled and is already in the steamer basket (thank you, barely caffeinated morning self!), and all you have to do is move it to the stove and turn on the heat...

The point is to free yourself from having to make decisions and develop a dinner strategy after a long day of work. If I had to do that every day, my brain would implode and I'd probably declare make-your-own-sandwich night or order delivery more times than I'd prefer. There's absolutely nothing wrong with sandwiches and delivery food (I adore both options and invoke them pretty often), but I think we all can benefit from as much culinary variety as we can manage, and improving our home cooking organizational and planning skills is a fine way to do that.

HOW TO USE THIS BOOK

At the risk of this becoming incredibly goofy and awkward, let's walk through a recipe together. How about the first one in the book, Eggplant Tian—my version of a classic French vegetable casserole that's usually baked forever in the oven, the cook pushing it down with a spatula every half hour or so. Here it's paired with a side dish of olive-marinated fresh mozzarella, but there are other accompaniments throughout the book that might go well with it too, so I've listed those just after the recipe title. If on any day another side dish in the book appeals to you more than the one that accompanies the recipe, use a cover flap to mark it.

After a little introduction, you'll see "THE PLAN," a skeleton version of the recipe that tells you the main tasks the recipe will ask you to complete in the morning and in the evening. You'll see that, to make this tian, in the morning you'll load up the cooker (pretty easy), and in the evening you'll be sautéing some bread crumbs (also easy, but it does require the stovetop).

Still on board with the tian? Okay! Round up the ingredients. The recipe instructions begin with your "MORNING" tasks. Do those, and set the slow cooker for eight hours on low. You've had a cup of coffee by now and are feeling energetic. Any other "MORNING" tasks listed? Nope, all clear. Check your side dish recipe. Anything you can do in the "MORNING"? Yep, go ahead and do those tasks, too.

Now, what I'd do before heading off to work is skim the "EVENING" instructions to see if you'll need any skillets or spoons or spatulas to finish up your meal when you get home. In this case, you can see you'll need a skillet and a spoon, so dig those out so they're ready when you walk in the door. You can even measure out your bread crumbs and display them—*hint, hint*—near the skillet. Keep this beautiful book propped open and out on the counter too.

When you get home, you'll be greeted by the ridiculously enticing aroma of basil and garlic and roasted peppers and fruity olive oil. You'll suddenly remember you put a tian in the slow cooker, and be pleased with your foresight. Don't forget there's a tangy-salty mozzarella salad marinating in the fridge; pull it out and set it on the table to warm up a bit, maybe sneaking a shred as you do—it's been a long day. You'll notice next to the stove a little cup of what looks like . . . bread crumbs? What the—? And you'll remember your plan: Quickly fry those up for a crunchy topping for your tian, which smells even better when you finally lift the lid of the slow cooker to take a peek. It's a little watery, which is understandable because it's been simmering here under a lid all day, so you scoop off some of the liquid: now, perfect. Let the tian settle a bit while you set plates and forks out and pour drinks, spread those toasty bread crumbs over the top, and dig in.

CHOOSING A SLOW COOKER

All the slow cooker main dishes in this book were developed for 3½- or 4-quart (3.3- or 3.8-L) slow cookers, which I find to be the most useful for a small family. Our family of three always has leftovers from dishes cooked in a cooker of this size, and rarely do I cook a slow cooker meal that requires more than three or four pounds (1.4 or 1.8 kg) of meat. I do use a larger, 6-quart (5.7-L) slow cooker for making stocks (pages 240–243), since it doesn't make much sense to prepare small batches of stock.

    If what you have now is a larger slow cooker, and you don't wish to donate that one to charity and replace it with a smaller model, consider increasing the quantities in these recipes by at least 50 percent to keep the ingredients from cooking too quickly.

    I've tried out many, many slow cookers over the years, and, honestly, the different makes and models are all pretty comparable in terms of the finished product, so you should just choose the one that has the features that are important to you: a countdown timer, say, or an automatic keep-warm setting, a lid that can be clamped down for leak-free transport (to the local bar if you live in the Midwest, for example), an extra-low "simmer" setting for more-than-eight-hour days, or an attractive housing.

    Probably the most important extra to consider is the automatic keep-warm feature, which is helpful in two common scenarios: If you're held up and can't get home to turn off the slow cooker at the eight-hour mark, the cooker will switch to warm to keep the dish at a safe and ready-to-eat temperature for several hours without overcooking. And if there's a dish that would be better if it didn't cook for the full eight hours, you can set the cooker for, say, six hours and it'll be fine if you're away from the kitchen for longer than that.

One feature that I do not find useful for my purposes is a stovetop-ready insert—that is, a pot that can be used on a burner to brown ingredients (or in the cooker itself on a "sear" or similar hot setting) and then transferred to the slow cooker housing (or turned down to low) to finish cooking. The inserts are always nonstick-finished, and that limits you to medium heat on the stovetop—I like more firepower when browning. It also means using nonstick-friendly tongs and spatulas, which I find irritating because they're not as stiff and sturdy as the stainless-steel ones. And nonstick pans are simply not as good at browning as cast-iron skillets or a heavy tri-ply sauté pan. But the main reason I don't brown in stovetop-ready inserts is this: If your goal is to let the dish cook for a full day with no attention, starting the ingredients out in an insert that's hot from the stovetop is a disadvantage—the food will come up to temperature more quickly and will be at much greater risk of overcooking. I prefer to brown in a skillet or sauté pan (deglazing will practically clean the pan anyway, so cleanup isn't much of an issue) and transfer the browned food to a good old-fashioned ceramic insert for the slow cooking part of the process.

So which one should you buy? Short version: Slow cookers in the 3½- to 4-quart (3.3- to 3.8-L) size vary in price from about twenty dollars to sixty dollars, though some fancy (attractive, multifeatured) models can be more expensive. Buy the one that seems right for you, and it'll work just fine.

Longer version: I currently own at least half a dozen of the suckers, and when I finish this book I'll be paring the collection down to one or two, so I suppose I should tell you which ones I'll probably be saving and why. I like the Cuisinart for a few reasons: On low, it cooks the lowest and slowest of all the cookers I've used, it has a countdown timer that shows me how much time is left in the cycle, and it auto-switches to the warm setting at the end of the set cooking time. I also like the Crock-Pot Smartpot: It too cooks quite slowly, and while it lacks a countdown timer, and the set time increments aren't always the ones I want to use, I like that to set it for eight hours on low you just push one button three times; it also, of course, has the auto-warm feature.

At the insistence of several food-writer friends of mine, I recently purchased and have been experimenting with a 6-quart (5.7-L) Instant Pot, which is a slow cooker, pressure cooker, rice cooker, yogurt incubator, gaming system, Wi-Fi hotspot, self-driving car, and Neptune probe all in one. I'll be retaining it along with the cookers mentioned above. Despite its 6-quart capacity, it has handled the recipes I've tried in it just the same as if they were cooked in a smaller traditional slow cooker (so feel free to use it for any of these recipes). It also does a great job making quark (page 253), yielding a consistently creamy cheese with little risk of overcooking.

OTHER USEFUL TOOLS

Immersion blender This is a game changer for the eight-hour slow cooker enthusiast. Not only can you easily make smooth blended soups right in the cooker insert, you can also quickly smooth out certain sauces that separate or cook unevenly over a long period of completely unattended time—to be perfectly honest, when you come home and lift the lid what you see inside might look a little . . . rough. Don't worry about it: As you'll notice in a lot of recipes for stews and curries and similar dishes, I'll suggest that you remove the solid ingredients from the pot, puree the sauce in the pot, and then return the solids to the sauce. The browned edges, the separated fats, the lumps all get reincorporated, and the fats emulsify with blending and thicken the sauce slightly—a bonus. You can do this with an upright blender—pour the liquid into the blender jar, let it cool for a few minutes, then put the lid on with the hole in the lid open and a towel over it to prevent an explosion—but an immersion blender will make the whole process so much easier, with much less cleanup. I strongly encourage you to acquire one if you don't have one already.

Slotted spoon or skimmer Many recipes here will ask you to remove the chunks of meat or vegetables from the slow cooker (without getting too fussy about retrieving every little bit, of course) so you can more easily season or puree the sauce. This is the tool you need for that, so be sure you have one on hand.

Large granite mortar and pestle I bought a granite mortar and pestle set a few years ago to up my Thai cooking game, and I now use it almost every day. For small quantities, it's less fuss than a food processor or blender (you don't have to stop and scrape down the sides of the bowl), and the heavy pestle and rough interior texture make efficient work of pounding solids into pastes or powders. Use a mortar and pestle for spices; toss a few cloves of garlic in and tap them to remove the skins (if you want to keep your cutting board uncontaminated by garlic oils); crush nuts and seeds for toppings and sauces; mix marinades; make seasoning pastes with fresh or frozen aromatics. You can find them pretty cheap at Asian grocery stores. My mortar has a well that's 4½ inches (11 cm) in diameter at the top, and it's a good size.

Mini food processor I use this frequently for pulsing quick salsas and tart or spicy sauces and toppings for freshening up rich stews from the slow cooker. You don't need one, but it sure makes things easier.

CHOOSING INGREDIENTS FOR LONG-HAUL SLOW COOKING

The beauty of the slow cooker is that you can transform less-expensive ingredients, like dried beans or tough cuts of meat, into delicious meals with little effort. While you can cook pretty much anything in a slow cooker (in my first book on the subject there's a salmon recipe and a brownie recipe, for crying out loud), if your goal is to let the dish cook for eight hours or longer with no intermediate attention there are some limitations on what you can use. All but the most hearty grains and vegetables will break down too much; very lean meats can overcook and become somewhat dry or grainy. Following are some of the ingredients to consider using in your eight-hour slow cooker dishes, and the ones I rely on most in the recipes in this book. If you want to adapt standard long-cooked recipes for the slow cooker, look for ones that feature these ingredients.

Dried beans If you're familiar with the way your particular beans cook in your particular slow cooker (see page 246), and are confident they'll be done in eight or so hours, go ahead and use dried beans in your dishes (but don't cook them with anything acidic, like tomatoes or wine or vinegar, or they won't soften properly). Otherwise, cook them separately (on the weekends, perhaps), so you can check on them occasionally and make sure they're not under- or overcooked, and add them at the end of cooking. In my experience, black beans, all types of white beans, pinto beans, and cranberry beans are reliably done (and not overdone) after eight hours, so you'll find those in some of the main dishes here. See page 246 for details about how to cook dried beans to keep in the fridge or freezer.

Lentils You can use just about any lentils in an eight-hour dish: Red lentils will break down almost completely and serve to thicken your dish; brown lentils will hold their shape a little more but also thicken the liquid a bit; green and black (beluga) lentils will stay firmer. Varieties popular in Indian cooking can be used too, of course: The smaller or split ones, without skins, will usually cook nicely in eight hours; the larger whole lentils (and beans) should be cooked separately in advance (so you can control the timing) and added to dishes at the end.

Grains Only the heartiest whole grains can withstand eight hours of slow cooking without breaking down completely: pot (hull-less but not pearled) barley (look for this in the bulk bins at the supermarket or in natural-foods stores), hard red or white wheat berries, rye berries, and spelt, for example. If you want a dish with very distinct, firm grains, and your recipe is vegetarian, replace some of the water in the recipe with ice to slightly delay the start of cooking (see page 42 for an example). Quicker-cooking grains, like millet and quinoa and white and brown rices, will become mushy over eight hours—good for thickening purposes or for porridges or congee (page 79), but not if you want individual grains to be apparent in the finished dish. Cook delicate grains separately and fold them in at the end or serve them on the side.

Roots and tubers Waxy-type potatoes like Yukon Gold will still hold their shape after eight hours; russet, or Idaho, potatoes will tend to break down but will absorb more of the flavor of the sauce or broth they're cooked in. Chunks of sweet potatoes will become very soft, and will not hold their shape well unless they're being cooked in a very liquid mixture (though they're excellent for sweetening and thickening purposes). Turnips cut into chunks will just barely hold their shape after eight hours. Carrots that are about the thickness of your thumb at the thick end will cook perfectly in eight hours—still with a little bite; cut them smaller and layer them in the bottom of the pot or make sure they're well covered by liquid if you want them quite soft.

Winter squashes Any of them, peeled (if needed), seeded, and cut into chunks or wedges, will work fine. Butternut squash chunks will become nice and tender and will break down just a bit at the edges.

Green vegetables Most green vegetables (green beans, peas, summer squash, asparagus, broccoli, and so on) will become very soft with a whole day's worth of cooking. Cook them separately, or adjust your expectations. Especially if you're going to puree them into a soup or sauce, you can cook hearty greens like kale, turnip greens, mustard greens, or collard greens all day (and with broccoli it won't matter if it's too soft if you're pureeing it anyway); if you want distinct pieces of the leaves, cook greens separately and add them in the evening. Add raw spinach at the last minute—the heat of the dish in the cooker will wilt the leaves in a few minutes' time.

Go as far into the cooking process in advance

(in the morning or on the night before)

as possible:

WASH AND SPIN-DRY greens, chop them, if needed, and keep them in the salad spinner or another container in the fridge so they're ready in the evening—I absolutely despise prepping greens right before finishing up a meal; it's so much easier to do that task while the cutting board and knife are out in the morning, and when you don't have a full day's work behind you already. And while the cutting board is out, go ahead and chop fresh herbs, scallions, or any other last-minute additions to your dish and stash them in the refrigerator.

MEASURE SPICES in advance (or at least dig them out of the cupboard and have them handy).

SET OUT ANY PANS and utensils you'll need for finishing the meal so they're ready to go in the evening; put a baking sheet in the oven so it'll be in there when you turn on the oven to preheat for roasted vegetables as soon as you get home from work. Plug in the immersion blender (see page 12) and have it waiting near the slow cooker with a slotted spoon and a bowl.

IF YOU'LL BE BREADING and frying anything in the evening—say, for fried okra (page 86) or for the crisp chicken topping on the congee (page 79)—go ahead and set up the breading station (minus the egg dip) with one plate of seasoned flour and another of bread crumbs, and have a plate lined with paper towels ready; pour the oil for frying into the pan.

PUT OIL AND CHOPPED garlic or spices—say, for a sautéed green side dish or for a spiced rice—in the skillet or saucepan in the morning and leave it on the stovetop; those will be fine at room temperature for the day.

Cauliflower Use large florets, which will become very soft but will hold up better than small florets; still they'll likely just fall apart as you spoon out the dish. I use cauliflower mostly in dals and soups, where it's fine if the florets sort of disintegrate into the liquid.

Onions Onions give off a lot of water as they cook throughout the day, which can throw off the consistency of your dish if you add them raw. In most recipes, and especially the ones that are meant to be more saucy than soupy, I prefer to brown the onions in a skillet, which cooks off some of that water (and also adds some nice browning flavor), before putting them in the slow cooker.

Chicken Choose thighs or leg quarters, with or without skin and bone. In eight hours, the meat of a drumstick will be falling off the bones, and because it might be difficult to extract from the dish that one tiny sharp bone from along the side of each leg you might wish to just stick to thighs. Chicken breast can dry out over long cooking, so I use it only in cases where the meat will be completely shredded into a soup or sauce and its leanness won't be an issue; I use boneless chicken breast because the breast has small bones that can become dislodged and hidden in the dish.

Turkey Choose legs, with or without skin and bone. Turkey breast will dry out a bit, but it's possible to use it if you're sure to add plenty of fat to the dish. If you have a slow cooker model that runs hot—if your dishes are consistently boiling or simmering vigorously after four hours or so—I'd avoid it.

Duck Choose leg quarters. Avoid duck breast, the meaty part of which is too lean.

Pork Choose shoulder (preferably Boston butt), short ribs, baby back ribs, country-style ribs (which are usually cut from the loin but tend to have enough fat for slow cooking), or smoked ham hocks or neckbone. Loin and tenderloin and most chops are pretty lean, so use with care. Smoked sausage, in an eight-hour dish, tends to give up most of its flavor to the broth, so I sear and add it at the end of cooking; fresh sausages will become very tender but most will retain their juiciness (you might have to experiment with different sausages to find one you like in the slow cooker—the more fat content, the better).

Beef Choose chuck, stew meat, flank, brisket, short ribs, shanks, or oxtails; ground beef needs to be parcooked (browned briefly on the stovetop) so it doesn't clump up unpleasantly in the cooker. Avoid most steaks, which are almost always better cooked hot and fast. Grass-fed beef may take longer to cook to absolute tenderness than grain-fed, so you might wish to factor that into your planning.

Lamb Choose shoulder, neck, or stew meat, boneless or bone-in; lamb leg or shoulder roasts are great in the slow cooker; ground lamb needs to be parcooked like ground beef. Avoid chops, which would be wasted in a slow cooker dish.

Goat Choose shoulder or stew meat, boneless or bone-in. Those are usually your only choices.

Ingredients that thicken slow cooker sauces or at least lessen the effects of long cooking in a closed, damp environment masa harina, toasted flour (see page 88), caramel-colored roux (see page 85; darker roux will add flavor but has little thickening power), curry roux (see page 136), flour-and-water slurry, beurre manié (equal parts flour and soft butter mashed together and stirred in bit by bit), grated unsweetened coconut, tomato paste, coconut milk powder, bits of stale bread or corn tortillas, Maria cookies (see page 91) or gingersnap cookies, mashed cooked beans or potatoes, filé powder (see page 85).

A note on tamarind: I call for Tamicon-brand concentrate—the very thick, dark, smooth paste—because it works especially well in slow cooker recipes, adding a ton of flavor without excess liquid. Otherwise, your best bet is "wet seedless" tamarind that comes in blocks: Break off a chunk and soak it in warm water to cover until softened, then push the paste through a sieve to remove stray seeds and fibers. It's not a concentrate like Tamicon; use at least ¼ cup for every 1 tablespoon Tamicon.

SLOW COOKER SAFETY

It may seem silly to say this, but I've been asked this question before, so, right off the bat: Yes, it's safe to leave the slow cooker turned on while you're not at home—it was designed specifically for that purpose. It doesn't need to be watched or attended as it cooks.

Countertop location The outer housing of the slow cooker can get pretty hot, so make sure nothing is touching or within a couple of inches of it. The annoyingly short cord is that way for electrical-safety reasons and you shouldn't use an extension cord with it.

Power outages If there's a power outage, the slow cooker will turn off and not come back on even if power is restored. This is a safety feature. If you weren't home when the power went out, you should discard the contents of the cooker—it might have cooled to an unsafe temperature. If you're home when the power fails and the food isn't done cooking yet, transfer it to a stovetop or grill-safe pot as soon as possible and finish cooking it over a burner (if you have a gas stove) or a grill. If the food is done cooking and the power goes out, eat it within two hours.

Doneness For the most part, in these recipes I don't bother giving details about how to tell if a dish made in the slow cooker is done. If it's been cooking for eight hours, *it's done.* The meat will almost certainly be much hotter than the minimum safe temperature, and there's nothing to worry about, safety-wise. For reference, though, in case you're adapting or using other recipes—and if you're cooking any of these for less than eight hours for some reason—the following are the recommended safe temperatures for meats, which you can check with an instant-read meat thermometer inserted into the thickest part and not touching a bone:

> chicken or turkey: 165°F (74°C)
> ground meats or mixtures, such as meatloaf: 165°F (74°C)
> beef or lamb roasts: 145°F (63°C)
> pork: 145°F (63°C)

Again, these are minimum safe temperatures. For the slow-cooked meats in this book, the temperature will and should be much greater by the end of the cooking time (tough cuts of beef and lamb, for example, will be safe but not tender at the temperature above, and may need cooking to as high as 190°F/88°C).

Reheating leftovers Don't use the slow cooker itself to reheat leftovers from the refrigerator; they won't come up to a safe temperature quickly enough. Reheat in a microwave oven (without the lid) or in a different pot on the stovetop.

Frozen foods Frozen vegetables and beans and grains are fine to use in the slow cooker. For the best results and utmost safety, avoid using frozen meats, though: They can thaw and cook unevenly, and may not come up to the correct temperature within a safe time frame.

Care and cleaning Avoid running cold water into a hot ceramic insert—the sudden temperature change could cause the ceramic to crack. Clean the insert and the lid with regular dish soap or in a dishwasher. I've done a lot of experimenting, shall we call it, in my slow cookers and have occasionally ended up with the absolute worst stuck-on, burned mess in the insert. An overnight soak and a good scrubbing with a scouring pad, sometimes with some baking soda, have done the trick every time. I never use plastic slow cooker liners, because the ceramic pots are easy enough to clean and the liners just seem like more trouble than they're worth.

Some ceramic inserts (never the lids) are safe to use in a conventional oven or microwave oven; check the manual that came with your machine. Ceramic inserts should never be put on a stovetop burner or under a broiler.

Don't submerge the housing in water to clean it. Just wipe off drips and spills with a damp rag or paper towel.

What if the food isn't done when I get back to the kitchen?

This is a highly unlikely scenario given the eight-hour cooking time for these recipes, but in the event you open the slow cooker lid and find that the beef or the beans, for example, are not as tender as you'd like (see page 246 for more about using dried beans), you have a couple of options: Turn up the cooker to high and have a snack while you wait it out, or transfer everything to a Dutch oven or similar pot and simmer it on the stovetop until it's to your liking. If you're using an InstantPot, just flip the valve on the lid to "sealing" and cook on high pressure for 10 minutes or so.

These recipes use so many spices !

(Because that's one of the best ways to extract deliciousness from the slow cooker.)

How do I cope ?

GO TO YOUR LOCAL Indian or Middle Eastern store or online and find a masala dabba, a round, shallow lidded tin with seven smaller lidless stainless-steel cups inside and a cute little spoon. Put your most frequently used spices in the cups and keep the whole tin handy on your counter or near your stovetop; it needs to be kept flat (to avoid spillage inside the tin) and—I can't stress this enough—within easy reach. My cooking process became much more streamlined and infinitely less hectic when I started using mine and had figured out which spices to keep in it, and I'd strongly recommend you try it.

HERE'S WHAT I KEEP in the cups: ground cumin, ground coriander, ground turmeric, paprika (sometimes hot, sometimes regular), whole cumin seeds, and brown mustard seeds. The seventh cup is variable, and will usually contain one of these: fennel seeds, ground fenugreek, whole coriander seeds, yellow mustard seeds, or ground cayenne. Crushed red pepper, ground cinnamon, garam masala (a dark spice blend often added to curries at the end of cooking), and dried hot red chiles are in separate jars in easy-access locations. Most of the rest of my spices are in freezer bags arranged more or less alphabetically in three plastic lidded containers in the cupboard. I refill the masala dabba and the freezer bags as needed from a bulk spices area of the pantry/laundry room.

Other Ideas for Rounding Out a Meal

- Good crusty white or whole wheat bread, dark German-style pumpernickel, or warmed pita bread

- Warmed ready-made Indian flatbreads from the freezer (naan, paratha, chapati...)

- Warmed flour or corn tortillas (see page 100)

- Cooked beans from the freezer (see page 246), heated with a little stock or water in a saucepan

- Cooked brown rice or hearty whole grains from the freezer (see page 250), heated in a steamer basket or sieve, covered, over boiling water

- Ready-made pierogies or dumplings from the freezer (no shame here, in my opinion—they are superconvenient and can be really good!), thawed for a few minutes in hot water, then drained and pan-fried until crisp (or cooked according to the package instructions)

- Baked potatoes or sweet potatoes (see page 15 for a slow cooker method if you have an extra machine, or use the oven)

- Plain Greek yogurt, quark (store-bought or homemade, page 253), or ricotta

- Sliced raw, cold vegetables (cucumbers, carrots, jicama, sugar snap peas, sweet peppers, romaine or other crisp lettuce leaves, Belgian endive spears). I'll sometimes serve spears of carrot, celery, jicama, or peppers in a container of crushed ice to keep them crisp and, well, cold.

- Tender greens tossed with fresh lemon juice or vinegar, olive oil, salt, and pepper

- Sliced ripe tomatoes or cherry tomatoes

- Corn on the cob, boiled for just a couple of minutes

- Edamame in the shell, boiled and then seasoned with salt and pepper or a spice blend

- Whole olives or chunks of hard cheese tossed with olive oil, citrus zest and juice, crushed red pepper, and dried herbs

- Hummus or any other bean puree

- Slices of a nice cheese

- Toasted spiced nuts and seeds

- A simple fruit salad with citrus juice and mint

CHAPTER 1

Vegetarian and Vegan

Eggplant Tian 28
Olive-marinated fresh mozzarella

Kale, Potato, and Almond Soup 29
Fried baguette

Baked Sweets and Russets 30
Herb salad

Miso-Ghee Corn Chowder 32
Tomato-furikake salad

Butternut Squash and Masa Soup 34
Spiced pepitas and chipotle quark

Summer Tomato Soup 36
Tangy potato salad

Classic Tofu-Mushroom Chili 38
Sautéed fresh poblanos and corn

Seared Tofu with
Spiced Mustard Greens 40
Sweet tomato chutney

Creamy Pot Barley with Butternut
Squash and Thyme 42
*Baby kale salad with dates
and pistachios*

Dal 1: Potatoes, Fresh Turmeric,
and Whole Spices 43
Spiced chopped vegetables

Dal 2: Cauliflower and Quinoa 45
Cardamom roasted sweet potatoes

Dal 3: Brown Lentils
and Spicy Tomato Masala 46
Cilantro yogurt dollop

Chipotle Chickpea Stew 47
*Sautéed green tomatoes with
bread crumb topping*

Hearty Sweet Potato and Chickpea
Stew with Sweet Spices 48
Almond-lemon pistou

Spicy Masala Chickpeas 50
Spinach labneh

Fresh Tomato, Pinto Bean,
and Ancho Chile Stew 51
Cucumber yogurt with hot cumin oil

Smoky Collards and
Black-Eyed Peas 52
Whole grain peach salad

Creamy Giant Limas with
Sun-Dried Tomatoes 55
Oven-fried eggs

Ribollita 56
Seared radicchio

Sagamité with Maple Syrup
and Butternut Squash 58
Garlic sautéed dandelion greens

White Bean–Tahini Soup
with Garlic Oil 59
Roasted tomatoes and croutons

Smoky Black Lentils and Beans 60
Seared halloumi and chile mince

White Bean, Corn,
and Chard Stew 62
Shortcut cheese puffs

Eggplant Tian

WITH *olive-marinated fresh mozzarella*
ALSO GOOD WITH *corn muffins* (PAGE 153) OR *almond couscous* (PAGE 195)

I included a similar tian in my first slow cooker book, but have since simplified my approach a lot. When you layer the ingredients, they'll come almost to the top of the cooker pot, but don't worry: They'll collapse and sink down after a couple of hours and their flavors will all meld, resulting in a dish that's much greater than the sum of its parts.

IN THE MORNING
Layer the ingredients
in the cooker.

IN THE EVENING
Fry the bread crumb
topping.

---

5 tablespoons (75 ml) olive oil

½ onion, sliced

Salt and freshly ground
black pepper

1 large (1¼-pound/570-g)
eggplant, peeled and
sliced ¼ to ½ inch (6 to
12 mm) thick

3 large roasted and peeled
red bell peppers, torn into
large pieces

6 plum tomatoes, sliced

2 large sprigs fresh basil,
stemmed

6 cloves garlic

1 cup (80 g) coarse bread
crumbs or panko

MORNING

Use 1 tablespoon of the oil to coat the slow cooker pot. Spread the onion in the bottom of the pot and sprinkle with salt and pepper. Arrange layers of the vegetables on top, seasoning each layer lightly with salt and pepper: first eggplant, then roasted peppers and tomatoes; then basil, eggplant, peppers and tomatoes, basil, and eggplant; and, finally, peppers and tomatoes on top. Tuck the garlic cloves in around the vegetables. Drizzle with 3 tablespoons of the oil. Cover and cook on low for 8 hours.

EVENING

In a large skillet or sauté pan, heat the remaining 1 tablespoon oil over medium heat. When it shimmers, add the bread crumbs and a pinch of salt and pepper and cook, stirring frequently, until golden and crunchy, 2 to 4 minutes.

If there's a lot of excess liquid in the cooker pot, use a large spoon to press down on the layers of vegetables and scoop it out without disturbing the layers too much. Spread the fried bread crumbs on top and serve.

Olive-marinated fresh mozzarella

10 oil-cured olives, pitted

1 clove garlic

Pinch of crushed red pepper

Juice of ½ lemon

2 tablespoons olive oil

8 ounces (225 g) fresh
mozzarella cheese

MORNING

With a mortar and pestle, pound the olives, garlic, and crushed red pepper to a paste (or use a chef's knife on a cutting board, then scrape into a bowl). Whisk in the lemon juice and oil. Tear the cheese into rough bite-size pieces, put them in a bowl, and toss with the olive dressing. Cover and refrigerate.

EVENING

Set the mozzarella out at room temperature for 10 minutes, then serve.

Kale, Potato, and Almond Soup

WITH *fried baguette*

ALSO GOOD WITH *tangy potato salad* (PAGE 36) OR *marinated bean and tomato salad* (PAGE 139)

This is a great way to get a whole lot of greens into a meal—the creamy potato in the soup is comforting and familiar, the lemon bright and fresh.

IN THE MORNING
Load the cooker.

IN THE EVENING
Add the spinach and lemon juice, puree the soup, and fry the almonds.

---

3 russet potatoes, chopped

1 cup (140 g) whole almonds

Salt

½ teaspoon freshly ground black pepper

1 bunch (about 10 ounces/280 g) kale

1 tablespoon olive oil

2 big handfuls baby spinach

2 teaspoons fresh lemon juice

MORNING

Put the potatoes, ½ cup (70 g) of the almonds, 1½ teaspoons salt, the pepper, and 6 cups (1.4 L) water in the slow cooker. Wash the kale, then gather it back into a bunch and cut the leaves crosswise into 1½-inch (4-cm) lengths. Add to the cooker, packing it down so it fits. Cover and cook on low for 8 hours.

MORNING OR EVENING

Coarsely chop the remaining ½ cup (70 g) almonds. In a skillet or sauté pan, heat the oil over medium-high heat. When it shimmers, add the almonds and cook, stirring, until they're lightly browned, 1 to 2 minutes. Set aside.

EVENING

Add the spinach and lemon juice to the soup and use an immersion blender to puree until it's as smooth as possible—this could take a few minutes. Season with more salt, if needed. Serve the soup, topping each serving with almonds.

Fried baguette

Baguette

Olive oil

Salt

EVENING

Cut the bread into 2-inch (5-cm) lengths, then split each piece in half horizontally. In a skillet or sauté pan (the one you cooked the almonds in is fine), heat the oil over medium-high heat. When it shimmers, add some of the bread in a single layer, cut side down, and fry until golden, 1 to 2 minutes. Sprinkle with salt and repeat to cook the remaining bread. Serve.

Baked Sweets and Russets

WITH *herb salad*
ALSO GOOD WITH *grizzled asparagus* (PAGE 201)
OR *garlic sautéed dandelion greens* (PAGE 58)

Why not make a baked potato or sweet potato the center of your meal? Add a protein-rich creamy sauce (no need for butter here), lemony spiced almond chunks, and something green, and it's a perfect light but satisfying meal.

IN THE MORNING
Foil-wrap the potatoes and, if you have time, make the almonds and tofu cream.

IN THE EVENING
Unwrap, split, and serve.

4 to 6 russet potatoes or sweet potatoes (as many as will fit in your cooker; you can fill it to the top)

Salt and freshly ground black pepper

For the tofu cream:

8 ounces (225 g) silken tofu

3 tablespoons fresh lemon juice

Grated zest of ½ lemon

1 tablespoon olive oil

¼ teaspoon salt

¼ teaspoon hot paprika

For the smoky almonds:

1 cup (140 g) whole almonds, coarsely chopped

2 tablespoons olive oil

1 teaspoon chipotle chile powder

½ teaspoon salt

Grated zest of 1 large lemon

MORNING

Wrap the potatoes tightly in aluminum foil (thin, not-heavyweight is easiest to use here) and arrange them in the slow cooker. Cover and cook on low for 8 hours.

MORNING OR EVENING

Make the tofu cream: Put all the ingredients in a blender or food processor and blend to combine. Transfer to a container, cover, and refrigerate until ready to serve.

Make the smoky almonds: Put all the ingredients in a skillet or sauté pan and toss to combine. Place over medium-high heat and cook, stirring and tossing frequently, until very fragrant (an understatement) and deeply browned, 4 to 5 minutes. The smaller almond bits and spices will become almost black, and that's okay. Scrape into a bowl and set aside at room temperature until ready to serve.

EVENING

Using tongs, remove the potatoes from the cooker, unwrap them, and split each down the center lengthwise. Season with salt and pepper and serve with the tofu cream and almonds.

Herb salad

4 ounces (115 g) baby lettuces

½ cup (30 g) packed fresh flat-leaf parsley leaves (no stems)

6 fresh basil tops, torn

Salt and freshly ground black pepper

Juice of 1 lemon

1 tablespoon olive oil

EVENING

Toss the lettuces, parsley, and basil in a large bowl; season with a couple of good pinches of salt and several grindings of pepper and use your hand to distribute the seasonings to every leaf. Squeeze in the lemon juice, drizzle in the oil, and toss well. Serve.

Miso-Ghee Corn Chowder

WITH *tomato-furikake salad*
ALSO GOOD WITH *honey-lemon raw red pepper relish* (PAGE 187) OR *green apple rojak* (PAGE 158)

The distinctive toasted-butter flavor of ghee nicely complements the sweetness of miso and corn in this summery soup.

IN THE MORNING
Sauté the onion and load up the cooker.

IN THE EVENING
Stir in the miso and crush some of the potatoes to thicken.

2 tablespoons ghee (page 234)

½ onion, diced

Salt and freshly ground black pepper

4 ears sweet corn

2 russet potatoes, peeled and cut into 1-inch (2.5-cm) chunks

4 cups (960 ml) vegetable stock (page 240) or water

2 tablespoons miso paste

3 scallions, sliced

MORNING

In a skillet or saucepan, heat the ghee over medium-high heat. When it is hot, add the onion and a pinch of salt and cook, stirring frequently, until translucent and golden, 5 to 7 minutes. Scrape the onion and ghee into the cooker. Cut the kernels from the corn cobs and put the kernels and two or three of the cobs in the slow cooker. Add the potatoes to the cooker. Pour in the stock. Cover and cook on low for 8 hours.

EVENING

Remove and discard the corn cobs. Stir the miso paste into the soup and season with salt and pepper. Use a spoon to break up some of the potatoes to thicken the chowder. Sprinkle with the scallions and serve.

Tomato-furikake salad

1 teaspoon rice vinegar

Salt

1 tablespoon olive oil

1 pint (10 ounces/280 g) cherry or grape tomatoes, cut in half

1 large sprig fresh basil

Generous sprinkling of furikake (see Note)

EVENING

In a medium bowl, whisk together the vinegar, a good pinch of salt, and the oil. Add the tomatoes to the bowl; tear in the basil leaves and toss to coat with the dressing. Sprinkle with plenty of furikake and serve.

NOTE: You can find furikake, a Japanese blend of seaweed, sesame seeds, and various other flavorings that's usually used to season rice, in the Asian section of a good supermarket, or in any Asian grocery store. In the latter, there will likely be lots of varieties to choose from; I like the ones with hijiki and a large percentage of sesame seeds, but I think any of them would be great here.

Butternut Squash and Masa Soup

WITH *spiced pepitas and chipotle quark*

ALSO GOOD WITH *marinated bean and tomato salad* (PAGE 139) OR *avocado-lime topping* (PAGE 76)

You can use any kind of winter squash here—red kuri, kabocha, pie pumpkin, Hubbard, acorn—or a combination of several if you have stray pieces of larger squash in your fridge...they'll each taste a bit different but they'll all cook up about the same. Feel free to add a carrot or two, or sweet potato.

IN THE MORNING
Sauté the onion and garlic and load up the cooker.

IN THE EVENING
Stir in the masa and puree the soup.

---

1 large (2½-pound/1.2-kg) butternut squash, peeled, seeded, and cut into large chunks

4 cups (960 ml) vegetable stock (page 240) or water

1 tablespoon olive oil

1 onion, chopped

Salt and freshly ground black pepper

2 cloves garlic, chopped

2 tablespoons masa harina

MORNING

Put the squash in the slow cooker with the stock.

In a large skillet or sauté pan, heat the oil over medium-high heat. When it shimmers, add the onion and a pinch of salt and cook, stirring frequently, until wilted and golden at the edges, 5 to 7 minutes. Add the garlic and cook for 1 minute longer. Scrape into the cooker. Pour 1 cup (240 ml) water into the skillet and stir to scrape up any browned bits, then pour into the cooker. Add 1 teaspoon salt and several grindings of pepper. Cover and cook on low for 8 hours.

EVENING

Ladle about 1 cup (240 ml) of the liquid into a small bowl and whisk in the masa, then scrape back into the cooker. With an immersion blender, puree the soup until very smooth. Season with more salt and pepper, if needed, then serve.

Spiced pepitas and chipotle quark

For the spiced pepitas:

- 1 tablespoon olive oil
- ½ cup (65 g) pepitas (hulled pumpkin seeds)
- ½ teaspoon ground cumin
- ½ teaspoon ancho chile powder
- Salt

For the chipotle quark:

- 1 cup (240 ml) quark (page 253) or plain Greek yogurt (preferably full-fat) or labneh
- 1 to 2 chipotle chiles in adobo, with some of the sauce
- Pinch of salt

MORNING OR EVENING

Make the spiced pepitas: In a medium skillet or sauté pan, heat the oil over medium heat. When it shimmers, add the pepitas, cumin, chile powder, and a good pinch of salt and cook, stirring, until most of the pepitas have expanded and the spices are fragrant, 1 to 2 minutes. Scrape into a small bowl and serve hot or leave on the counter and serve at room temperature.

MORNING OR EVENING

Make the chipotle quark: Puree all the ingredients in a mini food processor or blender (or finely mince the chipotles on a cutting board and stir them into the quark). Cover and refrigerate until ready to serve, up to 5 days.

HOW TO DEAL WITH THE REST OF THE CAN OF TOMATO PASTE OR CHIPOTLE CHILES

How many of you open a can of tomato paste or chipotle chiles in adobo (both of which appear more than once in this book), use a bit of it, cover the can and refrigerate it, and then forget about it until the can is rusty and the contents fuzzy green and you need another tablespoon of tomato paste or chipotles? I know my own self, and I am not conscientious enough to use those leftovers in a timely way, so I go ahead and take the time to tablespoon the tomato paste onto waxed paper and freeze it until firm, then transfer it to a freezer bag (it can be dropped into the slow cooker straight from the freezer). I'll mince or puree the extra chipotles and sauce in a mini food processor, or pound them in a mortar and pestle, and refrigerate the puree in a clean canning jar (which won't rust) or freeze it.

Summer Tomato Soup

WITH *tangy potato salad*

ALSO GOOD WITH *quesadillas sincronizadas* (PAGE 68) OR *whole grain peach salad* (PAGE 54)

It might seem odd to slow-cook good summer tomatoes for a simple soup like this one, but they stay fresh-tasting and summery even after a daylong stint in the slow cooker. For an exceptionally smooth and luscious soup worthy of dinner guests, either peel the tomatoes in the morning or strain the soup after you puree it in the evening.

IN THE MORNING
If you'd like, peel the tomatoes. Load up the cooker.

IN THE EVENING
Puree the soup and blend in the cream cheese, if using. If needed, strain the soup.

4½ pounds (2 kg) ripe tomatoes

2 (14- to 16-ounce/400- to 455-g) cans white beans, drained, or about 3 cups cooked and drained white beans (page 246)

1 large sprig fresh basil

1 cup (240 ml) vegetable stock (page 240)

Salt and freshly ground black pepper

3 tablespoons olive oil

2 tablespoons cream cheese (optional)

MORNING
If you're not planning to strain or food-mill the soup in the evening, you might wish to peel the tomatoes now (a serrated peeler is good for this). Coarsely chop the tomatoes and put them in the slow cooker with the beans, basil, stock, 1 teaspoon salt, and several grindings of pepper. Cover and cook on low for 8 hours.

EVENING
With an immersion blender, puree the soup until very smooth. If you'd like, pour the soup into a sieve set over a large bowl or pot and push it through with a rubber spatula (or pass it through a food mill fitted with the smallest-holed disk), discarding the seeds and bits of skin in the sieve, then return the soup to the cooker to reheat. Blend in the oil and the cream cheese, if using. Season with more salt and pepper, if needed, and serve.

Tangy potato salad

If you happen to have fresh lovage, mince some stalks and leaves and add them with the celery for the most delicious potato salad ever.

2 pounds (910 g) russet potatoes, cut into 1-inch (2.5-cm) pieces

Salt

6 tablespoons (90 ml) cider vinegar

2 tablespoons Dijon-style or Creole mustard

Lots of freshly ground black pepper

3 ribs celery, diced with leaves

½ sweet onion, diced

1 kosher dill pickle, finely diced

Put the potatoes in a large saucepan and cover with water. Add 2 teaspoons salt, bring to a boil, and cook until just tender, about 10 minutes.

While the potatoes are cooking, in a large bowl, whisk together the vinegar, mustard, ½ teaspoon salt, and the pepper. Drain the potatoes and add them, still hot, to the bowl and toss to coat, mashing a few of the potato pieces with a fork. Toss in the celery, onion, and pickle; season with more salt and pepper, if needed. Serve warm or let cool, cover, and refrigerate until evening and serve cold.

Classic Tofu-Mushroom Chili

WITH *sautéed fresh poblanos and corn*
ALSO GOOD WITH *chili garnishes* (PAGE 172), *broiled sweet onions* (PAGE 141),
OR *warm corn tortillas* (SEE PAGE 100)

Yes, this is an old-school tofu-as-beef-substitute chili, and maybe *chili* should properly be in quotation marks, but I think there's a place for different versions of the protein-plus-chile-and-cumin stew. Earthy mushrooms and lots of dark-red ancho chile powder, and a little hit of tamari at the end, give it a deep flavor.

Press the tofu to remove as much water as possible.

IN THE MORNING
Sauté the onion and mushrooms, then the tofu and spices.

IN THE EVENING
Serve.

2 tablespoons olive oil

½ large onion, diced

Salt

2 cloves garlic, minced

1 pound (455 g) mushrooms, finely chopped

1 pound (455 g) extra-firm tofu, pressed (see Note)

2 tablespoons ancho chile powder

2 teaspoons ground cumin

1 teaspoon chipotle chile powder

½ teaspoon dried oregano

1 (28-ounce/794-g) can crushed tomatoes

1 (14- to 15-ounce/400- to 430-g) can kidney beans, drained and rinsed, or about 1½ cups cooked and drained kidney beans (page 246)

Tamari or soy sauce (if needed)

MORNING

In a large skillet or sauté pan, heat 1 tablespoon of the oil over medium-high heat. When it shimmers, add the onion and a pinch of salt and cook, stirring frequently, until translucent, about 5 minutes. Add the garlic and mushrooms and turn the heat to high; cook, stirring frequently, until the mushrooms have released their liquid and it has mostly evaporated, about 5 minutes. Scrape into the slow cooker.

Return the skillet to medium heat, add the remaining 1 table-spoon oil, then crumble in the drained tofu. Cook for 1 minute, then add the ancho chile powder, cumin, chipotle chile powder, and oregano, stir for 30 seconds, and scrape into the cooker. Pour ½ cup (120 ml) water into the hot skillet, scraping up any browned bits, then pour the liquid into the cooker. Stir in the tomatoes, beans, and 1 teaspoon salt. Cover and cook on low for 8 hours.

Season with tamari, if needed, then serve.

NOTE: Cut the tofu into slabs ½ inch (12 mm) thick. Extract as much of the water from the tofu as possible, using one of these methods:

1. *Arrange the slices between paper towels on a plate and set another plate on top, weighted down with heavy pots or cans. Let drain for 30 minutes to 1 hour at room temperature, or up to overnight in the refrigerator, replacing the paper towels once or twice, if possible.*

2. *Arrange the slices on a plate and cook in a microwave oven for 3 minutes, place another plate on top to make a sandwich, and squeeze the plates together to drain off the excess liquid.*

Sautéed fresh poblanos and corn

You could use 2 cups (330 g) cooked and drained hominy (page 246) instead of the corn.

1 tablespoon

½ onion, diced

Salt and freshly ground black pepper

2 poblano chiles, seeded and diced

2 cups (270 g) fresh or frozen corn kernels

½ teaspoon ground cumin

EVENING

In a large skillet or sauté pan, heat the oil over medium-high heat. When it shimmers, add the onion and a pinch of salt and cook, stirring frequently, until translucent, about 5 minutes. Add the poblanos, corn, and cumin and cook, stirring, for 3 minutes. Add about ¼ cup (60 ml) water, increase the heat to high, and cook, stirring frequently, until it has mostly evaporated, about 2 minutes. Season with salt and pepper and serve.

Sweet tomato chutney

TO ACCOMPANY *Seared Tofu with Spiced Mustard Greens,* PAGE 40

Try leftovers on sandwiches, in tacos, on quesadillas, with scrambled eggs and cilantro, and so on.

1 tablespoon vegetable oil or ghee (page 254)

1 small shallot, thinly sliced

1 coin fresh ginger, thinly sliced

½ teaspoon brown mustard seeds

½ teaspoon cumin seeds

2 tablespoons cider vinegar

1 pint (10 ounces/280 g) cherry or grape tomatoes

1 tablespoon jaggery or brown sugar

½ teaspoon crushed red pepper, or to taste

Pinch of salt

MORNING OR EVENING

In a small saucepan, heat the oil over medium heat. When it shimmers, add the shallot, ginger, mustard seeds, and cumin seeds. Cook, stirring, 2 to 3 minutes. Add the remaining ingredients, cover, and cook, stirring occasionally, for about 5 minutes. (If making this more than 8 hours in advance, cover and refrigerate, then bring to room temperature before serving.)

Seared Tofu with Spiced Mustard Greens

WITH *sweet tomato chutney* (PAGE 39)
ALSO GOOD WITH *lightly spiced basmati rice* (PAGE 69) OR *cranberry-orange wild rice* (PAGE 114)

You'll have plenty of greens to go around, so, if you'd like, cook more tofu (a large griddle would be useful here) to serve more people or for a more substantial plate, or cook a pot of rice to round out the meal.

IN THE MORNING
Sauté the onion and load up the cooker.

IN THE EVENING
Puree the sauce, reheat the onion mixture, and sear the tofu.

---

2 bunches (1 pound/455 g) mustard greens, washed and finely chopped (remove stems thicker than a pencil)

3 tablespoons vegetable oil or ghee (page 254), or more, if needed

1 large onion, sliced

Salt

2 cloves garlic

2 teaspoons ground coriander

2 teaspoons paprika

1 teaspoon ground cumin

¼ teaspoon turmeric

1 teaspoon brown mustard seeds

2 to 3 tablespoons cream cheese

1 (14-ounce/400-g) block extra-firm tofu

MORNING

Pack the mustard greens into the slow cooker and pour in 1½ cups (360 ml) water.

In a large skillet or sauté pan, heat 1 tablespoon of the oil over medium-high heat. When it shimmers, add the onion and a good pinch of salt. Cook, stirring frequently, for 5 minutes, then add the garlic and cook for another 2 minutes. Scrape half of the onion mixture into the cooker over the greens. Sprinkle in the coriander, paprika, cumin, turmeric, and 1 teaspoon salt. Cover and cook on low for 8 hours.

Continue to cook the remaining onion mixture in the skillet over medium-low heat until very deeply browned and soft, adding a splash of water, if needed, to keep the onion from sticking, 10 to 15 minutes. Add the mustard seeds and set aside in the skillet until evening.

EVENING

Reheat the onion and mustard seed mixture.

Using an immersion blender, puree the ingredients in the cooker until very smooth, adding the cream cheese and blending to incorporate it. Season with salt, if needed, and cover to keep warm.

Cut the tofu into slabs or small squares ¼ to ½ inch (6 to 12 mm) thick and pat dry with a paper towel. In a large skillet or sauté pan (or using a large griddle), heat the remaining 2 tablespoons oil over medium-high heat. When it shimmers, add the tofu in a single layer (work in batches if necessary, with more oil) and cook without disturbing it until nicely browned, 3 to 5 minutes. With a thin metal spatula, turn the tofu and brown the other side, then transfer to the puree in the cooker. Top with the sautéed onion and serve.

Creamy Pot Barley with Butternut Squash and Thyme

WITH *baby kale salad with dates and pistachios*
ALSO GOOD WITH *quick-cooked shredded collards* (PAGE 161) OR *seared radicchio* (PAGE 56)

I was determined to figure out how to make a risotto-type dish with barley in the required eight hours, and after three or four attempts I finally hit on two key elements: using ice to slow the start of cooking, so the barley would be less likely to overcook (it's okay if it does; it's just that the texture is a little more interesting when there are distinct barley grains in the mix), and folding tangy buttermilk into the barley just before serving (it gives the dish a lightness that it was lacking in my previous versions using cream).

IN THE MORNING
Brown the onion and garlic and load up the cooker.

IN THE EVENING
Stir in the buttermilk.

1½ cups (300 g) pot barley (that is, hull-less but not pearled)

2 cups (320 g) diced peeled butternut squash (½-inch/12-mm pieces)

3 sprigs fresh thyme

Salt and freshly ground black pepper

1 tablespoon olive oil

½ onion, diced

2 cloves garlic, chopped

2 cups (310 g) ice cubes

6 tablespoons (90 ml) buttermilk

Parmesan cheese

MORNING

Rinse the barley in a sieve under running water, then dump it into the slow cooker. Add 3 cups (720 ml) water, the squash, thyme, 1½ teaspoons salt, and several grindings of pepper.

In a skillet or sauté pan, heat the oil over medium-high heat. When it shimmers, add the onion and a pinch of salt and cook, stirring frequently, until deeply browned, about 7 minutes, adding the garlic in the last 2 minutes. Scrape into the cooker and add the ice. Cover and cook on low for 8 hours.

EVENING

Remove and discard the thyme stems. Gently fold in the buttermilk, season with more salt and pepper, if needed, and serve with a generous sprinkling of shaved or grated Parmesan on top.

Baby kale salad with dates and pistachios

1 tablespoon fresh lemon juice

½ teaspoon salt

¼ cup (60 ml) olive oil

5 ounces (140 g) baby kale

½ cup (60 g) pitted dates, coarsely chopped

3 tablespoons shelled pistachios, chopped

EVENING

In a large salad bowl, whisk together the lemon juice and salt, then gradually whisk in the oil until the dressing is emulsified. Add the kale and toss with your hand to coat. Top with the dates and pistachios and serve.

Dal 1:
Potatoes, Fresh Turmeric, and Whole Spices

WITH *spiced chopped vegetables*
ALSO GOOD WITH *fresh sweet mango and date relish* (PAGE 99) OR *sweet tomato chutney* (PAGE 39)

For even more fresh turmeric flavor and color, go ahead and grate a second thumb-size piece on top of the finished dal.

IN THE MORNING
Sauté the aromatics and load up the cooker.

IN THE EVENING
Stir in the salt and lemon juice.

2 cups (about 380 g) mixed lentils and hearty grains (I like half yellow split peas, a quarter red lentils, and a quarter hard red wheat berries)

8 ounces (255 g) small Yukon Gold potatoes, cut in half

1 tablespoon ghee (page 254) or vegetable oil

½ onion, diced

2 cloves garlic, chopped

4 coins fresh ginger, chopped

2 teaspoons brown mustard seeds

1 teaspoon cumin seeds

1 or 2 jalapeño or serrano chiles, split but kept in one piece

1 thumb-size piece fresh or frozen turmeric root

Salt

Juice of ½ lemon, or to taste

MORNING

Put the lentils and grains in a sieve and rinse under running water. Dump into the slow cooker and add the potatoes and 6 cups (1.4 L) water.

In a skillet or sauté pan, heat the ghee over medium-high heat. When it shimmers, add the onion, garlic, ginger, mustard seeds, and cumin seeds and cook, stirring, until the onion is translucent, about 5 minutes. Scrape into the cooker and add the chiles. Scrape the peel off the turmeric root (use a small spoon for this), then finely grate it into the cooker. Cover and cook on low for 8 hours.

EVENING

Season the dal with salt and stir in the lemon juice. Serve.

Spiced chopped vegetables

Save time in the evening by chopping all the vegetables in the morning—refrigerate the onion, garlic, and ginger in one container, the cabbage and carrot in another.

1 tablespoon ghee (page 254) or vegetable oil

½ onion, diced

2 cloves garlic, chopped

2 coins fresh ginger, chopped

Salt

1 teaspoon ground coriander

1 teaspoon paprika

½ teaspoon brown mustard seeds

½ teaspoon cumin seeds

¼ teaspoon turmeric

½ head cabbage (any kind; about 14 ounces/400 g), cored and finely chopped

1 carrot, diced

½ cup (75 g) shelled peas

1 cup (180 g) chopped tomato

EVENING

In a large deep skillet or sauté pan, heat the ghee over medium-high heat. When it shimmers, add the onion, garlic, ginger, and a pinch of salt and cook, stirring for about 5 minutes. Add the spices and stir for 1 minute. Add the cabbage and carrot, salt to taste, and 1 cup (240 ml) water, stir, cover, and cook for 10 minutes, stirring in the peas and tomatoes in the last 2 minutes.

Dal 2: Cauliflower and Quinoa

WITH *cardamom roasted sweet potatoes*
ALSO GOOD WITH *lemon kale* (PAGE 124) OR *plain yogurt*

Usually I use whole spices in a dal and temper them in ghee or oil before adding them, either in the beginning of the cooking process or just before serving, but sometimes there just isn't time for even that little bit of extra prep work, so I'm including this very simple but tasty version that requires little more than loading and unloading the slow cooker. If you'd like, fry some eggs to serve alongside.

IN THE MORNING
Load the slow cooker.

IN THE EVENING
Serve.

2 cups (about 380 g) mixed lentils and hearty grains (I like half red lentils, a quarter toor dal or other firm pulse, and a quarter barley)

¼ cup (45 g) quinoa

6 cups (1.4 L) vegetable stock (page 240) or water, or a combination

2 teaspoons ground coriander

1 teaspoon ground cumin

½ teaspoon paprika

¼ teaspoon turmeric

½ small head cauliflower, broken into large chunks

1 or 2 jalapeño or serrano chiles, split but kept in one piece

Salt

MORNING

Rinse the lentils and grains and quinoa in a sieve under running water, drain, and put in the slow cooker. Add the stock, then whisk in the coriander, cumin, paprika, and turmeric. Add the cauliflower and chiles. Cover and cook on low for 8 hours.

EVENING

Season with salt, if needed, then serve, ladling the chiles into the bowls of those who want more heat.

Cardamom roasted sweet potatoes

This recipe is based on one for roasted cauliflower in Suvir Saran's fantastic book American Masala. *I sometimes toss a handful of fresh curry (neem) leaves in with the vegetables for roasting.*

2 large sweet potatoes, peeled and cut into ¾-inch (2-cm) chunks

2 tablespoons olive oil

2 teaspoons coriander seeds

1 teaspoon cardamom seeds

1 teaspoon cumin seeds

¼ teaspoon whole black peppercorns

½ teaspoon salt

MORNING OR EVENING

Put the sweet potatoes in a large bowl and toss with the oil. With a mortar and pestle, coarsely crush the coriander seeds, cardamom seeds, cumin seeds, and peppercorns. Toss the spices with the sweet potatoes to coat evenly. Cover and refrigerate if doing this in the morning.

EVENING

Preheat the oven to 400°F (205°C) and put a rimmed baking sheet in the oven to heat.

Remove the hot baking sheet from the oven and spread the sweet potatoes on it in a single layer, then sprinkle with the salt. Roast until nicely browned, 20 to 25 minutes. Serve.

Dal 3: Brown Lentils and Spicy Tomato Masala

WITH *cilantro yogurt dollop*
ALSO GOOD WITH **bok choy brown basmati rice** (PAGE 111) OR **lemony seared okra** (PAGE 229)

If you don't have time to make the masala in the morning, you can mix up and fry it in the evening and stir it into the cooked lentils just before serving.

IN THE MORNING
Pound together the aromatics and fry them.

IN THE EVENING
Season with salt and serve.

---

1 pound (455 g) brown lentils

1-inch (2.5-cm) piece fresh ginger, peeled and sliced

2 jalapeño or serrano chiles, chopped

1 teaspoon crushed red pepper

2 teaspoons hot paprika

1 teaspoon turmeric

1 teaspoon cumin seeds

½ teaspoon brown mustard seeds

Pinch of asafoetida (optional, see Note)

1 cup (180 g) peeled and diced tomato

1 tablespoon ghee (page 254) or vegetable oil

Salt

MORNING

Rinse the lentils in a sieve under running water. Dump into the slow cooker and add 7 cups (1.7 L) water.

With a mortar and pestle, pound the ginger, chiles, and crushed red pepper to a coarse paste (or use a mini food processor). Stir in the paprika, turmeric, cumin seeds, mustard seeds, asafoetida, if using, and tomato. In a small skillet or sauté pan, heat the ghee over medium-high heat. When it shimmers, add the tomato mixture and cook, stirring frequently, until fragrant and a shade darker, 2 to 3 minutes, then scrape into the cooker. Pour 1 cup (240 ml) water into the hot skillet, scraping up any browned bits, then pour the liquid into the cooker and stir well. Cover and cook on low for 8 hours.

EVENING

Season with about 2 teaspoons salt, or to taste. To thicken the liquid, either whisk the lentils briskly or hit them briefly with an immersion blender. Serve.

NOTE: Asafoetida, also called hing, is a spice made from dried and ground gum from the root of an herb plant. It's available in Indian and Middle Eastern grocery stores—often displayed behind glass at the counter. Asafoetida is extremely pungent (I keep my bottle tightly sealed in a plastic bag, and only use a dash or two of it at a time), but its flavor mellows with heat to a slight, hard-to-define undertone of funkiness; it's often used as a stand-in for onion and garlic. If you don't have it, just omit it.

Cilantro yogurt dollop

½ cup (120 ml) plain Greek yogurt (preferably full-fat)

½ cup (20 g) chopped fresh cilantro

Salt

MORNING OR EVENING

Stir the yogurt, cilantro, and a couple of pinches of salt together in a small bowl. Cover and refrigerate if doing this in the morning. Serve cold.

Chipotle Chickpea Stew

WITH *sautéed green tomatoes with bread crumb topping*
ALSO GOOD WITH *cumin spiced millet* (PAGE 231) OR *simple garlic spinach* (PAGE 224)

This may be my ideal fall vegetarian meal: spicy and warming, tangy and nutty, and deeply satisfying. A dollop of plain Greek yogurt goes nicely with it too.

IN THE MORNING
Puree the chipotles and tomatoes and load up the cooker. If you have time, make the peanut sauce.

IN THE EVENING
Stir in the cilantro.

5 chipotle chiles in adobo, with some of the sauce

1 (14.5-ounce/411-g) can diced, whole, or crushed tomatoes

2 (14- to 15-ounce/400- to 430-g) cans chickpeas, drained and rinsed, or about 3 cups cooked and drained (page 246)

1 large sweet potato, peeled and cut into 1-inch (2.5-cm) chunks

1 large russet potato, peeled and cut into 1-inch (2.5-cm) chunks

½ cup (120 ml) chunky natural peanut butter

Juice of 1 lime, or more to taste

Salt

2 tablespoons chopped fresh cilantro

MORNING
Put the chipotles, tomatoes, and 1½ cups (360 ml) water in the slow cooker and use an immersion blender to puree the mixture until smooth (or puree in a blender and transfer to the cooker). Add the chickpeas and sweet and russet potatoes. Cover and cook on low for 8 hours.

MORNING OR EVENING
In a small bowl, whisk together the peanut butter, lime juice, and about 6 tablespoons (90 ml) water, or enough to make a pourable sauce. Season with salt. Cover and refrigerate if doing this in the morning, then bring to room temperature or warm in a small pan or the microwave oven before serving.

EVENING
Stir the cilantro into the stew and season with salt, if needed. Serve the stew with the peanut sauce for drizzling.

Sautéed green tomatoes with bread crumb topping

3 tablespoons vegetable oil

½ cup (40 g) coarse bread crumbs

Salt

½ teaspoon brown mustard seeds

1 pound (455 g) green tomatoes, cut into 1-inch (2.5-cm) chunks

EVENING
In a large skillet or sauté pan, heat 2 tablespoons of the oil over medium-high heat. When it shimmers, add the bread crumbs and a pinch of salt and stir well. Cook, stirring and tossing constantly, until nicely browned, 2 to 3 minutes. Scrape into a bowl and set aside.

Return the skillet to medium-high heat and add the remaining 1 tablespoon oil. Add the mustard seeds, then the tomatoes and a good pinch of salt, and toss well. Cover and cook, tossing occasionally, until the tomatoes have softened and are nicely browned but still hold their shape, about 7 minutes. Transfer to a serving bowl and top with the bread crumbs. Serve.

Hearty Sweet Potato and Chickpea Stew with Sweet Spices

WITH *almond-lemon pistou*

ALSO GOOD WITH *quickie cilantro-lime topping* (PAGE 81) OR *spinach and garlic rice* (PAGE 91)

You'll have a little leftover spice blend—save it and use it to season roasted vegetables or as a rub for grilled chicken or steak.

IN THE MORNING
Brown the onion, garlic, and spices.

IN THE EVENING
Serve.

---

1 tablespoon olive oil

1 onion, chopped

Salt

2 cloves garlic, chopped

4 teaspoons sweet spice blend (see Note), or more, if needed

3 sweet potatoes (about 1½ pounds/680 g), peeled and cut into ¾- to 1-inch (2- to 2.5-cm) pieces

2 russet potatoes (about 14 ounces/400 g), peeled and cut into ¾- to 1-inch (2- to 2.5-cm) pieces

1 (14- to 15-ounce/400- to 430-g) can chickpeas, drained and rinsed, or about 1½ cups cooked and drained (page 246)

2 tablespoons tomato paste

3 cups (720 ml) vegetable stock (page 240) or water

MORNING

In a large skillet or sauté pan, heat the oil over medium-high heat. When it shimmers, add the onion and a pinch of salt and cook, stirring occasionally, until the onion is nicely browned, about 7 minutes. Add the garlic and stir for 1 minute. Add the spice blend and stir for 15 to 30 seconds, until very fragrant and deep brown, then scrape into the slow cooker. Pour ½ cup (120 ml) water into the hot skillet, scraping up any browned bits, then pour the liquid into the cooker. Add the sweet and russet potatoes, chickpeas, tomato paste, stock, and ½ teaspoon salt. Cover and cook on low for 8 hours.

EVENING

Add more salt, if needed, and stir gently; the sweet potatoes will break up a bit and thicken the stew. Serve.

NOTE: To make the spice blend, combine the following in a cup with a fork: 2 teaspoons sweet paprika; 1 teaspoon each of ground coriander, ground cardamom, ground ginger, and ground cinnamon; ½ teaspoon freshly ground black pepper; ¼ teaspoon turmeric; ¼ to ½ teaspoon ground cayenne (to taste).

Almond-lemon pistou

⅔ cup (95 g) whole almonds

1 cup (40 g) chopped fresh basil with tender stems

Grated zest and juice of 1 small lemon

¼ cup (60 ml) olive oil

½ teaspoon salt

MORNING OR EVENING

In a skillet or sauté pan over medium heat, toast the almonds, tossing frequently, until dark brown in spots, 3 to 4 minutes. Transfer to a plate and let cool.

Put the basil, lemon zest and juice, oil, and salt in a mini food processor, add the cooled almonds, and pulse until finely minced and combined—it'll be like pesto. Transfer to a small serving bowl. If doing this in the morning, cover and refrigerate, and bring to room temperature (if you have time) before serving.

Spicy Masala Chickpeas

WITH *spinach labneh*
ALSO GOOD WITH *avocado-lime topping* (PAGE 76) OR *Mom's naan* (PAGE 109)

This is based on a recipe for Punjab-style chickpeas by Heather Carlucci that I first saw on Luisa Weiss's blog *The Wednesday Chef* a few years ago and have been making frequently ever since. I like this simplified process: Over the hours in the slow cooker, the sauce darkens and browns a bit at the edges, adding layers of flavor with no effort on your part.

IN THE MORNING
Puree the masala (aromatics and spices) and load the cooker.

IN THE EVENING
Serve.

½ onion, chopped

1 shallot, chopped

3 cloves garlic

5 coins fresh ginger

1 jalapeño or serrano chile, chopped

1 tomato, choppped, or ½ cup (120 ml) crushed tomatoes

2½ teaspoons ground cumin

2 teaspoons ground coriander

2 teaspoons paprika

1 teaspoon ground cayenne

½ teaspoon ground cinnamon

¼ teaspoon turmeric

1½ teaspoons salt

2 (14- to 16-ounce/400- to 455-g) cans chickpeas, drained and rinsed, or about 3 cups cooked and drained (page 246)

1 lemon, cut into wedges

MORNING

Put all the ingredients except the chickpeas and lemon in the slow cooker with ½ cup (120 ml) water and use an immersion blender to puree until smooth (or do this in a blender or food processor and transfer the puree to the cooker). Stir in the chickpeas. Cover and cook on low for 8 hours.

EVENING

Season with more salt, if needed, and serve with lemon wedges on the side.

Spinach labneh

6 ounces (170 g) frozen chopped spinach

1 cup (240 ml) labneh (see Note)

¼ teaspoon salt

Good pinch of ground cumin (optional)

MORNING OR EVENING

Put the spinach in a sieve and rinse under cold water to thaw it. Squeeze to remove all the liquid—then squeeze some more; you want it to be very dry and crumbly. Put the spinach on a cutting board and use a sharp knife to finely chop it. Transfer to a bowl and stir in the labneh, salt, and cumin, if using, with a fork, breaking up the clumps of spinach as you go. Serve, or cover and refrigerate until evening.

NOTE: You can buy very good labneh in Middle Eastern grocery stores, or easily make your own: Line a fine-mesh sieve with two layers of rinsed and squeezed cheesecloth, set it over a bowl, and dump in a 32-ounce (907-g) container of plain Greek yogurt (preferably full-fat). Let drain in the refrigerator for as long as you can, up to a couple of days, until it's very thick, almost like cream cheese. Transfer to a container and keep in the fridge. Save the whey, if you'd like, for smoothies, or to use in place of water in soups or bread doughs.

Fresh Tomato, Pinto Bean, and Ancho Chile Stew

WITH *cucumber yogurt with hot cumin oil*
ALSO GOOD WITH *shortcut cheese puffs* (PAGE 63) OR *warmed corn tortillas* (SEE PAGE 100)

This is a simplified version of Deborah Madison's famous Zuni Stew, a big pot of pinto beans and vegetables, with handfuls of shredded cheese stirred in just before serving. Her stew also includes chunks of zucchini or yellow squash, but I prefer to leave those out so the flavors are more pure and clear. If you'd like, though, feel free to sauté some squash and fold it into the stew in the evening.

IN THE MORNING
Puree and food-mill
the tomatoes.

IN THE EVENING
Stir in the cilantro
and cheese.

1 pound (455 g) dried pinto
beans

6 plum tomatoes

2 cups (290 g) fresh or frozen
sweet corn kernels

1 teaspoon dried epazote
(see Note, page 63)

2 teaspoons ancho chile
powder

1 teaspoon ground coriander

1 teaspoon ground cumin

Freshly ground black pepper

2 dried ancho chiles, seeded

Salt

½ cup (20 g) chopped fresh
cilantro

1 cup (115 g) shredded
Monterey Jack cheese,
or more, if you'd like

MORNING

Rinse the beans in a sieve under running water, then dump them into the slow cooker. Coarsely chop the tomatoes and puree them in a blender (or in a deep container using an immersion blender), then pass them through a food mill set over the cooker, discarding the seeds and bits of peel (or peel the tomatoes—a serrated peeler works well—and puree them, but don't bother with the food mill). Add the corn, epazote, chile powder, coriander, cumin, several grindings of black pepper, and 5 cups (1.2 L) water. With kitchen shears, snip the ancho chiles into small pieces into the cooker. Cover and cook on low for 8 hours.

EVENING

Season with salt to taste (about 2 teaspoons) and more pepper, if needed. Stir in the cilantro and cheese and serve.

Cucumber yogurt with hot cumin oil

10 ounces (280 g) English
cucumber (about ½ large),
very thinly sliced into
rounds

½ teaspoon kosher salt

¾ cup (180 ml) plain Greek
yogurt (preferably full-fat)

1 tablespoon olive oil

1 teaspoon cumin seeds

Good pinch of ancho chile
powder or paprika

Flaky sea salt

EVENING

In a bowl, sprinkle the cucumber with the kosher salt and toss. Let stand for 15 minutes, then drain and squeeze out excess liquid. Add the yogurt and transfer to a serving dish.

In a small pan, cook the oil and cumin over medium heat, stirring until the cumin is darkened a shade, 2 to 3 minutes. Add the chile powder and immediately spoon the spiced oil over the yogurt. Sprinkle with flaky salt and serve.

Smoky Collards and Black-Eyed Peas

WITH *whole grain peach salad*
ALSO GOOD WITH *corn muffins* (PAGE 153) OR *fried okra* (PAGE 86)

A one-two punch from smoked paprika and chipotle chile powder infuses the black-eyed peas and their cooking liquid with a flavor profile that's more complex and nuanced than it would be if you used just one or the other. When you lift the lid in the evening, you'll see that some of the collards will be peeking out of the stock and turning a bit brown—that's fine; just push them back down when you stir in the salt, and they'll meld together with the rest of the dish.

IN THE MORNING
Sauté the onion and garlic and load up the cooker.

IN THE EVENING
Add salt.

1 tablespoon olive oil

1 onion, diced

2 cloves garlic, chopped

1½ teaspoons smoked paprika, or more to taste

½ teaspoon chipotle chile powder

5 cups (1.2 L) vegetable stock (page 240) or water

1½ cups (250 g) dried black-eyed peas

1 large bunch (1 pound/455 g) collard greens, including stems, chopped

Salt

MORNING

In a large skillet or sauté pan, heat the oil over medium-high heat. When it shimmers, add the onion and cook, stirring, until translucent, about 5 minutes. Add the garlic, smoked paprika, and chile powder and stir for 1 minute. Pour in 1 cup (240 ml) of the stock and scrape up any browned bits. Scrape the onion mixture into the slow cooker.

Rinse the black-eyed peas and add them to the cooker, along with the remaining 4 cups (960 ml) stock and the collards, pushing the collards down into the stock as well as you can. Cover and cook on low for 8 hours.

EVENING

Gently stir in salt to taste (about 2 teaspoons) and let cook for 5 or more minutes to allow the beans to absorb the salt. Add more smoked paprika, if needed, and serve.

RECIPE CONTINUES...

Whole grain peach salad

If you can't find excellent ripe peaches, use mangoes instead.

- **1 cup (170 g) quinoa (well rinsed) or other whole grain (see Note)**
- **Salt and freshly ground black pepper**
- **2 tablespoons fresh lemon juice**
- **1 teaspoon maple syrup or honey**
- **1 small shallot, thinly sliced**
- **3 tablespoons olive oil**
- **2 ripe peaches, diced**
- **2 small sprigs fresh basil**

MORNING

Put the quinoa in a 2-quart (2-L) saucepan and add 1 ¼ cups (300 ml) water and a pinch of salt. Bring to a boil over high heat, stir once, then cover and cook over the lowest heat for 15 minutes, or until tender. Dump into a fine-mesh sieve and rinse under cold running water to cool completely; drain very well.

While the quinoa is cooking, in a medium bowl, whisk together the lemon juice, maple syrup, ½ teaspoon salt, several grindings of pepper, the shallot, and oil. Add the peaches and quinoa and toss to coat with the dressing. Cover and

EVENING

Tear in the basil leaves, toss, season with more salt, if needed, and serve.

NOTE: The quinoa can be replaced with either 3 cups (455 g) cooked hearty grains (if frozen, thaw by rinsing them in a fine-mesh sieve) or one of these quick-cooking grains:

Bulgur: Bring the salted water to a boil, add 1 cup (140 g) fine or medium bulgur, cover, and cook on the lowest heat for 15 minutes.

Couscous: Bring 1½ cups (360 ml) salted water to a boil with 2 teaspoons olive oil, add 1 cup (195 g) whole wheat couscous, cover, remove from the heat, and let stand for 5 minutes.

Creamy Giant Limas with Sun-Dried Tomatoes

WITH *oven-fried eggs*

ALSO GOOD WITH *olive-marinated fresh mozzarella* (PAGE 28) OR *spinach-Gruyère toasts* (PAGE 194)

This dish is inspired by one I tested for Julia Sherman for her book *Salad for President*. The creamy, falling-apart lima beans suspended in emulsified broth and fruity olive oil with tart dried tomatoes are revelatory. If you have ground sumac on hand, definitely sprinkle some over the whole dish for another layer of contrasting tartness.

IN THE MORNING
Load up the cooker.

IN THE EVENING
Fold in the sun-dried tomatoes.

1 pound (455 g) dried large lima beans

¼ cup (60 ml) olive oil (drained from sun-dried tomatoes if there's extra in the jar)

1 large sprig fresh rosemary

⅓ cup (35 g) oil-packed sun-dried tomatoes, coarsely chopped

Salt and freshly ground black pepper

1 small sweet onion, very thinly sliced

Paprika and/or ground sumac

Lemon wedges

MORNING

Rinse the beans and put them in the slow cooker with the oil, rosemary, and 6 cups (1.4 L) water. Cover and cook on low for 8 hours.

EVENING

Gently stir in the sun-dried tomatoes and season with salt and plenty of pepper to taste. Scatter the raw onion over the top and sprinkle with paprika. Serve with the lemon wedges alongside for squeezing over individual servings.

Oven-fried eggs

1 tablespoon ghee (page 254) or vegetable oil

4 eggs

Salt and freshly ground black pepper

EVENING

Preheat the oven to 400°F (205°C). Put the ghee on a small rimmed baking sheet and put it in the oven to heat up. Let the pan with the ghee heat for 5 to 10 minutes after the oven is up to temperature so it's very hot.

Carefully remove the hot pan from the oven, tilt it to coat the bottom with ghee, and crack the eggs onto the pan with as much space between them as possible. Sprinkle with salt and pepper. Bake until the whites are set, the edges are crisp, and the yolks are thickened, about 4 minutes. Remove the eggs from the pan with a metal spatula and serve.

Ribollita

WITH *seared radicchio*

ALSO GOOD WITH *lemon kale* (PAGE 124) OR *quick-cooked shredded collards* (PAGE 161)

Here again I'm lucky to have the opportunity to improve on a recipe I developed for my first slow cooker book. This ribollita, a traditional Italian bread soup, is much less fussy and more aggressively flavorful—don't skimp on the black pepper.

IN THE MORNING
Load up the cooker.

IN THE EVENING
Fold in the bread and tomatoes and season the soup.

8 ounces (255 g) dried white beans

8 ounces (255 g) dried cranberry beans

2 large carrots, cut into ½-inch (12-mm) pieces

2 ribs celery with leaves, cut into ½-inch (12-mm) pieces

1 Yukon Gold or peeled russet potato, diced

½ onion, diced

2 cloves garlic, crushed

1 large sprig fresh rosemary

2 cups (140 g) cubed crusty bread

2 tomatoes, chopped

Salt and freshly ground black pepper

MORNING
Rinse the white and cranberry beans in a sieve under running water. Dump them into the slow cooker and add the carrots, celery, potato, onion, garlic, rosemary, and 8 cups (2 L) water. Cover and cook on low for 8 hours.

EVENING
Turn the cooker to high. Fold in the bread and tomatoes. Season the soup with salt and plenty of pepper, cover, and cook until the bread and tomatoes have broken down somewhat and the bread has thickened the soup, about 15 minutes. Serve.

Seared radicchio

1 head radicchio (about 12 ounces/340 g total)

2 tablespoons olive oil

Salt and freshly ground black pepper

EVENING
Trim the bottom of the radicchio head and cut the head into wedges that are about 1½ inches (4 cm) thick on the widest side, keeping the core intact. Put on a plate and rub the oil all over the wedges, keeping them as wedge-like as possible, and sprinkle with salt (about ½ teaspoon total) and several grindings of pepper. Heat a large skillet or sauté pan over medium-high heat. When a drop of water on the surface evaporates immediately, it's hot enough. Add the radicchio, cut side down, in a single layer (you might need to do this in two batches) and cook without disturbing them for 2 to 3 minutes, until deeply browned. Using tongs or a thin metal spatula, turn the wedges and brown the other cut side. Remove to a platter or serving bowl and serve.

Sagamité with Maple Syrup and Butternut Squash

WITH *garlic sautéed dandelion greens*
ALSO GOOD WITH *herb salad* (PAGE 31) OR *oven-fried eggs* (PAGE 55)

My friend Leda told me about a meal she'd had in an upscale field-to-table restaurant in Canada, and on the menu was a word I'd never encountered before: *sagamité*. Sagamité comes up in European colonizers' accounts of the foods prepared by Native Americans and Canadian First Peoples, and is most often described as a porridge of Indian corn (either nixtamalized or parched), sometimes with beans or a little wild game or fat, and chunks of pumpkin or other hard squashes, and sometimes sweetened. This is my interpretation, based on those descriptions (though not, I should say, on one Jesuit's description centuries ago of sagamité as being comparable to wallpaper paste). I was surprised by how well these elements came together in a delicious, hearty, and, I might add, kid-pleasing meal.

IN THE MORNING
Load up the cooker.

IN THE EVENING
Cook the grits and fold them into the beans with the maple syrup.

1½ cups (290 g) dried pinto beans

½ large butternut squash, peeled and cut into large chunks

1 teaspoon dried epazote (see Note, page 63)

2 teaspoons salt, or to taste

⅔ cup (115 g) hominy grits

2 tablespoons maple syrup, plus more for serving

MORNING
Rinse the beans under running water, then dump them into the slow cooker and add the squash, epazote, and 6 cups (1.4 L) water. Cover and cook on low for 8 hours.

EVENING
Stir in the salt, then ladle about 2½ cups (600 ml) of the liquid from the cooker into a small saucepan and bring to a boil over high heat. Whisk in the grits and cook until tender and thick, adding more liquid, if needed, about 10 minutes. Scrape the cooked grits into the cooker and gently fold them into the beans and squash and add the maple syrup. Serve with more syrup on the side for drizzling.

Garlic sautéed dandelion greens

If you're not concerned about keeping the meal vegetarian, I'd highly recommend using schmaltz (page 251) in place of the olive oil.

1 tablespoon olive oil

2 cloves garlic, minced

1 bunch (about 14 ounces/400 g) mature dandelion greens, chopped

Salt

EVENING
Heat the oil and garlic in the skillet over medium-high heat, stirring. Cook about 2 minutes, then add the greens and a good pinch of salt. Cook, tossing with tongs, until the leaves with the thickest stems are just tender, 3 to 5 minutes. Serve hot.

White Bean–Tahini Soup with Garlic Oil

WITH *roasted tomatoes and croutons*
ALSO GOOD WITH *lemon kale* (PAGE 124) OR *carrot-top pesto* (PAGE 165)

In very-long-cooked dishes, the sharp edge of garlic's flavor can be lost—slow-cooked garlic has its own appeal, of course, but sometimes I want that strong bite. Here I sauté the garlic and drizzle the sizzling hot garlic oil into the creamy soup just before serving.

IN THE MORNING
Load up the cooker.

IN THE EVENING
Scoop out excess liquid, add the tahini, puree the soup, and make the garlic oil.

---

1 pound (455 g) dried Great Northern beans

6 cups (1.4 L) vegetable stock (page 240) or water

Pinch of crushed red pepper

3 tablespoons tahini

Salt and freshly ground black pepper

2 tablespoons olive oil

2 cloves garlic, minced

MORNING
Rinse the beans in a sieve under running water. Dump them into the slow cooker and add the stock and crushed red pepper. Cover and cook on low for 8 hours.

EVENING
Ladle out and discard excess liquid, if there is any—the stock should just cover the cooked beans. Stir the tahini into the soup. With an immersion blender, puree about half of the beans to thicken the soup. Season with salt and plenty of black pepper.

In a small sauté pan, heat the oil over medium heat. When it shimmers, add the garlic and cook, stirring, until golden, about 3 minutes. Scrape the hot garlic oil into the soup. Serve.

Roasted tomatoes and croutons

1 pound (455 g) cherry tomatoes

4 cups (200 g) cubed crusty bread (in ¾-inch/2-cm pieces)

2 tablespoons olive oil

½ teaspoon salt

Freshly ground black pepper

1 sprig fresh basil

EVENING
Preheat the oven to 450°F (230°C). Put a rimmed baking sheet in the oven to heat.

In a large bowl, toss together the tomatoes and bread, then drizzle with the oil and sprinkle with the salt and several grindings of pepper, tossing well. Spread the mixture on the hot baking sheet and roast until the tomatoes have collapsed and the bread is golden, 15 to 20 minutes. Tear in the basil, use a large spatula to transfer to a serving dish or platter, and serve.

Smoky Black Lentils and Beans

WITH *seared halloumi and chile mince*

ALSO GOOD WITH *spinach labneh* (PAGE 50) OR *cucumber yogurt with hot cumin oil* (PAGE 51)

Black, or beluga, lentils are well worth seeking out—they hold their shape and add great texture to long-cooked dishes like this stew.

IN THE MORNING
Cook the onion
and spices.

IN THE EVENING
Stir in the tomatoes.

1 tablespoon olive oil

1 onion, diced

2 teaspoons hot paprika

½ teaspoon smoked paprika, or more to taste

1 teaspoon ground cumin

1 cup (200 g) black (beluga) lentils

1 cup (185 g) dried black beans

½ cup (120 ml) crushed tomatoes

1 tablespoon tomato paste

Salt

MORNING

In a large skillet, heat the oil over medium-high heat. When it shimmers, add the onion and cook, stirring frequently, until translucent, about 5 minutes. Stir in the hot and smoked paprikas and the cumin and stir for 15 seconds. Pour in 1 cup (240 ml) water and scrape up any browned bits. Scrape the mixture into the slow cooker.

Put the lentils and beans in a sieve and rinse under running water, then dump into the cooker. Pour in 5 cups (1.2 L) water. Cover and cook on low for 8 hours.

EVENING

Turn the cooker to high and stir in the tomatoes, tomato paste, and about 2 teaspoons salt (or more to taste); add more smoked paprika, if needed. Cover until heated through, then serve.

Seared halloumi and chile mince

You can serve this as a topping for the lentils and beans dish or as a side.

1 bunch fresh cilantro or parsley, chopped

1 to 2 jalapeño or serrano chiles, chopped, seeded if you'd like less heat

3 sweet mini peppers, seeded and chopped

Juice of ½ lime

Salt

10 ounces (280 g) halloumi cheese, cut into slabs ¼ inch (6 mm) thick

MORNING OR EVENING

Put the cilantro, chiles, sweet peppers, lime juice, and a good pinch of salt in a mini food processor and pulse to finely mince (or use a chef's knife and mince the cilantro, chiles, and peppers together on a cutting board, then transfer to a bowl and stir in the lime and salt). Cover and refrigerate if doing this in the morning.

EVENING

Heat a large nonstick pan or griddle over medium heat. When a drop of water on the surface evaporates almost instantly, add the cheese slices in a single layer (in batches if necessary) and cook without disturbing them until nicely browned, 1 to 2 minutes. Flip with a thin spatula and brown the other side. Serve the cheese topped with the chile mince.

White Bean, Corn, and Chard Stew

WITH *shortcut cheese puffs*
ALSO GOOD WITH *almond couscous* (PAGE 195)
OR *dark bread, eggplant quark, and pickled beet stems* (PAGE 218)
—*either use beet greens instead of chard below or pickle the chard stems*

There's really nothing fancy about this dish; it's simple and satisfying just as it is, but also quite adaptable—feel free to add spices to the chard just before you scrape it into the cooker: Cracked toasted coriander would be nice, as would a good pinch of ground cayenne or crushed red pepper, or a spoonful of cumin seeds and mustard seeds.

IN THE MORNING
Load up the cooker.
Chop the chard and mince the garlic in the morning or evening.

IN THE EVENING
Sauté the chard and fold it into the stew.

1½ cups (310 g) dried navy beans

3 cups (410 g) frozen sweet corn kernels

1 teaspoon dried epazote (see Note)

½ onion, diced

½ large bunch Swiss chard

1 clove garlic

Salt and freshly ground black pepper

1 tablespoon olive oil

Rinse the beans and put them in the slow cooker with the corn, epazote, onion, and 4 cups (960 ml) water. Cover and cook on low for 8 hours.

MORNING OR EVENING

Coarsely chop the chard, including the stems, and mince the garlic. If doing this in the morning, cover and refrigerate.

EVENING

Turn the cooker to high and season the stew with salt and pepper.

In a large skillet or sauté pan, heat the oil over medium-high heat. When it shimmers, add the chard and garlic and a pinch of salt and cook, tossing with tongs, until just tender, 5 to 7 minutes, adding a splash of water, if needed, to keep the leaves from sticking. Gently fold into the stew. Serve.

NOTE: Dried epazote (a fragrant herb) is available in Mexican markets and in good supermarkets. Try to get epazote "de comer," as it'll say on the label—this kind has fewer tough stems to pick out.

Shortcut cheese puffs

Makes 24

I love pão de queijo, the little Brazilian cheese rolls, but they're kind of a pain to make, and I can never get the consistency just right. These rolls, made in a mini muffin tin from a thin batter, are more like chewy, cheesy popovers but satisfy a similar craving. If you have leftovers, they're fantastic warmed up the next morning and eaten with coffee.

1 cup (240 ml) milk

½ cup (120 ml) vegetable oil

1 large egg

2 cups (240 g) tapioca flour (tapioca starch)

4 ounces (115 g) grated Parmesan cheese

EVENING

Preheat the oven to 400°F (205°C). Spray a mini muffin tin with cooking oil spray.

In a blender, combine all the ingredients. Pour into the muffin tin wells, filling them almost to the top. Bake until puffed and golden, about 20 minutes. Loosen the edges with a thin knife and pop the puffs out of the pan. Serve warm.

CHAPTER 2

Chicken, Turkey, and Duck

Caldo de Pollo 66
Yellow tomato ají

Chicken Soup with Tomatillos 68
Quesadillas sincronizadas

Chicken and Spinach Curry 69
Lightly spiced basmati rice

Shredded Chicken and White Bean Chili
with Roasted Poblanos 71
Mini faux pupusas

Chicken Soup with Fresh Turmeric and
Galangal 74
Fried bean thread noodles

Tortilla Stew 76
Avocado-lime topping

Whole Grain Congee with
Crisp Panko Chicken 78
Sweet chile-garlic sauce

Chicken and Red Rice 81
Quickie cilantro-lime topping

Chicken and Andouille Jambalaya 82
Chayote with garlic buttered bread crumbs

A Chicken Gumbo 85
Fried okra

Romanian-Style Chicken and Noodles 88
Pan-seared green beans

Chicken in Shortcut Mole 90
Spinach and garlic rice

Chicken "Cobbler" 94
Two peas with marjoram

Chicken Tikka Masala 98
Fresh sweet mango and date relish

Chicken Tinga 100
Quick-pickled vegetables

Chicken with Coconut Milk
and Achiote 103
Seared peppers

Chicken with Tart Pineapple,
Coconut, and Cashews 106
Basic coconut rice

Fried Nuts and Seeds Chicken Curry 108
Mom's naan

Kasoori Methi Chicken 110
Bok choy brown basmati rice

Tarragon and Crème Fraîche Chicken 112
Cranberry-orange wild rice

Chicken Mull 115
Collard slaw

Chicken with Sour Cherries, Caramelized
Onions, and Lots of Dill 116
Fancy saffron-butter basmati rice

Chicken with Spanish Chorizo
and Peppers 118
Garlic- and tomato-rubbed grilled bread

Herb Butter–Braised Turkey Breast 120
Butter-roasted mixed potatoes

Duck Confit with White Beans
and Leeks 123
Lemon kale

Caldo de Pollo

WITH *yellow tomato ají*

ALSO GOOD WITH *fried bean thread noodles* (PAGE 74) OR *quick-pickled vegetables* (PAGE 102)

This is similar to the chicken soup served at one of my favorite restaurants, Tulcingo del Valle, a small storefront Mexican place in far-western Hell's Kitchen in Manhattan. It's the kind of soup that you might crave when you're feeling under the weather—it's brothy and comforting, with simple, clear flavors.

IN THE MORNING
Load up the cooker.

IN THE EVENING
Remove and discard the chicken bones, strain the broth, if desired, and add the spinach.

2 carrots, peeled and cut into 1- to 1½-inch (2.5- to 4-cm) pieces

1 large russet potato, peeled and cut into 1- to 1½-inch (2.5- to 4-cm) pieces, or about 5 baby Yukon Gold potatoes, halved

2 large bone-in chicken breast halves, skin pulled off and excess fat trimmed

2 small ears sweet corn, husked and cut into 2-inch (5-cm) lengths

5 to 6 cups (1.2 to 1.4 L) good-quality chicken or turkey stock (page 240)

2 small zucchini, cut into chunks

1 tablespoon olive oil

Salt and freshly ground black pepper

Large handful of baby spinach

MORNING

Layer the carrots, potato, chicken, and corn in the slow cooker and pour in enough stock to cover the chicken (it doesn't have to cover the corn). Cover and cook on low for 8 hours.

EVENING

Turn the cooker to high. Using a slotted spoon, transfer the chicken to a bowl. If the broth is murky, spoon out the vegetables too, then ladle the broth through a fine-mesh sieve into a pot and return it to the cooker. Pull the chicken meat off the bones and return it to the cooker, along with the vegetables. Stir in the spinach, season with salt and pepper.

In a large sauté pan, heat the oil over high heat. When it shimmers, add the zucchini in a single layer and season with salt and pepper. Cook, tossing occasionally, until golden and just tender, adding a little water if it starts to stick to the pan, 5 to 7 minutes. Add the zucchini to the soup and serve.

Yellow tomato ají

This is based on a recipe on the *My Colombian Recipes* blog for the more traditional version of ají made with gooseberries. If tart-sweet gooseberries are available, try using them instead of the tomatoes, or use a combination of the two.

1 pint (10 ounces/280 g) yellow cherry tomatoes or coarsely chopped sweet yellow tomatoes

¼ cup (30 g) diced sweet onion

1 habanero chile, seeded and chopped (wear gloves or otherwise avoid touching the cut surfaces with your hands)

1½ tablespoons sugar

½ teaspoon salt, or to taste

½ bunch fresh cilantro, including tender stems, chopped

Juice of 1 lime

MORNING OR EVENING

Put the tomatoes, onion, chile, sugar, salt, and ¼ cup (60 ml) water in a 2-quart (2-L) saucepan and cook over high heat until the tomatoes are very soft and are breaking down, 5 to 7 minutes. Add the cilantro and lime juice and use an immersion blender to puree the sauce until smooth. If doing this in the morning, transfer to a covered container and refrigerate. Bring the salsa to room temperature before serving.

Chicken Soup with Tomatillos

WITH *quesadillas sincronizadas*

ALSO GOOD WITH **warm corn tortillas** (SEE PAGE 100) OR **cumin spiced millet** (PAGE 231)

We should use more tomatillos! They're even easier to use in soups like this one than tomatoes—you don't have to worry about their being underripe, and they don't need peeling or coring.

IN THE MORNING
Load up the cooker.

IN THE EVENING
Puree the soup and add the cilantro and cayenne.

1½ pounds (680 g) tomatillos (about 8 large), husked, rinsed, and cut in half

1 to 2 jalapeño or serrano chiles, chopped

2 cloves garlic, chopped

3 cups (720 ml) good-quality chicken or turkey stock (page 240)

2 pounds (910 g) well-trimmed boneless, skinless chicken thighs

Salt and freshly ground black pepper

1 cup (40 g) chopped fresh cilantro

½ teaspoon ground cayenne, or to taste

MORNING

Put the tomatillos, chiles, garlic, and stock in the slow cooker. Arrange the chicken on top and sprinkle with a little salt and several grindings of pepper. Cover and cook on low for 8 hours.

EVENING

Using a slotted spoon, transfer the chicken to a bowl—it'll be very tender, and it's okay if some bits of chicken remain in the pot or some vegetables come with the chicken. With an immersion blender, puree the tomatillo mixture until smooth, blending in the cilantro and cayenne. Return the chicken to the soup. Season with more salt and cayenne, if needed, then serve.

Quesadillas sincronizadas

For each quesadilla:

2 (6-inch/15-cm) flour tortillas

⅓ to ½ cup (1½ to 2 ounces/ 40 to 55 g) shredded melty cheese, such as Monterey Jack or extra-sharp cheddar

Pinch of salt

1 thin slice deli ham, torn into pieces (optional)

EVENING

If you're making more than one quesadilla at a time, heat a large griddle or several skillets or sauté pans over medium heat until hot. Lay down the first tortilla for each quesadilla on the griddle and spread with half of the cheese and a pinch of salt. Top with the ham, if using (make sure to leave some space between the ham pieces), then the remaining cheese and the second tortilla. Cook, pressing down gently with a spatula, until the cheese has started to melt, the two tortillas stick together, and the bottom is browned, 2 to 3 minutes. Flip and brown the other side, then remove to a cutting board and let cool for a minute (to let the cheese settle so it doesn't ooze too much). Cut into wedges and serve.

Chicken and Spinach Curry

WITH *lightly spiced basmati rice*
ALSO GOOD WITH *Mom's naan* (PAGE 109) OR *cardamom roasted sweet potatoes* (PAGE 45)

This is a streamlined version of the classic chicken saag restaurant dish, and is great as is. If you're inclined to complicate things to add a little more nuance, toss a dried red chile or two into the cooker with the chicken, and add about 1 teaspoon each of cumin seeds and brown mustard seeds to the onion in the last few minutes of cooking.

IN THE MORNING
Load up the cooker.

IN THE EVENING
Sauté the onion.
Puree the sauce, mixing in the cream cheese.

---

1 tablespoon ground coriander

1 tablespoon paprika

2 teaspoons ground cumin

1 teaspoon turmeric

Salt

2 pounds (910 g) well-trimmed boneless, skinless chicken thighs

3 cloves garlic

3 serrano chiles, chopped, seeded if you'd like less heat

5 coins fresh ginger

2 (10- to 12-ounce/280- to 340-g) packages frozen chopped spinach

2 tablespoons ghee (page 254) or vegetable oil

1 onion, thinly sliced

4 tablespoons (55 g) cream cheese

MORNING

In a cup, combine the coriander, paprika, cumin, turmeric, and 2 teaspoons salt. Put the chicken in the slow cooker and toss with the spice mixture to coat. Add the garlic, chiles, and ginger. Break up the frozen spinach and arrange it on top of the chicken. Cover and cook on low for 8 hours.

EVENING

In a large skillet or sauté pan, heat the ghee over medium-high heat. Add the onion and a pinch of salt and cook, stirring occasionally, until the onion is tender, evenly browned, and crisp on the edges, 8 to 10 minutes.

Meanwhile, using a slotted spoon, transfer the chicken to a bowl (it's okay if spinach comes with it, but try to leave the garlic, chiles, and ginger in the cooker). With an immersion blender, puree the sauce and mix in the cream cheese. Return the chicken to the sauce, top with the sautéed onion (fold it in, if you wish), and serve.

Lightly spiced basmati rice

1 tablespoon ghee (page 254) or vegetable oil

1 teaspoon cumin seeds

3 green cardamom pods, lightly crushed

3 whole cloves

2 cups (360 g) basmati rice, rinsed well in a sieve

Salt

EVENING

In a 2-quart (2-L) saucepan, cook the ghee, cumin, cardamom, and cloves over medium heat until fragrant, about 2 minutes. Add the rice and stir for 30 seconds. Add 2½ cups (600 ml) water and a good pinch of salt, increase the heat to high, and bring to a boil. Stir once to unstick any grains from the bottom of the pan, then cover and cook over the lowest heat for 14 minutes, or until the water is absorbed and the rice is tender. Let stand, covered, for about 3 minutes, then pick out the cardamom and cloves, if you'd like (they usually float and then settle on top of the rice), and fluff the rice with a spatula or fork and serve.

Shredded Chicken and White Bean Chili with Roasted Poblanos

WITH *mini faux pupusas*

ALSO GOOD WITH *fried plantains* (PAGE 214) OR *chili garnishes* (PAGE 172)

When poblanos are in season, roast a bunch of them at a time, peel and chop them, then put them in the freezer so you can just pop them—still frozen is fine—into stews like this one.

IN THE MORNING
Sauté the onion and garlic (and roast the poblanos if you need to) and load up the cooker.

IN THE EVENING
Shred the chicken and season the chili.

1 tablespoon olive oil

½ onion, diced

Salt and freshly ground black pepper

1 clove garlic, chopped

½ teaspoon ground cumin

4 large poblano chiles, roasted, peeled, and seeded (see Note), then diced (about 1¼ cups/230 g)

1½ pounds (680 g) boneless, skinless chicken breasts, cut into large chunks

4 cups (960 ml) chicken or turkey stock (page 240)

1 cup (210 g) dried navy beans

½ cup (20 g) chopped fresh cilantro, or 1 cup (30 g) finely chopped spinach

3 scallions, sliced

Juice of ½ lime

RECIPE CONTINUES...

MORNING

In a skillet or sauté pan, heat the oil over medium-high heat. When it shimmers, add the onion and a pinch of salt and cook, stirring frequently, until the onion is translucent, about 5 minutes. Add the garlic and cumin and stir for 1 minute. Pour in ½ cup (120 ml) water and scrape up any browned bits, then scrape the mixture into the slow cooker. Add the poblanos, chicken, and stock. Rinse the beans in a sieve under running water and add them to the cooker. Cover and cook on low for 8 hours.

EVENING

Using two forks, shred the chicken. Stir in the cilantro, scallions, and lime juice and season with salt and pepper; cover and let stand for a few minutes to allow the beans to absorb some salt. Serve.

NOTE: To roast poblanos, put them on a baking sheet and broil until the tops are blistered and blackened in spots, then turn them over and broil on the other side. Transfer to a bowl, cover, and let steam for 10 minutes; rub off the peels and pull out the stems and seeds.

Mini faux pupusas

Makes 8 (3½- to 4-inch/9- to 10-cm) pupusas

When I'm in a hurry or lazy, I just mix the cheese right into the dough. For a slightly less faux version, shape the dough into balls, then poke a hole in the center to make a "pinch bowl"; stuff as much shredded cheese as you can inside, then close up the dough ball, flatten, and cook as below.

1 cup (115 g) masa harina

¾ cup (180 ml) warm water

¼ teaspoon salt

1 cup (115 g) shredded Monterey Jack cheese, with or without peppers

Put the masa harina in a medium bowl and stir in the warm water and salt to make a soft dough. Knead in the cheese. Shape the dough into eight Ping-Pong–size balls, then flatten into 3 ½- to 4-inch (9- to 10-cm) rounds with your palm. If doing this in the morning, arrange the rounds on a plate (layers separated with plastic wrap or waxed paper), cover with plastic wrap, and refrigerate.

Heat a large cast-iron griddle (or use a skillet or sauté pan and work in batches) over medium-high heat. When a drop of water on the surface evaporates immediately, it's hot enough. Arrange the masa rounds on the griddle and cook until the bottom is brown-flecked, about 4 minutes, then flip and brown the other side, pressing down gently on the top with a spatula; the pupusas will puff up a bit in spots (and probably ooze a little cheese, which is fine). Serve hot.

Chicken Soup with Fresh Turmeric and Galangal

WITH *fried bean thread noodles*

ALSO GOOD WITH *lemongrass rice* (PAGE 211) OR *pandan water* (PAGE 149)

Lots of fresh turmeric gives this coconut milk–enriched soup a brilliant yellow color and a pleasant bittersweet flavor. You can use 1 teaspoon ground turmeric if you don't have fresh, but know that you can keep turmeric root in the freezer almost indefinitely—it's actually easier to peel and slice or grate when it's frozen.

IN THE MORNING
Make the seasoning paste and sauté it.

IN THE EVENING
Puree the liquid, fold in the spinach, and season the soup to taste.

3-inch (7.5-cm) piece fresh or frozen galangal, peeled and chopped

2 thumb-size pieces fresh or frozen turmeric, peeled and chopped

2 stalks lemongrass, tops and tough outer leaves removed, chopped

2 cloves garlic, chopped

3 dried red chiles, preferably Thai, torn into pieces

1 small (5.6-ounce/165-ml) can coconut milk (⅔ cup/165 ml)

2½ cups (600 ml) chicken or turkey stock (page 240) or water

Salt

1 large tomato, peeled, seeded, and torn (about ¾ cup/125 g)

2 pounds (910 g) well-trimmed boneless, skinless chicken thighs, cut into small pieces

2 kaffir lime leaves, torn in several places but kept whole

4 ounces (115 g) baby spinach

1 tablespoon fish sauce, or to taste

Juice of ½ lime, or to taste

1 teaspoon sugar, or to taste

Fresh Thai chiles, thinly sliced

MORNING

Using a granite mortar and pestle, pound the galangal, turmeric, lemongrass, garlic, and dried chiles together to a paste (or pulse in a mini food processor).

Put about half of the coconut milk (the thick stuff from the top of the can, if possible) in a small skillet or sauté pan and place over medium-high heat. When it's bubbling at the edges, scrape in the galangal paste. Cook and stir until the paste is dryish and starting to stick to and brown in the skillet, about 3 minutes, then scrape it into the slow cooker. Pour ½ cup (120 ml) water into the hot skillet, scraping up any browned bits, then pour the liquid into the cooker, along with the remaining coconut milk and the stock. Stir in ½ teaspoon salt, the tomato, chicken, and lime leaves. Cover and cook on low for 8 hours.

Turn the cooker to high. Use a slotted spoon to transfer the chicken, tomato, and lime leaves to a bowl. With an immersion blender, puree the broth until smooth. Return the chicken and vegetables to the cooker and stir in the spinach. Season with fish sauce, lime juice, and sugar to taste. Serve with a small bowl of sliced fresh chiles on the side.

Fried bean thread noodles

Vegetable oil

2 or 3 bundles of dried bean thread (saifun) noodles

Pour at least 1½ inches (4 cm) of oil into a very dry deep saucepan and place over medium-high heat; heat to about 400°F (205°C) on a candy thermometer. Line a tray with paper towels or a paper bag and have a slotted spoon or skimmer handy.

Break the noodle bundles roughly in half. (You might want to do this over a large bowl or the sink to catch stray broken bits.) When the oil is hot, drop one half-bundle at a time into the oil; the noodles should immediately expand to fill the pan and rise to the surface of the oil—press down on the mass of noodles gently with the slotted spoon to make sure all the noodles are puffed, then remove them to the paper towels to drain. The noodles should be in the oil for 5 to 7 seconds at most. Repeat with the remaining noodles. Serve atop soups or salads. (When the oil is cool, strain it into a clean dry container and save for another use.)

Tortilla Stew

WITH *avocado-lime topping*

ALSO GOOD WITH *chilled radish chips* (PAGE 134) OR *chili garnishes* (PAGE 172)

This is a fine way to use up any stale corn tortillas you might have in the back of the fridge. Here you'll stir half of the tortillas into the soup to thicken the broth, and lightly fry the other half to use as a crunchy-salty topping.

IN THE MORNING
Load the cooker and, if you have time, fry half of the tortilla strips for the topping.

IN THE EVENING
Stir in the unfried tortilla strips and the cilantro.

2½ pounds (1.2 kg) well-trimmed boneless, skinless chicken thighs, cut into chunks

1 tablespoon ground cumin

1 tablespoon ancho chile powder

1 tablespoon dried oregano, preferably Mexican

Salt

2 cups (480 ml) chicken stock (page 240)

1 cup (165 g) peeled and chopped tomatoes

Vegetable oil

8 corn tortillas, stacked, cut in half, then cut into strips about ¼ inch (6 mm) wide

2 tablespoons chopped fresh cilantro

MORNING

Put the chicken in the slow cooker. In a cup, stir together the cumin, chile powder, oregano, and 1½ teaspoons salt, then sprinkle over the chicken and toss to coat. Pour in the stock and add the tomatoes. Cover and cook on low for 8 hours.

MORNING OR EVENING

In a large skillet or sauté pan, heat about ⅛ inch (3 mm) of oil over medium heat. When it shimmers, add half of the tortilla strips. Cook, stirring with a slotted spoon, until nicely browned and crisp, 3 to 5 minutes. With the spoon, transfer to paper towels to drain and sprinkle with salt. Set the fried and unfried strips aside.

EVENING

Turn the cooker to high, stir the unfried tortilla strips into the stew, cover, and cook until the tortillas are softened and you're ready to serve. Serve the soup with the fried tortilla strips on the side for topping.

Avocado-lime topping

2 Hass avocados, peeled, pitted, and diced

Juice of 1 lime

¼ cup (10 g) chopped fresh cilantro

Salt

EVENING

Toss the avocados in a bowl with the lime juice and cilantro; season with salt to taste. Serve.

Leftover stew?

Make a tacky-but-homey enchilada casserole: Preheat the oven to 400°F (205°C). Shred leftover drained chicken (reserve 1 cup/240 ml of the stew liquid) and add cooked and drained black beans to make 1½ cups (360 ml). Heat 9 corn tortillas on a hot griddle or in a skillet or sauté pan over medium-high heat until pliable. Lightly oil a 7 by 11-inch (17.5 by 28-cm) baking dish and layer the tortillas (cut to fit as necessary) and chicken and beans in the baking dish. Combine the reserved stew liquid and 1 cup (240 ml) crushed tomatoes, season with salt to taste, and pour over the casserole. Cover with as much shredded Monterey Jack or cheddar cheese as you feel is appropriate and bake until bubbly, about 30 minutes. Let settle for a few minutes before scooping out servings.

Whole Grain Congee with Crisp Panko Chicken

WITH *sweet chile-garlic sauce*
ALSO GOOD WITH *green apple rojak* (PAGE 158)
OR *grizzled asparagus* (PAGE 201)

Use a good homemade stock here, if possible, because its flavor will be the basis of this simple porridge. I like the nutty, textured quality of whole grains in this dish, but feel free to use white rice or a combination of white and brown rice. And if frying chicken at the last minute is not something you want to tackle on an evening, a handful of just about any leftover meat pulled from the bone, or from a store-bought rotisserie chicken, is a perfectly acceptable substitute.

IN THE MORNING
Load up the cooker and, if you have time, prep the chicken and set up your frying station.

IN THE EVENING
Pan-fry the chicken.

---

1 cup (about 190 g) whole grains: farro, pearled or pot barley, brown jasmine rice, or a combination

2 quarts (2 L) good-quality stock, such as beef stock (page 243) or chicken or turkey stock (page 240), or a combination

1 tablespoon Shaoxing wine

1 tablespoon minced fresh ginger

2 well-trimmed skinless, boneless chicken breasts

¼ cup (30 g) all-purpose flour

Salt and freshly ground black pepper

1 cup (80 g) panko bread crumbs, or more, if needed

1 large egg

About 6 tablespoons (90 ml) vegetable oil

Chinese light soy sauce

3 scallions, thinly sliced

¼ cup (10 g) chopped fresh cilantro

Toasted sesame seeds

MORNING

Rinse the grains in a sieve under running water, then dump them into the slow cooker. Add the stock, wine, and ginger. Cover and cook on low for 8 hours.

MORNING OR EVENING

Cut the chicken into strips ½ inch (12 mm) thick. If doing this in the morning, put in a covered container and refrigerate. Put the flour in a medium bowl or on a plate and sprinkle with a pinch of salt and a grinding of black pepper. Put the panko in a second bowl or plate. Line a plate with paper towels and set aside.

EVENING

In a small bowl, whisk the egg together with 1 tablespoon water and a pinch of salt; set it near the flour and panko. In batches, toss the chicken strips in the flour to coat, then in the egg, then in the panko. In a large skillet or sauté pan, heat half of the oil over medium-high heat. When it shimmers, add half of the chicken strips. Cook, turning with tongs, until browned all over and cooked through, about 5 minutes total; transfer to the paper towels to drain. Grab a paper towel with the tongs and wipe out the pan to remove any blackened bits. Cook the remaining chicken. If you'd like, coarsely chop the chicken strips on a board (it makes for easier eating, if a less attractive bowl).

Whisk the rice mixture in the cooker and season with soy sauce to taste. Serve in bowls, topped with the fried chicken, scallions, cilantro, and sesame seeds.

RECIPE CONTINUES...

Sweet chile-garlic sauce

With the widely available Fresno chiles, this makes a slightly hot but not blistering sauce. If you want more heat, replace some or all of the sweet bell pepper with an equal weight of hot peppers, replace the Fresno chiles with red jalapeño or serrano chiles, if you have them, or just stir in a little ground cayenne.

- **10 ounces (280 g) fresh hot red chiles, such as Fresno**
- **1 (7 ounces/200 g) red bell pepper**
- **2 cloves garlic**
- **½ cup (120 ml) cider vinegar or distilled white vinegar**
- **¼ cup (55 g) sugar**
- **1 teaspoon salt**

MORNING

Stem and seed the chiles and pepper, and coarsely chop them and the garlic. Put the chiles, pepper, and garlic in a food processor and pulse until finely minced. Transfer to a saucepan and add the vinegar, sugar, and salt. Bring to a boil (watching the pan to make sure it doesn't boil over), then lower the heat and simmer briskly, stirring occasionally, until much of the liquid has reduced, about 10 minutes. If you'd like, use an immersion blender to puree the sauce—tilt the pan so you can submerge the blender head. Transfer to a clean heatproof, nonreactive container (such as a canning jar), let cool for a few minutes, then cover and refrigerate for up to several weeks.

Chicken and Red Rice

WITH *quickie cilantro-lime topping*
ALSO GOOD WITH *two peas with marjoram* (PAGE 97) OR *seared peppers* (PAGE 104)

If you have rice left over from another meal, this is a good way to use it. Otherwise, just cook 1 cup (185 g) rice in 1½ cups (355 ml) water, either in the morning or evening.

IN THE MORNING
Load the cooker.

IN THE EVENING
Add the cooked rice.

2 pounds (910 g) well-trimmed boneless, skinless chicken thighs

2 teaspoons ground cumin

2 teaspoons paprika

1 teaspoon dried oregano

1½ teaspoons salt, or more to taste

1 (14.5-ounce/411-g) can crushed tomatoes

3 cups (615 g) cooked long-grain rice

MORNING
Put the chicken in the slow cooker. In a cup, mix together the cumin, paprika, oregano, and salt, then sprinkle the mixture over the chicken and toss to coat. Fold in the tomatoes. Cover and cook on low for 8 hours.

EVENING
Turn the cooker to high. Season with more salt, if needed, then gently fold in the rice, cover until heated through, then serve.

Quickie cilantro-lime topping

½ bunch fresh cilantro, chopped

1 jalapeño chile, chopped, seeded if you'd like less heat

½ onion, chopped

Juice of 1 lime

Salt

MORNING OR EVENING
In a mini food processor, pulse the cilantro, jalapeño, onion, and lime juice until very finely chopped, scraping the side of the bowl once or twice. Season with salt to taste. Cover and refrigerate if making this in the morning. Serve cold or at room temperature.

Chicken and Andouille Jambalaya

WITH *chayote with garlic buttered bread crumbs*
ALSO GOOD WITH *quick-cooked shredded collards* (PAGE 161) OR *fried okra* (PAGE 86)

Instead of—or in addition to—the andouille, which is quickly sautéed and added in the evening, you could use peeled and deveined shrimp, either whole or diced.

IN THE MORNING
Sauté the onion and load up the cooker.

IN THE EVENING
Cook the andouille and rice and fold them into the chicken mixture.

1½ to 2 pounds (680 to 910 g) well-trimmed boneless, skinless chicken thighs

1 (28-ounce/794-g) can whole tomatoes

1 tablespoon vegetable oil

1 onion, diced

Salt

2 cloves garlic, chopped

2 to 3 teaspoons Cajun seasoning blend (one that includes salt is fine)

2 ribs celery, cut into ¾-inch (2-cm) pieces

1 green bell pepper, cut into ¾-inch (2-cm) pieces

1½ cups (275 g) long-grain white rice

1 (6- to 8-ounce/170- to 225-g) link andouille sausage, diced

MORNING
Put the chicken in the slow cooker and add the tomatoes and their juices, crushing them with your hand as you add them.

In a large skillet or sauté pan, heat the oil over medium-high heat. When it shimmers, add the onion and a pinch of salt and cook, stirring, until translucent, about 5 minutes. Add the garlic and cook for 1 minute, then scrape into the cooker. Add the Cajun seasoning, celery, and bell pepper. Cover and cook on low for 8 hours.

EVENING

Season the sauce in the cooker with salt or more Cajun seasoning, if needed.

Put the rice in a sieve and rinse very well under running water. In a 2-quart (2-L) saucepan over medium-high heat, cook the sausage, stirring frequently, until nicely browned, 2 to 3 minutes. Transfer to the cooker. Ladle 2 cups (480 ml) of the liquid from the cooker into the hot saucepan and stir in the rice. Bring to a boil, then cover and cook over the lowest heat until the rice is tender and has absorbed all the liquid, 15 to 18 minutes (it won't be fluffy like regular cooked rice); add a little more liquid as it cooks, if needed. Gently fold the cooked rice into the chicken mixture in the cooker (the chicken will fall apart into bite-size pieces) and serve.

Chayote with garlic buttered bread crumbs

Sautéed chayote, also called mirliton, has an appealing crisp texture, but is fairly bland—hence the large quantity of garlic here in the crunchy bread crumb topping.

2 chayote squashes (about 1½ pounds/680 g)

3 tablespoons unsalted butter

3 cloves garlic, minced

½ cup (40 g) coarse bread crumbs

Salt

MORNING OR EVENING

Peel the chayote (hold it with a paper towel as you do—it'll be slippery), then cut it in half through the dent in the bottom. Scrape out the seed and pithy center with a spoon. Cut each half in half lengthwise, then slice ¼ inch (6 mm) thick. Put in a container and refrigerate if doing this in the morning.

EVENING

In a large skillet or sauté pan, melt 2 tablespoons of the butter over medium-high heat. Add the garlic, then the bread crumbs and a pinch of salt and cook, stirring, until deeply browned, 2 to 3 minutes. Scrape into a bowl and set aside.

Return the skillet to medium-high heat, add the remaining 1 tablespoon butter, the chayote, and ½ teaspoon salt, and cook, tossing frequently, until tender but still crisp, about 5 minutes. Toss in the garlic bread crumbs, then transfer to a serving bowl and serve.

A Chicken Gumbo

WITH *fried okra*

ALSO GOOD WITH *tangy potato salad* (PAGE 36) OR *retro garlic bread* (PAGE 164)

If you have toasted flour left over from the Romanian chicken stew on page 88, you can use about 6 tablespoons (about 35 g) of it here instead of the roux, though it will yield a somewhat less dark and rich gumbo. I find that gumbo is great on its own, but if you have the energy you might wish to cook a pot of long-grain white or brown rice and serve a small scoop in each bowl to ladle the gumbo around.

IN THE MORNING
Brown the chicken and make the roux.

IN THE EVENING
Blend the roux into the liquid and season the gumbo.

2 pounds (910 g) well-trimmed boneless, skinless chicken thighs, cut into large pieces

1 teaspoon dried thyme

Salt and freshly ground black pepper

1 to 2 tablespoons plus ½ cup (120 ml) vegetable oil

½ onion, diced

1 (28-ounce/794-g) can whole tomatoes with their juice

2 small ribs celery, cut into ½-inch (12-mm) pieces

4 ounces (115 g) smoked ham, pulled into shreds or chopped (you can cut the meat off a ham hock, if you'd like)

1 bay leaf

1 green bell pepper, cut into 1-inch (2.5-cm) pieces

½ cup (65 g) all-purpose flour

Ground cayenne and/or Cajun seasoning blend

Filé powder (see Note)

MORNING

Toss the chicken with the thyme, several pinches of salt, and several grindings of pepper. In a large skillet or sauté pan, heat the 1 tablespoon oil over medium-high heat. When it shimmers, add the chicken (work in batches if necessary) and cook, turning with a thin metal spatula, until the pieces are browned on one or two sides, about 5 minutes per batch. Transfer to the slow cooker.

To the skillet, add the onion and a little more oil, if needed, and cook over medium heat until just softened, about 3 minutes. Pour some of the tomato juices from the can into the hot skillet, scraping up any browned bits, then scrape into the cooker and add the tomatoes, crushing them with your hand as you do. Add the celery, ham, and bay leaf and put the bell pepper on top of everything. Cover and cook on low for 8 hours.

RECIPE CONTINUES...

Make a roux: In a large clean and dry skillet or sauté pan, combine the remaining ½ cup (120 ml) oil and the flour. Place over medium heat and cook, stirring almost constantly with a heatproof spatula and/or a whisk, until it's the color of coffee with just a touch of cream, about 15 minutes—be careful not to splash it onto yourself or others (it's hot), and watch it closely so it doesn't burn. Scrape into a heatproof bowl and let cool completely.

EVENING

Using a slotted spoon, remove most of the solid ingredients (chicken, vegetables) from the gumbo to a bowl. Pour off the layer of excess oil that will have risen to the top of the roux, then use an immersion blender to blend the sludgy roux into the liquid in the cooker. Return the chicken and vegetables to the cooker, season with more salt and cayenne and/or Cajun seasoning, if needed, and serve with a small bowl of filé so people can add it to their gumbo if they'd like.

NOTE: If you have access to sassafras trees and a microwave oven or dehydrator, it's definitely worth making your own filé; it is so much more flavorful and vibrant than store-bought (though the thickening power is about the same, and filé is available in most grocery stores in the spice section).

Pick tender young sassafras leaves, rinse well, and pat dry. To dry in a microwave oven: In batches, arrange the leaves in a single layer between two paper towels, set the sandwich on the turntable, and cook on full power in 15- to 30-second bursts until the leaves are crisp and completely dry. Grind in a spice mill or with a mortar and pestle and, if you'd like, sift it to remove any little bits of ribs or stems.

Fried okra

This makes a skilletful, which should be plenty for 3 or 4 people who are also eating bowls of hearty gumbo. If you want to double the recipe, you'll have to do it in two skillets, or in two batches, straining or replacing the cooking oil to remove little blackened bits.

¼ cup (30 g) all-purpose flour

¼ cup (45 g) fine cornmeal

½ teaspoon salt, plus more for sprinkling

Good pinch ground cayenne

1 cup (240 ml) buttermilk or half-and-half

8 ounces (255 g) okra, stems trimmed off, cut into rounds ¾ inch (2 cm) thick

Vegetable oil for shallow-frying

MORNING

In a medium bowl, combine the flour, cornmeal, salt, and cayenne. Toss the okra in the buttermilk, drain, then toss in the flour mixture to coat, then spread on a waxed paper–lined tray and put in the freezer. Set a plate lined with paper towels near the stovetop and pour about ⅛ inch (3 mm) oil into a large skillet or sauté pan and set aside for evening.

EVENING

Heat the oil over medium-high heat. When it shimmers, add the frozen okra and cook, gently stirring with a slotted spoon every couple of minutes, until nicely browned all over, 5 to 7 minutes. Transfer to the paper towels to drain, sprinkle with salt, and serve.

Romanian-Style Chicken and Noodles

WITH *pan-seared green beans*

ALSO GOOD WITH *simple garlic spinach* (PAGE 224) OR *Parmesan roasted broccoli spears* (PAGE 182)

I read about this dish (in the same category as paprikash and the Albanian dish called çervish or qervish) in Clifford A. Wright's invaluable collection of classic recipes, *Real Stew*. Thickened with coffee-dark toasted flour and subtly fragrant with allspice, this makes a comforting winter meal over noodles or rice.

IN THE MORNING
Sauté the onions. If you have time, toast the flour.

IN THE EVENING
Whisk in the flour and cook the noodles.

---

2 pounds (910 g) well-trimmed boneless, skinless chicken thighs

1 tablespoon hot paprika

Salt and freshly ground black pepper

1 tablespoon unsalted butter

2 onions, sliced

½ teaspoon allspice berries

1 cup (240 ml) white wine

4 tablespoons (60 ml) tomato paste

1 bay leaf

12 tablespoons all-purpose flour

Wide egg noodles

MORNING

Put the chicken in the slow cooker and toss it with the paprika and ¾ teaspoon salt.

In a large skillet or sauté pan, melt the butter over medium-high heat. Add the onions, allspice, a pinch of salt, and several grindings of pepper and cook, stirring frequently, until the onions are tender and a little wilted, about 5 minutes. Pour in the wine and cook for 5 minutes longer, then scrape the onion mixture into the cooker over the chicken. In a cup, stir together the tomato paste and 1 cup (240 ml) water and pour over the onions. Tuck in the bay leaf. Cover and cook on low for 8 hours.

MORNING OR EVENING

Place a small skillet or sauté pan over medium-high heat and add the flour. Cook, stirring and tossing frequently (then constantly toward the end), for 7 to 10 minutes, until the flour is very fragrant and the color of a coffee with two creams. Transfer to a piece of waxed paper if doing this in the morning.

EVENING

Bring a large pot of salted water to a boil. Add the noodles and cook until al dente; drain.

Turn the cooker to high. Using a slotted spoon, transfer the chicken to a bowl. Sift the toasted flour into the sauce in the cooker a little at a time and stir or whisk it in, adding just enough to thicken the sauce slightly, about 6 tablespoons. (Save the remainder for another use, such as the gumbo on page 85.) Season the sauce with more salt and pepper, if needed, then return the chicken to the sauce and serve over the noodles.

Pan-seared green beans

1 tablespoon unsalted butter

12 ounces (340 g) green beans, trimmed

Salt

EVENING

In a large skillet or sauté pan, melt the butter over medium-high heat. Add the green beans, spreading them as evenly as possible in the pan, and sprinkle with a pinch of salt. Cook for 2 minutes without disturbing them, then toss, sprinkle with salt, and cook for 2 minutes longer.

Pour in ¼ cup (60 ml) water, cover, and cook for 4 minutes, then uncover and cook, tossing occasionally, until the beans are tender and blackened in spots, about 3 minutes longer. Serve.

Handy stew thickeners, clockwise from tip right: toasted flour, filé powder, stale corn tortillas, dried unsweetened coconut, masa harina, coconut milk powder.

Chicken in Shortcut Mole

WITH *spinach and garlic rice*
ALSO GOOD WITH *cumin spiced millet* (PAGE 231)
OR *brown rice and peas* (PAGE 235; OMIT THE COCONUT MILK AND ALLSPICE)

I've made wonderfully complex mole sauces that required several rounds of straining and blending and three solid days in the kitchen to complete, and I've used bottled store-bought mole that was convenient but nothing to write home about flavor-wise. This, I think, is a compromise between the two: It has exactly what I want in a mole (a little heat, bitterness, a slight sweetness, a silky texture, and, if you use the hoja de santa, a subtle herby fragrance), but is much less work than you'd expect.

IN THE MORNING
Rehydrate and puree the chiles and sauce ingredients.

IN THE EVENING
Add the cookies and puree again.

4 pounds (1.8 kg) bone-in chicken thighs, skin pulled off and excess fat trimmed

2 ounces (55 g) dried guajillo chiles (about 8), stemmed and broken into pieces

6 dried chiles de árbol, stemmed

3 cups (720 ml) boiling water

2 tablets Abuelita Mexican chocolate (see Notes)

½ cup (120 ml) unsweetened peanut butter

½ onion, chopped

3 cloves garlic, chopped

2 teaspoons salt, or more to taste

Palm-size piece dried hoja santa (optional, see Notes)

6 to 8 plain Maria cookies (see Notes)

Avocado, lime, and queso fresco (optional, for serving)

MORNING
Put the chicken in the slow cooker. Put the dried guajillos and chiles de árbol in a blender and pour the boiling water over them. Let soak for at least 10 minutes, until the chiles are softened. Add the chocolate, peanut butter, onion, garlic, salt, and hoja santa, if using, and puree until very smooth. Set a fine-mesh sieve over the cooker and pour in the chile puree, pushing the puree and liquid through with a spatula; discard the bits of skin and seeds in the sieve. Turn the chicken to coat with the sauce. Cover and cook on low for 8 hours.

EVENING

Turn the cooker to high. Using a slotted spoon, transfer the chicken to a bowl (pull out and discard the bones, if you'd like). Using an immersion blender, puree the sauce again, crumbling in the cookies, until very smooth. Add enough cookies to thicken and sweeten the mole to your liking. Season with more salt, if needed, then return the chicken to the mole and serve.

NOTES: You can find Abuelita in most supermarkets, either in the Mexican foods section or with the hot chocolate and cocoa mixes.

Hoja santa is an herb that adds a mild anise flavor to simmered sauces like this one; look for it in Mexican grocery stores.

Crisp, bland, lightly sweetened Maria cookies (sometimes labeled "Marie biscuits") are readily available in most supermarkets, with the Mexican foods.

Spinach and garlic rice

- **1½ cups (275 g) long-grain white rice**
- **4 ounces (115 g) spinach**
- **1 cup (40 g) chopped fresh cilantro (optional)**
- **1 tablespoon olive oil**
- **2 cloves garlic, chopped**
- **¾ teaspoon salt**

EVENING

Rinse the rice well in a sieve under running water and set aside to drain.

Put the spinach, cilantro, and 2 cups (480 ml) water in a blender and puree until fairly smooth.

In a 2-quart (2-L) saucepan, heat the oil over medium-high heat. When it shimmers, add the garlic and cook, stirring, until golden, about 1 minute. Add the rice and stir for 30 seconds, then add the salt and the spinach mixture, scraping as much of it from the blender as you can. Stir well and bring to a boil over high heat. Stir again, cover, and cook on the lowest heat for 15 to 20 minutes, until the rice is tender (check after 15 minutes; much of the spinach will have floated to the top, but that's fine—just dig a few grains out with a fork to test them). Remove from the heat and let stand for 3 minutes, then fold and fluff with a spatula or fork and serve.

Chicken "Cobbler"

WITH *two peas with marjoram*
ALSO GOOD WITH *herb salad* (PAGE 31) OR *lemon kale* (PAGE 124)

While the natural recipe to put here would be chicken and dumplings, in which a soft, biscuit-like dough is dropped directly onto the simmering chicken stew and then steamed until done, I like the version in my first slow cooker book so much I don't even want to change it. But I think this cobbler is even better. The stew is a classic flour-thickened and cold-weather-vegetable-heavy affair, and the topping—though you don't even have to put it on top—is a contrasting fluffy, crusty cheddar biscuit.

This might seem like a complicated recipe, but it's simpler than it looks. You can even substitute bakery-bought biscuits for homemade, or just leave them off and serve the hearty stew as is, perhaps with some good bread.

IN THE MORNING
Brown the chicken and onion. If you have time, mix the biscuit dry ingredients and refrigerate.

IN THE EVENING
Finish and bake the drop biscuits. Thicken the stew, if needed.

For the stew:

¼ cup (30 g) all-purpose flour, or more, if needed

Salt and freshly ground black pepper

2 pounds (910 g) well-trimmed boneless, skinless chicken thighs, each cut roughly in half

½ onion, diced

1 tablespoon schmaltz (page 251) or olive oil

1½ cups (360 ml) chicken or turkey stock (page 240)

2 carrots, diced

2 ribs celery, diced

1 Yukon Gold or peeled russet potato, diced

1 bay leaf

¼ cup (13 g) chopped fresh parsley

For the drop biscuits:

2½ cups (320 g) all-purpose flour

1 tablespoon baking powder

½ teaspoon salt

4 tablespoons (55 g) unsalted butter, cut into pieces

4 ounces (115 g) extra-sharp cheddar cheese, shredded

1⅓ cups (315 ml) half-and-half or milk

RECIPE CONTINUES...

Start the stew: In the slow cooker, combine the flour, 1 teaspoon salt, and several grindings of pepper. Toss the chicken and onion in the mixture to coat. In a large skillet or sauté pan, heat the schmaltz over medium-high heat. When it shimmers, add half of the chicken and onion and cook, turning occasionally, until the chicken is golden on both sides, about 5 minutes total. Scrape into a bowl and brown the remaining chicken and onion mixture (it's okay if some of the flour dredge remains in the cooker). Return all of the chicken and onion to the cooker. Pour ½ cup (120 ml) of the stock into the hot skillet, scraping up any browned bits, then pour the liquid into the cooker. Add the carrots, celery, potato, bay leaf, and the remaining 1 cup (240 ml) stock. Cover and cook on low for 8 hours.

Start the drop biscuits: In a medium bowl, combine the flour, baking powder, and salt. Add the butter and pinch it in with your fingertips. Add the cheese and toss to combine. If doing this in the morning, put the bowl in the refrigerator.

Finish the drop biscuits: Preheat the oven to 400°F (205°C). Line a baking sheet with parchment paper. Stir the half-and-half into the flour mixture until just incorporated—don't overmix the dough. Drop six to eight mounds of the dough onto the prepared baking sheet. Bake until golden, 15 to 17 minutes.

Finish the stew: Fold in the parsley. Season the stew with salt and lots of pepper. If it's very liquid, ladle some of the liquid into a bowl and whisk in 2 or more tablespoons flour, then gently stir it back into the stew.

Two peas with marjoram

1 tablespoon butter or olive oil

4 ounces (115 g) sugar snap peas, each cut in half on the diagonal

12 ounces (340 g) shelled fresh or frozen English peas

Scant ½ teaspoon salt

A couple of small sprigs fresh marjoram

In a large skillet or sauté pan, melt the butter over medium-high heat. Add the sugar snap peas, English peas, and salt and cook, tossing frequently, until all the peas are just tender, about 5 minutes. Add about 2 tablespoons water at the end of cooking, and tear in the marjoram. Serve immediately.

Chicken Tikka Masala

WITH *fresh sweet mango and date relish*

ALSO GOOD WITH *sweet tomato chutney* (PAGE 39) OR *Mom's naan* (PAGE 109)

I really, really wanted to get this recipe right, because it's such a crowd-pleasing favorite that in its non–slow cooker forms relies a great deal on techniques and processes that don't necessarily translate to slow cookerdom. I went through probably half a dozen trials and finally came up with something I was quite happy with. Then my friend Leda tried out my recipe for her husband and her mother-in-law, who are accomplished cooks from Hyderabad. They were *not impressed*; they had some helpful suggestions, and I headed back to the kitchen for more experimenting. The results, I have to admit, were worth it.

IN THE MORNING
Sauté the aromatics and spices.

IN THE EVENING
Blend in the yogurt and cook the rice.

- 1 tablespoon ground coriander
- 2 teaspoons paprika
- 1 teaspoon ground cumin
- 1 tablespoon vegetable oil or ghee (page 254)
- 3 coins fresh ginger, chopped
- 2 cloves garlic, chopped
- 1 jalapeño or serrano chile, chopped, seeded if you'd like less heat
- 1 (14.5-ounce/411-g) can diced tomatoes with their juices
- 2 pounds (910 g) well-trimmed boneless, skinless chicken thighs
- ½ cup (120 ml) plain Greek yogurt (preferably full-fat)
- ¼ cup (60 ml) heavy cream
- 2 tablespoons chopped fresh cilantro (optional)
- 2 cups (360 g) basmati rice
- Pinch of salt

MORNING

In a small cup, combine the coriander, paprika, and cumin. In a large skillet or sauté pan, heat the oil over medium heat. When it shimmers, add the ginger, garlic, and chile and cook, stirring, for 1 to 2 minutes, until fragrant and the garlic is just starting to brown. Add the spices and stir for 30 seconds. Remove from the heat and add the tomatoes and their juices, stirring to mix all the aromatics into the tomatoes. Scrape the mixture into the slow cooker and add the chicken, turning to coat it with the sauce and then folding the thighs on themselves and tucking them into a single layer in the pot. Cover and cook on low for 8 hours.

HAVE SLICED AND MINCED GINGER READY

If all the meals in which I use ginger (I do use it a lot) involved first peeling and mincing or slicing or grating fresh ginger, I'd be much better friends with the local pizza delivery people. When I have a moment and the energy, I'll peel a big hand of ginger with the edge of a spoon. I'll slice half of it into coins, put them in a canning jar, cover them with something in the Shaoxing/dry sherry/vermouth family, put the lid on, and stick the jar in the refrigerator, where the ginger will keep almost indefinitely. I'll then just fish out coins with a fork, give them a quick rinse, and use them as if they were fresh. The rest of the ginger I'll chop up and put in the mini food processor with a little water, pulse to finely mince it, then dollop teaspoon- or tablespoon-size mounds on a piece of waxed paper and freeze them until solid; then I'll peel the mounds off the paper and store them in a freezer bag. The ginger can be used straight from the freezer in most cases.

EVENING

Turn the cooker to high. Using a slotted spoon, transfer the chicken to a bowl (it will be very tender and almost falling apart, and it's okay if some of the vegetables come with it, and if small bits of chicken remain in the cooker). With an immersion blender, blend the yogurt and cream into the sauce in the cooker until smooth. Stir in the cilantro, if you'd like. Return the chicken to the sauce and cover while you cook the rice.

Put the rice in a sieve and rinse very well under running water. Dump into a 2-quart (2-L) saucepan and add 2¼ cups (540 ml) water and a good pinch of salt. Bring to a boil over high heat, stir once to unstick any grains from the bottom of the pan, then cover and cook over the lowest heat for 14 minutes, or until all the water is absorbed and the rice is tender. Let stand, covered, for 3 minutes, then fluff with a fork or spatula. Serve with the chicken.

Fresh sweet mango and date relish

2 small ripe mangoes, preferably Ataulfo, peeled and diced

2 tablespoons fresh lime juice

1 teaspoon sugar

1 heaping teaspoon minced fresh mint

¼ cup (35 g) finely chopped dates

MORNING

Combine all the ingredients in a bowl and mash some of the mangoes a bit with a fork. Cover and refrigerate until ready to serve (up to 2 days).

Chicken Tinga

WITH *quick-pickled vegetables*
ALSO GOOD WITH *spinach and garlic rice* (PAGE 91) OR *chili garnishes* (PAGE 172)

This is one of the few recipes in which it's possible to use chicken breasts (eight hours in the slow cooker is not easy on that lean cut): The meat is shredded after cooking and the stew is saucy enough that the breasts can withstand a bit of overcooking. However, feel free to substitute thighs, or even pork shoulder.

IN THE MORNING
Load up the cooker.

IN THE EVENING
Shred the chicken and warm the tortillas.

½ **large onion, diced**

2 **cloves garlic, chopped**

½ **(7-ounce/198-g) can chipotle chiles in adobo, pureed or minced, with sauce**

2 **tablespoons tomato paste**

1½ **cups (360 ml) chicken stock (page 240) or water**

2 **pounds (910 g) boneless, skinless chicken breasts**

Salt and freshly ground black pepper

Corn or flour tortillas, warmed (see Note)

MORNING
Put the onion, garlic, chipotles, tomato paste, stock, chicken, 1 teaspoon salt, and several grindings of pepper in the slow cooker. Cover and cook on low for 8 hours.

EVENING
Using two forks, shred the chicken in the cooker. Taste and season with more salt and pepper, if needed. Serve the tinga with the warm tortillas.

NOTE: The easiest way to warm tortillas—flour or corn—is to use a large cast-iron griddle and heat several at once, or use one or two skillets or sauté pans. Heat the griddle or skillet until a drop of water on the surface evaporates immediately. Put the tortilla on the dry griddle and cook for a minute or two, flip and cook for another minute or two, then flip one more time and press on the tortilla gently with a spatula or the back of a spoon to help it puff up a bit (this seems counterintuitive, but it works). Stack the tortillas in a towel-lined bowl, fold the towel over to keep them warm, and repeat.

If you're lacking griddle space or time, heat two tortillas at once in the same spot: Put two stacked tortillas down on the griddle and cook for a minute, then flip the stack over. While the second tortilla cooks on the bottom, flip the top tortilla so the uncooked side is facing up. Flip the stack again, and now flip the tortilla that's on top. Flip the stack one more time, and both tortillas will be heated on both sides.

RECIPE CONTINUES...

Quick-pickled vegetables

This makes about a quart or liter of vegetables, more than you'll need for a single family meal, but they keep well in the fridge and are excellent to have on hand for snacking, stuffing into sandwiches or quesadillas, or serving alongside any dish that needs a vinegary-tart accent.

About 1 pound (455 g) mixed vegetables, such as 2 Persian cucumbers, 4 small carrots, ½ red onion, and 1 serrano chile

1½ cups (360 ml) rice vinegar

2 teaspoons salt

2 teaspoons sugar

MORNING

Cut the vegetables into sticks about 2 inches (5 cm) long and ½ inch (12 mm) thick at the widest. Pack them into a quart- or liter-size canning jar or other heat-proof, nonreactive container. In a small saucepan, bring the vinegar, salt, and sugar to a boil, stirring to dissolve the salt and sugar, then pour it over the vegetables and press them down to cover them with the pickling liquid. Let cool to room temperature, then cover and refrigerate until evening. Serve cold. The pickles will keep for several weeks in the refrigerator.

Chicken with Coconut Milk and Achiote

WITH *seared peppers*
ALSO GOOD WITH *collard slaw* (PAGE 115) OR *brown rice and peas* (PAGE 235)

Stewed chicken with achiote, a spice that is used more for color than anything else (it's what gives cheddar cheese its orange tint), is a staple of Central and South American home cooking. Most versions I've seen do feature coconut milk, but you could try it with a cup (240 ml) or so of chicken stock (page 240) instead.

IN THE MORNING
Load up the cooker.

IN THE EVENING
Cook the rice and puree the sauce.

1 (13.5-ounce/400-ml) can coconut milk

1 cup (125 g) chopped sweet peppers

1 shallot, chopped

1 teaspoon ground achiote (annatto)

1 teaspoon ground cumin

1 teaspoon ancho chile powder

2 teaspoons adobo seasoning, such as Goya (see Note)

2 pounds (910 g) well-trimmed boneless, skinless chicken thighs

2 cups (370 g) long-grain white rice

Salt

2 tablespoons chopped fresh cilantro

MORNING

In the slow cooker, combine the coconut milk, sweet peppers, shallot, achiote, cumin, chile powder, and adobo, then add the chicken and turn to coat it with the coconut milk mixture. Cover and cook on low for 8 hours.

EVENING

Put the rice in a sieve and rinse very well under running water. Dump into a 2-quart (2-L) saucepan and add 2 ¼ cups (540 ml) water and a good pinch of salt. Bring to a boil over high heat, stir once to unstick any grains from the bottom of the pan, then cover and cook over the lowest heat for 14 minutes, or until all the water is absorbed and the rice is tender. Let stand, covered, for 3 minutes, then fluff with a fork or spatula.

Using a slotted spoon, transfer the chicken to a bowl. With an immersion blender, puree the sauce in the cooker. Season with more salt, if needed, and stir in the cilantro. Return the chicken to the sauce and serve with the rice.

NOTE: Goya adobo sin pimenta is one of the very few store-bought spice blends I use, simply because it's so efficient and versatile (and no more expensive than making your own). I was somewhat validated to see it being dusted liberally all over the griddled meats at my favorite taco and torta lunch counter in Port Chester, New York. (Could be that's why it's my favorite.) You can substitute 1 teaspoon salt, ½ teaspoon onion powder, ½ teaspoon granulated garlic, and a pinch of dried oregano.

RECIPE CONTINUES...

Seared peppers

4 Anaheim peppers, seeded

2 red, orange, or yellow bell peppers, seeded

1 sweet onion

2 tablespoons olive oil

Salt

MORNING OR EVENING

Cut the Anaheim and bell peppers and onion into ½-inch (12-mm) strips. Cover and refrigerate if doing this in the morning.

EVENING

In a large skillet or sauté pan, or two medium ones, heat the oil over high heat. When it's almost smoking, add the peppers and onion and a good pinch of salt and cook, tossing frequently, until the peppers and onion are nicely charred in spots and just tender, 5 to 7 minutes. Serve hot.

Chicken with Tart Pineapple, Coconut, and Cashews

WITH *basic coconut rice*

ALSO GOOD WITH *soy-steamed broccoli* (PAGE 199) OR *lemongrass rice* (PAGE 211)

A few months ago, in a Malaysian cookbook (see page 162) I read about a curry-like dish with sour carambola (starfruit) as the base, and ever since then my local (and even nonlocal) grocery stores have declined to restock the starfruit area of the "exotic" produce section—I've yet to try it. I was taken by the idea of using a tart fruit in a savory dish, though, so I came up with this one in which chicken is cooked in a puree of fresh pineapple, aromatics, and thickening ingredients like dried coconut and cashews.

Blend the sauce
ingredients.
If you have time,
toast the coconut
for the topping.

IN THE EVENING
Puree the sauce again.

1 stalk lemongrass, tops
and tough outer leaves
removed, chopped

5 coins peeled fresh ginger,
chopped

2 cloves garlic, chopped

6 tablespoons (30 g) grated
unsweetened coconut

½ cup (65 g) roasted unsalted
cashews

1 tablespoon paprika

2 teaspoons ground coriander

1 teaspoon ground cumin

Salt

¼ pineapple, peeled, cored,
and chopped

½ (13.5-ounce/400-ml) can
coconut milk

2 tablespoons brown sugar,
or more to taste

1 tablespoon tamarind
concentrate, such as
Tamicon brand, or more to
taste

3 to 4 pounds (1.4 to 1.8 kg)
well-trimmed skinless
chicken thighs, with or
without the bones

MORNING

In a good blender or a food processor, combine the lemongrass,
ginger, garlic, 3 tablespoons of the
coconut, the cashews, paprika,
coriander, cumin, and 2 teaspoons
salt and blend until finely ground,
scraping down the side of the bowl
as needed. Add the pineapple,
coconut milk, brown sugar, and
tamarind and blend until smooth.
Pour into the slow cooker, add the
chicken, and turn to coat. Cover
and cook on low for 8 hours.

MORNING OR EVENING

In a small saucepan, toast the
remaining 3 tablespoons coconut
over medium heat, stirring constantly, until golden and fragrant,
about 3 minutes, then scrape into a
small bowl and set aside.

EVENING

Using a slotted spoon, transfer the
chicken to a bowl (pull out and
discard the bones, if you'd like).
With an immersion blender, puree
the sauce in the cooker until very
smooth. Season with more brown
sugar or tamarind, if needed (it
should be more tart than sweet),
return the chicken to the cooker,
and serve, sprinkled with the
toasted coconut.

Basic coconut rice

*If you want to use up the can of
coconut milk from the recipe above,
use ½ (13.5-ounce) can coconut milk
and 1 full can water instead of the
other way around; it'll be a lighter
dish but won't leave you with an
opened can.*

2 cups (390 g) medium-grain
rice, such as Calrose rice

1 (13.5-ounce/400-ml) can
coconut milk

Salt

EVENING

Put the rice in a sieve and rinse
very well under running water.
Dump into a 2-quart (2-L) saucepan and add the coconut milk, ½
can (200 ml) of water, and a good
pinch of salt. Bring to a boil over
high heat, stir once to unstick
any grains from the bottom of the
pan, then cover and cook over the
lowest heat for 14 minutes, or until
most the liquid is absorbed and the
rice is tender. Let stand, covered,
for 5 minutes, then fluff with a fork
or spatula and serve.

Fried Nuts and Seeds Chicken Curry

WITH *Mom's naan*

ALSO GOOD WITH *lemony seared okra* (PAGE 229) OR *bok choy brown basmati rice* (PAGE 111)

Fragrant with coriander and cinnamon, and enriched by coconut milk and fried nuts and sesame seeds, this is a special dish. The pale white sauce is lovely just pureed and spooned over the chicken, but for a more refined dish consider straining it for a velvety smooth mouthfeel.

IN THE MORNING
Fry the nuts and seeds.

IN THE EVENING
Puree the sauce.

½ onion, chopped

2 cloves garlic, chopped

5 coins fresh ginger, chopped

2 pounds (910 g) well-trimmed boneless, skinless chicken thighs

1 cup (about 130 g) nuts, such as whole almonds and/or whole cashews or halves and pieces

1 tablespoon vegetable oil or ghee (page 254)

1 tablespoon sesame seeds

1 tablespoon coriander seeds

1 teaspoon cumin seeds

½ teaspoon ground cinnamon

⅛ teaspoon ground cloves

A few gratings of nutmeg

1 (13.5-ounce/400-g) can coconut milk

Salt

MORNING

Put the onion, garlic, ginger, and chicken in the slow cooker. In a skillet or sauté pan, toast the nuts over medium heat, stirring, until just golden, about 3 minutes, then add the oil, sesame seeds, coriander seeds, cumin seeds, cinnamon, cloves, and nutmeg and stir until golden and fragrant, 1 to 2 minutes. Scrape into the cooker. Pour the coconut milk into the skillet and stir to scrape up any browned bits; bring to a boil, cook for 1 minute to reduce slightly, then pour into the cooker and add ¾ teaspoon salt. Cover and cook on low for 8 hours.

EVENING

Using a slotted spoon, transfer the chicken to a serving dish. With an immersion blender, puree the sauce in the cooker. Season with more salt, if needed, then spoon the sauce over the chicken (ladle it through a sieve, if you'd like a smoother sauce) and serve.

Mom's naan

Or, rather, my cheater's version: Mom uses a sourdough starter for hers, but I rarely think far enough ahead for that.

- 3½ cups (450 g) all-purpose flour, or more, if needed
- 1 cup (240 ml) warm water
- 2 teaspoons sugar
- 2 teaspoons instant yeast
- 2 tablespoons olive or vegetable oil
- ½ cup (120 ml) plain Greek yogurt (preferably full-fat)
- 1½ teaspoons salt
- Melted ghee or unsalted butter (optional)

MORNING

Put the flour in the bowl of a stand mixer (or a large bowl), make a well in the center and add the water, sugar, yeast, oil, and yogurt to the well. Mix with the dough hook (or by hand), adding the salt as you mix. Knead in the mixer on low speed (or by hand on a work surface) for 5 (or 10) minutes, until smooth, adding a little more flour, if needed. Transfer to a work surface and form into a ball. Cut into eight wedges and put the wedges on a floured baking sheet; cover with plastic wrap and set aside at cool room temperature or in the refrigerator for 8 hours.

EVENING

Preheat the oven to 450°F (230°C) and put a baking sheet in the oven to heat.

Using a small rolling pin or your hands, on a floured work surface, flatten the wedges into rough triangles about ¼ inch (6 mm) thick. Working quickly, remove the hot baking sheet from the oven, slap four of the naan triangles onto it (they should just fit), and return the sheet to the oven. Bake until nicely browned and puffed in spots, about 10 minutes, then remove to a bowl, brush with melted ghee if desired, and cover to keep warm while you reheat the baking sheet and shape and bake the remaining naan.

Kasoori Methi Chicken

WITH *bok choy brown basmati rice*
ALSO GOOD WITH *quick-cooked shredded collards* (PAGE 161) OR *Mom's naan* (PAGE 109)

You can certainly leave out the kasoori methi, a dried herb that's available in any Indian grocery store, but it gives this spiced tomato-based sauce such an unusual, fragrant headiness that I'd say it's well worth seeking out.

IN THE MORNING
Puree the sauce ingredients and load the cooker.

IN THE EVENING
Puree the sauce again.

1 (28-ounce/794-g) can whole tomatoes

1 small onion, chopped

3 coins fresh ginger

2 cloves garlic, chopped

2 teaspoons ground cumin

1 teaspoon ground coriander

½ teaspoon ground turmeric

2 tablespoons dried kasoori methi (fenugreek leaves)

Salt

2 pounds (910 g) well-trimmed boneless, skinless chicken thighs

Sliced fresh hot chiles

Lemon wedges

MORNING

Put the tomatoes, onion, ginger, garlic, cumin, coriander, turmeric, kasoori methi, and a large pinch of salt in the slow cooker. Use an immersion blender to puree the mixture; rinse off the blender head but keep it handy for evening use. Nestle the chicken thighs in the tomato mixture. Cover and cook on low for 8 hours.

EVENING

Using a slotted spoon, transfer the chicken to a bowl. Puree the sauce again with the immersion blender and season with salt to taste. Return the chicken to the cooker and cover until ready to serve. Serve with chiles and lemon wedges on the side.

Bok choy brown basmati rice

1 cup (180 g) brown basmati rice

Salt

1 tablespoon vegetable oil

1 coin fresh ginger, minced

1 teaspoon cumin seeds

8 ounces (225 g) bok choy, chopped

MORNING

Put the rice in a sieve and rinse under cold running water. Dump into a medium saucepan, add a pinch of salt and cold water to cover by about 1 inch (2.5 cm), and bring to a boil. Lower the heat and simmer for 15 minutes. Drain well in the sieve and rinse under cold running water and drain again. Rinse the pan with cold water to cool it down, then fill it with about 1 inch (2.5 cm) water and put a collapsible steamer basket in the pan. Dump the rice into the steamer basket. Cover and refrigerate.

EVENING

Transfer the rice pot from the refrigerator to the stovetop. Still covered, bring the water in the bottom to a boil and steam the rice until tender, about 15 minutes.

Meanwhile, in a large deep sauté pan or skillet, heat the oil over medium heat until it shimmers. Add the ginger and cumin and stir for 30 seconds. Add the bok choy and a generous pinch of salt and cook, stirring frequently, until the leaves are wilted and the thicker stems are just tender, 5 to 8 minutes. Remove from the heat. Carefully lift the steamer basket of rice from the pan and dump the rice into the bok choy. Turn with a spatula to combine the rice with the bok choy. Taste and season with salt, if needed. Serve.

LEFTOVER KASOORI METHI SAUCE?

If you have 2 cups (480 ml) or more (or if you can supplement whatever you have with a little more tomato puree), use it the next day in a quick stir-fry. In a large sauté pan or skillet, heat a slick of vegetable oil over medium-high heat until it shimmers. Cut half a block of extra-firm tofu into cubes and add them to the oil in a single layer. Cook undisturbed until nicely browned on the bottom, then turn with a metal spatula and brown one or two other sides. Remove to a plate. Return the pan to medium-high heat and add a little more oil, along with whatever cut-up vegetables you'd like (try diced summer squash and small cauliflower florets) and a pinch of salt; sauté until just tender, then pour in the leftover sauce and bring to a simmer. Sprinkle in some frozen peas and frozen sweet corn, then return the tofu to the pan and heat through. Serve with rice.

Tarragon and Crème Fraîche Chicken

WITH *cranberry-orange wild rice*
ALSO GOOD WITH *pan-seared green beans* (PAGE 89) OR *garlic braised broccoli rabe* (PAGE 193)

This is a fairly fancy dish that would be wonderful for a Friday-night dinner party. Just a touch of tangy, thick cream, stirred in at the end, gives the flavorful sauce a rich, velvety consistency (a hit with the immersion blender is essential here to smooth out and emulsify the sauce, which will have separated during the day). Spoon it over a mixture of wild rice and brown rice scented with orange and cranberries, and perhaps toss a few cold-weather lettuces in lemon juice and olive oil to serve alongside.

IN THE MORNING
Brown the chicken and shallots and load up the cooker.

IN THE EVENING
Stir the crème fraîche and more dried tarragon into the chicken sauce.

2 tablespoons olive or vegetable oil

2 pounds (910 g) well-trimmed boneless, skinless chicken thighs

2 heaping teaspoons dried tarragon

Salt and freshly ground black pepper

2 shallots, thinly sliced

2 tablespoons brandy (optional)

2 tablespoons crème fraîche

RECIPE CONTINUES...

In a large skillet or sauté pan, heat 1 tablespoon of the oil over medium-high heat until it shimmers. Sprinkle the chicken thighs with 1 heaping teaspoon of the tarragon, several pinches of salt, and several grindings of pepper, then add to the pan, folded into little bundles with the smooth side out (the way they're often packaged in the store) so they fit in the pan. Cook until nicely browned on the bottom, 3 to 5 minutes, then use tongs to turn them over and brown the opposite side. Transfer them to the slow cooker, still shaped into their compact bundles.

Return the pan to medium heat and add the remaining 1 tablespoon oil. Add the shallots and a pinch of salt and cook, stirring frequently, until softened and lightly browned, about 3 minutes, then add the brandy (if using) and 1 cup (240 ml) water and stir up any browned bits from the pan. Scrape into the cooker. Cover and cook on low for 8 hours.

EVENING

Using a slotted spoon or tongs, remove the chicken to a bowl (along with some of the shallots). Stir the crème fraîche and remaining 1 heaping teaspoon tarragon into the sauce in the cooker and season with salt and pepper to taste. Return the chicken to the sauce and serve.

Cranberry-orange wild rice

¾ cup (135 g) brown rice

¾ cup (130 g) wild rice

Salt

¼ cup (35 g) dried cranberries

Grated zest of ½ orange

Freshly ground black pepper

1 teaspoon unsalted butter (optional)

MORNING

Put the brown and wild rices in a sieve and rinse under running water. Dump into a medium saucepan, add a large pinch of salt and cold water to cover by about 1 inch (2.5 cm), and bring to a boil. Lower the heat and simmer for 15 minutes. Drain well in the sieve and rinse under cold running water and drain again. Rinse the pan with cold water to cool it down, then fill it with about 1 inch (2.5 cm) of water and put a collapsible steamer basket in the pan. Dump the rice into the steamer basket. Sprinkle the cranberries and orange zest over the rice, cover, and refrigerate.

EVENING

Transfer the rice pot from the refrigerator to the stovetop. Still covered, bring the water in the bottom to a boil and steam the rice until tender, about 15 minutes. Lift the steamer basket out of the pot and dump the rice into a large bowl, fluffing it with a spoon or rubber spatula and incorporating the cranberries and orange zest. Add salt to taste, a few grindings of pepper, and the butter, if you'd like. Transfer to a serving bowl and serve.

Chicken Mull

WITH *collard slaw*

ALSO GOOD WITH *smothered butter beans* (PAGE 173) OR *garlic sautéed dandelion greens* (PAGE 58)

This recipe is based on one by my friend Eric Wagoner in Athens, Georgia. Feel free to add a couple of carrots or celery ribs to the broth and discard them with the chicken bones when you pull the meat. I like to use chicken parts with the bone in here because the bones enrich the broth, but if you have it you could use a good chicken or turkey stock (page 240) instead of the water and substitute boneless thighs; then you could just shred the meat right in the pot.

IN THE MORNING
Load up the cooker.

IN THE EVENING
Shred the chicken and remove the bones, then stir in the crackers and remaining ingredients.

4 pounds (1.8 kg) chicken thighs, skin pulled off

½ onion, in one piece

1½ sleeves saltines

1 teaspoon cracked black pepper, plus more for serving

2 tablespoons unsalted butter

3 tablespoons half-and-half

Vinegar-based hot sauce

MORNING
Put the chicken, onion half, and 2 quarts (2 L) water in the slow cooker. Cover and cook on low for 8 hours.

EVENING
Using a slotted spoon, transfer the chicken to a bowl and discard the onion half. When the chicken is just cool enough to handle (or wear kitchen gloves or use tongs to work with the chicken while it's hot), pull out and discard the bones and any large pieces of fat and gristle. Coarsely shred the meat and return it to the broth in the cooker. Crumble in the crackers and stir in the cracked pepper, butter, and half-and-half. You shouldn't have to add any salt. Serve with hot sauce and more cracked pepper.

Collard slaw

Juice of ½ lemon

½ teaspoon salt, or more to taste

1 tablespoon olive oil

4 cups (170 g) finely shredded collard greens (any stems or ribs thicker than a pencil removed)

1 carrot, grated

Crushed red pepper

MORNING OR EVENING
In a large bowl, whisk together the lemon juice, salt, and oil. Pile in the collards and carrot and toss with your hands to coat with the dressing, massaging the greens and carrot a bit to soften them. Season with crushed red pepper. Cover and refrigerate if doing this in the morning, or serve right away.

Chicken with Sour Cherries, Caramelized Onions, and Lots of Dill

WITH *fancy saffron-butter basmati rice*
ALSO GOOD WITH *cumin spiced millet* (PAGE 231) OR *almond couscous* (PAGE 195)

I've lost track of this dish's origin story—Was I thinking Persian when I first made this? Indian? Moroccan?—but it's shown up frequently on our table in the last year or so, for the best reasons: My family loves it, it's fairly unfussy, and it requires only a couple of fresh ingredients (chicken, dill).

You can certainly use boneless, skinless chicken thighs here instead of whole ones—use about 2 pounds (910 g) or a little more. And if you prefer a sweeter complement to the turmeric chicken, use golden raisins or diced dried apricots, figs, or dates in place of the sour cherries—they'll all be great.

IN THE MORNING
Brown the chicken.
If you have time,
caramelize the onions.

IN THE EVENING
Fold in the onions and dill.

---

1 teaspoon paprika

½ teaspoon turmeric

Salt and freshly ground black pepper

3 pounds (1.4 kg) bone-in, skin-on chicken thighs, trimmed of excess skin and fat

1 teaspoon plus 1 tablespoon olive oil

¼ cup (35 g) dried sour cherries

2 sweet onions, diced

½ cup (25 g) chopped fresh dill, including tender stems

MORNING

In a cup, combine the paprika, turmeric, 1 ½ teaspoons salt, and several grindings of pepper. Put the chicken in the slow cooker and toss it with the spice mixture to coat. In a large skillet or sauté pan, heat 1 teaspoon oil over medium-high heat. Add the chicken, skin side down, and cook until the skin is nicely browned and has rendered a good deal of fat, about 5 minutes. Using tongs, transfer the thighs to the slow cooker, nestling them in the pot skin side up. Pour the fat from the skillet, then pour ½ cup (120 ml) water into the hot skillet, scraping up any browned bits. Pour into the cooker around the thighs. Scatter the cherries over the chicken. Cover and cook on low for 8 hours.

MORNING OR EVENING

To the chicken-browning pan, add the remaining 1 tablespoon oil and place over medium heat. Add the onions and a good pinch of salt and cook, stirring occasionally and lowering the heat and/or adding a splash of water, if needed, to keep the onions from sticking and burning, until they are nicely browned and very soft, about 20 minutes. If doing this in the morning, scrape into a container, cover, and refrigerate.

EVENING

Using a slotted spoon, transfer the chicken to a bowl, then fold the onions and dill into the sauce in the cooker, season with salt and pepper, if needed, then return the chicken to the sauce and heat through. Serve.

LEFTOVER CHICKEN?

Make flatbread sandwiches: Warm pitas or large flour tortillas or any similar flatbread on a griddle or in the oven. Dollop creamy herb dressing (page 175) down the center of each, top with shreds of the chicken (I like it best cold from the fridge, but you could warm it up if you prefer), thinly sliced cucumber and tomato, and a handful of lettuce, roll up, and serve, perhaps with roasted potatoes (page 120) or warmed-up saffron-butter rice if you have any left.

Fancy saffron-butter basmati rice

2 cups (360 g) basmati rice

2 teaspoons salt

Pinch of saffron

4 tablespoons (55 g) unsalted butter

¼ cup (60 ml) plain Greek yogurt (preferably full-fat)

1 teaspoon thinly sliced fresh mint (optional)

MORNING OR EVENING

Rinse the rice very well in a sieve under running water. Dump into a 3-quart (3-L) saucepan and add 1 teaspoon salt and enough water to cover the rice by 2 inches (5 cm). Bring to a boil, stirring occasionally to keep grains from sticking to the pan; lower the heat and simmer briskly for 10 minutes.

Put the remaining 1 teaspoon salt, the saffron, and 2 tablespoons of the butter (cut into pieces) in a heatproof bowl. When the rice has simmered for 10 minutes, ladle ¼ cup (60 ml) of the hot cooking water into the saffron-butter bowl. Drain the rice in the sieve and cool under running water. Set aside over the cooled saucepan, covered with the pan lid, in the refrigerator if doing this in the morning.

EVENING

With a fork or whisk, stir the yogurt into the saffron butter, whisking until smooth. In the saucepan, melt the remaining 2 tablespoons butter over medium heat, swirling the pan to coat the bottom and partway up the sides. Gently spoon in the parboiled rice, letting it mound up in the center in a cone shape, then drizzle the saffron butter–yogurt mixture evenly all over the rice. Cover the saucepan, with a clean kitchen towel underneath the lid and its corners folded over the top, and continue to cook over medium heat for 15 minutes.

Wet a towel and lay it out on a heatproof surface. Move the hot pan to the towel and let stand for 5 minutes. Uncover, fluff, and spoon out the rice, dislodging the crusty bottom layer (the tahdig) and equitably distributing the pieces. If you'd like, sprinkle with the mint. Serve.

Chicken with Spanish Chorizo and Peppers

WITH *garlic- and tomato-rubbed grilled bread*

ALSO GOOD WITH *crusty rolls* (PAGE 155) OR *simple garlic spinach* (PAGE 224)

I went on a Spanish food kick when our local grocery store had a brilliant couple-of-months-long promotion of imported Spanish foods. (I might have gone a little overboard when, at the end of the event, all the pantry items were marked down by like 95 percent.) This simple dish, flavored mostly by funky cured chorizo, was one result. It's great with a cut-up rabbit, incidentally, but rabbit can't go the full eight hours without toughening a bit, so maybe save that variation for a weekend dinner.

IN THE MORNING
Briefly cook the chorizo and brown the chicken.

IN THE EVENING
Sauté the peppers and garlic.

- 1 teaspoon plus 1 tablespoon olive oil
- 4 ounces (115 g) Spanish chorizo picante, cut into ½-inch (12-mm) pieces
- 3 pounds (1.4 kg) well-trimmed boneless, skinless chicken thighs
- Salt and freshly ground black pepper
- ½ cup (120 ml) red wine
- 1 (14.5-ounce/411-g) can crushed tomatoes
- 2 tablespoons tomato paste
- 3 Cubanelle or other mild but not too sweet peppers (about 12 ounces/340 g), cut into 1-inch (2.5-cm) pieces
- 2 cloves garlic, minced

MORNING

In a large skillet or sauté pan, heat the 1 teaspoon oil over medium-high heat. Add the chorizo and cook until it's rendered some of its fat, about 2 minutes, then use a slotted spoon to transfer it to the slow cooker.

To the skillet, add half of the chicken and sprinkle with salt and several grindings of pepper. Cook, turning occasionally, until lightly browned on both sides, about 5 minutes total. Transfer to the cooker, season and brown the rest of the chicken, and transfer it to the cooker too; try to tuck the chicken in snugly so the thighs hold their shape as they cook. Pour the wine into the skillet, scraping up any browned bits, boil for about 3 minutes to reduce it, then pour into the cooker. Add the tomatoes, tomato paste, and a good pinch of salt. Cover and cook on low for 8 hours.

EVENING

In a large skillet (the one you used for browning is fine), heat the 1 tablespoon oil over medium-high heat. When it shimmers, add the peppers and garlic and a pinch of salt and cook, tossing occasionally, until just softened and nicely browned in spots, about 5 minutes. Stir into the chicken in the cooker. Add salt and pepper, if needed, then serve.

NEVER MEASURE TABLESPOONS OF OIL

Put olive and vegetable oils in a squeeze bottle with a fine tip or in a cleaned wine bottle with a liquor-pouring spout, which you can find at supermarkets or liquor stores. The first time you use the oil, measure out a tablespoon (into an actual measuring spoon) while counting seconds. Next time, just squeeze or pour out the oil directly into the pan or bowl for the appropriate number of seconds. (In my case it's four seconds per tablespoon.)

NEVER PEEL GARLIC—WELL, OKAY, RARELY PEEL GARLIC

When you have a few extra minutes, peel a head of garlic all at one time, then put the peeled cloves in an airtight container or freezer bag and stash them in the vegetable drawer of your refrigerator, where they'll keep for a couple of weeks. This will save so much time and hassle when all you need is a clove or two at a time. *Saveur* posted a video online showing how to peel a whole head of garlic (I do two heads at a time) in less than ten seconds, and I've been using this method ever since. Tap the top of the head with a heavy pan to separate the cloves, sweep everything into a bowl, turn an identical bowl over the first to make a lid, hold the bowls together tightly, and shake the garlic up and down in the bowls *vigorously* for fifteen to thirty seconds. Uncover and pick out the peeled cloves.

Garlic- and tomato-rubbed grilled bread

6 thick slices crusty, holey bread (ciabatta works well here)

Olive oil

Salt

1 large clove garlic, cut in half

½ small tomato

EVENING

Heat a grill pan over medium-high heat. When a drop of water on the surface evaporates almost immediately, it's hot enough. Brush the bread slices on both sides with oil and sprinkle with salt. Place on the grill pan and cook, pressing down on them with a spatula to ensure maximum surface contact, until dark grill marks show up, 2 to 3 minutes; flip and brown the other side.

Skewer the garlic halves with a fork and rub the cut sides all over the surface of the bread, then rub with the cut tomato. Serve.

Herb Butter–Braised Turkey Breast

WITH *butter-roasted mixed potatoes*
ALSO GOOD WITH *basil zucchini* (PAGE 191) OR *celery, spinach, and Parmesan salad* (PAGE 185)

Turkey breast is not something I often reach for when considering a slow cooker meal, because it can dry out over the long cooking time, but if you add enough—*a lot of*—herb butter it stays fairly juicy and makes a great basis for a simple meal. And it's even better as leftovers.

IN THE MORNING
Debone the turkey, make the herb butter, and spread it over the turkey in the cooker.

IN THE EVENING
Slice or pull the turkey.

1 whole turkey breast, the two breast halves cut off the bone (see Note)

Salt and freshly ground black pepper

½ cup (1 stick/115 g) unsalted butter, softened

1 large sprig fresh basil, stemmed, leaves torn into pieces

MORNING

Put the deboned turkey breast halves in the slow cooker (nestle them in snugly) and pour ¼ cup (60 ml) water into the cooker around them.

In a bowl, mash the butter together with the basil and ½ teaspoon salt and several grindings of pepper. Spread the butter all over the tops of the breast halves. Cover and cook on low for 8 hours.

EVENING

Using a slotted spoon or two sturdy spatulas, transfer the turkey to a carving board and thickly slice or pull the meat into serving-size pieces. Spoon some of the liquid from the cooker over the meat and serve.

Butter-roasted mixed potatoes

3 large Yukon Gold potatoes, cut into 1½-inch (4-cm) chunks

1 sweet potato, cut into 1½-inch (4-cm) chunks

3 tablespoons melted herb butter, skimmed from the surface of the liquid in the turkey pot or made fresh

Salt and freshly ground black pepper

EVENING

Preheat the oven to 450°F (230°C). Put a baking sheet in the oven to heat.

In a large bowl, toss the Yukon Gold and sweet potatoes with the butter and a couple of pinches of salt and grindings of pepper. Spread in a single layer on the hot baking sheet and roast until nicely browned on the bottoms and tender throughout, about 15 minutes. Serve.

NOTE: Save the bones to make a wonderful turkey stock (page 240) in a large slow cooker.

Leftover butter-braised turkey?

You almost certainly don't need any instructions for open-faced broiled turkey sandwiches, but: crusty bread, spicy mustard or a chunky schmear of Branston pickle, drizzle of butter from the turkey, pile of pulled turkey, shredded Jack or sliced brie or other melty cheese, black pepper. Put on a baking sheet and broil until heated through, melted, and crusty, about 5 minutes. Serve with a simple green salad.

Duck Confit with White Beans and Leeks

WITH *lemon kale*

ALSO GOOD WITH *garlic braised broccoli rabe* (PAGE 193) OR *crusty rolls* (PAGE 155)

Confit—duck cooked very slowly in its own fat (or in this case in whatever fats you can scrounge together to cover the legs)—can be used in so many ways, but I've always loved it with fragrant leeks and creamy white beans. You'll have some duck left over to experiment with: Try some in a simple pasta dish with lots of herbs and a touch of stock and cream, or shred it and mix with the rendered fat and more salt and pepper to make rillettes to spread on toasts as an appetizer.

IN THE MORNING

Load up the cooker to make the confit.

IN THE EVENING

Sauté the leeks and beans, and pull the confit from the bones (saving half of it in the refrigerator, covered in fat, for another use).

3 pounds (1.4 kg) duck leg quarters (thigh and drumstick together; about 6 quarters)

Salt and freshly ground black pepper

Big handful fresh thyme sprigs, plus more for garnish

1½ cups (360 ml) fat, such as duck fat, schmaltz (page 251), or olive oil, or a combination

1 large or 2 small leeks, white and light green parts only

1 clove garlic

½ cup (120 ml) white or rosé wine

About ½ cup (120 ml) chicken stock (page 240) or water

2 (14- to 15-ounce/400- to 430-g) cans white beans, drained and rinsed, or about 3 cups cooked and drained white beans (page 246)

3 tablespoons oil-packed sun-dried tomatoes, drained and torn

MORNING

Put the duck legs in the slow cooker and season with 1½ teaspoons salt and several grindings of pepper. Nestle them into the cooker in two layers, tucking in the thyme sprigs. Pour or dollop the fat over everything. Cover and cook on low for 8 hours.

MORNING OR EVENING

Cut the leek in half lengthwise and rinse well under running water, fanning the layers to get all the sand out from between them. Cut crosswise into ¼-inch (6-mm) slices. Thinly slice the garlic. Put the leeks and garlic in a container and refrigerate if doing this in the morning.

EVENING

Using a slotted spoon or tongs, remove half of the duck from the fat in the cooker and set aside to cool slightly.

RECIPE CONTINUES...

In a large deep skillet or sauté pan, heat 1 tablespoon of the fat from the cooker over medium-high heat. When it starts to sputter, add the leeks and garlic and cook, stirring frequently, until the leeks are tender and beginning to stick to the skillet, about 3 minutes. Pour in the wine, scraping up any browned bits, then add the stock, beans, and sun-dried tomatoes, lower the heat to medium, and bring to a gentle simmer.

Pull the meat from the duck bones in bite-size pieces, discarding the bones and skin; you should have about 1¼ cups (175 g) meat from half of the legs. Add it to the beans, season with more salt and pepper, if needed, and add a little more stock or water if the pan seems too dry. Cook to just heat through, then transfer to a serving dish, sprinkle with a few fresh thyme leaves, and serve.

When you have a moment after supper, pull the meat from the remaining duck legs and put it in a container. Cover with fat skimmed from the liquid in the cooker, put the lid on, and refrigerate for up to 1 week.

Lemon kale

1 large bunch (about 12 ounces/340 g) kale

Salt

Grated zest of ½ small lemon

Juice of 1 small lemon

1 small clove garlic (optional)

Good pinch of crushed red pepper

1 tablespoon olive oil

MORNING

Wash the kale and pull or cut out any stems or ribs thicker than a pencil. Tear the leaves into bite-size pieces and put them in a bowl. Sprinkle with ½ teaspoon salt and use your hand to massage it into the kale. Add the lemon zest and juice, finely grate in the garlic, if using, and add the crushed red pepper and oil. Toss to combine, cover, and refrigerate until evening.

CHAPTER 3

Pork

Basic "Roast" Pork and Rice

WITH *spicy tomatillo salsa*
ALSO GOOD WITH *all-purpose tomato salsa* (PAGE 140)
OR *marinated bean and tomato salad* (PAGE 139)

Feel free to experiment with this recipe, using different spices, different grains as accompaniments, even a different meat (my friend Leda made this using a bone-in lamb leg roast, for example, and was happy with the results).

IN THE MORNING
Load up the cooker.

IN THE EVENING
Cook the rice and slice or pull the pork.

2 teaspoons salt

2 teaspoons ancho chile powder

½ teaspoon ground cayenne

1 (3½- to 4-pound/1.6- to 1.8-kg) bone-in pork butt

2 cups (370 g) long-grain white rice

MORNING

In a cup, combine the salt, chile powder, and cayenne, then rub the mixture all over the pork. Put the pork in the slow cooker, fat side down. Cover and cook on low for 8 hours.

EVENING

Put the rice in a sieve and rinse very well under running water. Dump into a 2-quart (2-L) sauce-pan and add 2 ¼ cups (540 ml) water and a good pinch of salt. Bring to a boil over high heat, stir once to unstick any grains from the bottom of the pan, then cover and cook over the lowest heat for 14 minutes, or until all the water is absorbed and the rice is tender. Let stand, covered, for 3 minutes, then fluff with a fork or spatula.

Using tongs or two wide metal spatulas, remove the pork to a carving board. Slice or pull the meat from the bone, discarding any large pockets of fat. Serve, spooning some of the cooking liquid from the cooker over the meat.

Spicy tomatillo salsa

1 pound (455 g) tomatillos, husked and rinsed

4 ounces (115 g) jalapeño or serrano chiles, stems cut off

½ onion, cut into thick slices

2 cloves garlic, unpeeled

1 cup (40 g) chopped fresh cilantro

1 teaspoon salt

MORNING OR EVENING

Preheat the broiler to high and set a rack about 6 inches (15 cm) from the heat source.

Arrange the tomatillos, jalapeños, onion slices, and garlic on a rimmed baking sheet. Broil until the vegetables are softened and the tomatillos and jalapeños are charred in spots, about 15 minutes. Let cool for a few minutes. Peel the garlic. Transfer all the vegetables to a blender and add the cilantro and salt. Blend until chunky-smooth. Serve warm, or let cool, cover, and refrigerate; bring to room temperature before serving. The salsa will keep for at least 5 days in the refrigerator.

Porter Pork Roast

WITH *chunky rosemary applesauce*
ALSO GOOD WITH *skillet potatoes* (PAGE 190) OR *two peas with marjoram* (PAGE 97)

There's something about dark beer and pork that's so appealing: the bitterness of the beer cutting through the unctuousness of the meat, the wide range of flavors from so few ingredients.

IN THE MORNING
Sear the pork roast.

IN THE EVENING
Slice and serve.

---

1 (3-pound/1.4-kg) boneless pork shoulder roast

Salt and freshly ground black pepper

1 (12-ounce/360-ml) bottle of porter beer

1 large sprig fresh rosemary

MORNING

Season the pork all over with about 1½ teaspoons salt and plenty of pepper. Heat a large skillet or sauté pan over high heat. When it's hot, add the pork and cook, turning with tongs, until nicely browned on most sides, about 7 minutes total. Transfer to the slow cooker. Pour most of the beer into the hot skillet, scraping up any browned bits, then pour into the cooker. Nestle the rosemary alongside the roast. Cover and cook on low for 8 hours.

EVENING

Using tongs or two sturdy metal spatulas, transfer the roast to a carving board. Cut into thick slices with a sharp chef's knife (or pull the meat into serving-size pieces) and arrange on a platter. Spoon liquid from the cooker over the pork and serve.

Chunky rosemary applesauce

4 large sweet apples, peeled, if desired, and diced

1 teaspoon minced fresh rosemary

Pinch of salt

Juice of ½ lemon

1 tablespoon maple syrup

MORNING OR EVENING

Put all the ingredients in a saucepan with 1 cup (240 ml) water, bring to a boil, then lower the heat and simmer, stirring occasionally, until the apples are soft and breaking apart, about 15 minutes, adding a little more water if it seems too dry. Mash some of the apples against the side of the pan with a wooden spoon or spatula. If doing this in the morning, set aside, covered, until evening and reheat over medium heat, stirring frequently and adding some water, if needed, just before serving.

"Pulled Pork"

WITH *yogurt-dressed coleslaw*
ALSO GOOD WITH *collard slaw* (PAGE 115) OR *tangy potato salad* (PAGE 36)

With apologies to those of you who know real pork barbecue, this is not it. But it can certainly help ease the cravings of expat southeasterners—say, those living in a northern city apartment with no access to a good barbecue joint, much less a decent home smoker setup.

IN THE MORNING
Brown the pork.

IN THE EVENING
Pull the pork from the bones and puree the sauce.

1 (5- to 6-pound/2.3- to 2.7-kg) bone-in Boston butt pork roast

Salt and freshly ground black pepper

½ sweet onion, chopped

4 cloves garlic

1 (6-ounce/170-g) can tomato paste

½ cup (120 ml) crushed tomatoes

½ cup (120 ml) cider vinegar

¾ cup (110 g) raisins

2 teaspoons hot paprika

Soft split sandwich buns

MORNING

Season the pork all over with about 2 teaspoons salt and plenty of pepper. In a large skillet or sauté pan over high heat, cook the pork until nicely browned on several sides, turning with tongs or a carving fork, about 10 minutes total. It's okay if it doesn't quite fit in the pan—just do your best to brown it in your largest skillet.

Meanwhile, put the onion, garlic, tomato paste, crushed tomatoes, vinegar, raisins, and paprika in the slow cooker and stir. Transfer the browned pork roast to the cooker. Pour ½ cup (120 ml) water into the hot skillet and stir to scrape up any browned bits, then scrape the liquid into the cooker. Cover and cook on high for 8 hours.

EVENING

Using tongs or a carving fork and sturdy metal spatula, transfer the pork to a large baking pan.

With an immersion blender, puree the sauce in the cooker. With two forks or any other utensils that work for you, remove and discard the pork bones and any large pieces of fat, then shred the meat and return it to the sauce in the cooker to reheat. Serve on buns.

Yogurt-dressed coleslaw

This is a very straightforward slaw—I like to keep things pretty standard when pulled pork is involved. Serve it on the sandwiches, Virginia-style, or on the side.

3 tablespoons plain Greek yogurt (preferably full-fat)

¼ cup (60 ml) cider vinegar

1 teaspoon prepared mustard

1 teaspoon sugar

½ teaspoon celery seed

1 teaspoon salt, or more to taste

Freshly ground black pepper

1 small head green cabbage

1 large carrot

MORNING OR EVENING

In a large bowl, whisk together the yogurt, vinegar, mustard, sugar, celery seed, salt, and lots of pepper. Quarter, core, and finely shred (or food-processor) the cabbage. Peel and grate the carrot and add the cabbage and carrot to the bowl with the dressing. Toss to coat. Cover and refrigerate until ready to serve.

Derek's Red Posole

WITH *chilled radish chips*

ALSO GOOD WITH *chili garnishes* (PAGE 172) OR *mini faux pupusas* (PAGE 72)

Instead of rehydrating the chiles and tomatoes, you can use about 1½ cups (360 ml) chili base (page 244); just stir in water or stock to make about 2½ cups (600 ml) and add a little cayenne or more ancho chile powder and grate in some garlic when you add it to the slow cooker.

IN THE MORNING
Rehydrate the chiles, blend, and strain into the cooker.

IN THE EVENING
Stir in the hominy and radish tops.

2 ounces (55 g) dried guajillo and/or New Mexico chiles (about 8), stemmed and snipped into pieces with scissors

6 dried chiles de árbol, stemmed

6 sun-dried tomatoes

5 cloves garlic

3 cups (720 ml) boiling water

2 pounds (910 g) pork shoulder or country-style ribs, cut into 1½- to 2-inch (4- to 5-cm) chunks

1 teaspoon dried epazote (see Note, page 63)

1 teaspoon dried oregano, preferably Mexican

2 teaspoons ancho chile powder

1½ teaspoons salt, or more to taste

About 4⅓ cups (710 g) cooked and drained hominy (page 246), or one 25-ounce/709-g can) hominy

Tops from 1 bunch radishes, washed well and chopped (optional)

Lime wedges

MORNING

Shake out as many of the guajillo seeds as possible (but don't lose your mind over it). Put the guajillo and árbol chiles, sun-dried tomatoes, and garlic in a blender and pour the boiling water over them. Let soak for at least 10 minutes, until the chiles are softened. Puree until very smooth. Set a fine-mesh sieve over the slow cooker and pour in the chile puree, pushing the puree and liquid through with a spatula; discard the bits of skin and seeds in the sieve.

Stir in the pork, epazote, oregano, chile powder, and salt. Cover and cook on low for 8 hours.

EVENING

Turn the cooker to high and stir in the hominy and radish tops, if using. Cover and heat through. Season with more salt, if needed, and serve with lime wedges.

RECIPE CONTINUES...

Chilled radish chips

When very thinly sliced radishes are chilled in ice water for a few hours they curl into a scoop shape and become incredibly crisp and crunchy—a refreshing accompaniment to anything spicy. Keep them in the water in the fridge for up to 5 days and use them to scoop hummus, guacamole, or other dips.

1 bunch radishes, tops cut off (save the tops for the posole)

Salt

Ground cayenne (optional)

MORNING

With a mandoline or a Y-shaped vegetable peeler, slice the radishes paper-thin. Put in a container and cover with ice and cold water. Cover and refrigerate until ready to serve.

EVENING

Drain the slices, sprinkle with salt and cayenne, if desired, and serve.

Curried Pork Loin

WITH *roasted squash and Scotch bonnet sauce*
ALSO GOOD WITH *brown rice and peas* (PAGE 235) OR *chayote with garlic buttered bread crumbs* (PAGE 83)

Pork loin is very lean, and can easily toughen in the slow cooker, so here it's cooked in plenty of rich, flavorful liquid—coconut milk and tomato infused with aromatics and spice.

IN THE MORNING
Brown the pork, deglaze the skillet, and load the cooker.

IN THE EVENING
Hit the pork sauce with the immersion blender.

---

2 pounds (910 g) pork loin, cut into 1-inch (2.5-cm) chunks

Salt and freshly ground black pepper

2 teaspoons Madras or other hot curry powder

1 tablespoon vegetable oil

1-inch (2.5-cm) piece fresh ginger, chopped

2 cloves garlic, chopped

1 (13.5-ounce/400-ml) can coconut milk

1 fresh or frozen Scotch bonnet chile

1 large tomato, peeled and diced, or 2 canned tomatoes, diced

MORNING
Sprinkle the pork with several pinches of salt and grindings of black pepper and the curry powder. In a large skillet or sauté pan, heat the oil over medium-high heat until it shimmers. Add the pork in a single layer and cook, turning occasionally with a metal spatula, just until the spices are fragrant and the surface of the pork has lost its raw pink color, about 4 minutes. Scrape into the slow cooker.

Return the pan to medium heat and add the ginger, garlic, and most of the can of coconut milk (put the rest in the refrigerator for evening), stirring to scrape up any browned bits from the pan. Boil for 1 minute, then scrape into the slow cooker. Use a paring knife to slit the chile in one or two places, keeping it whole, and add it to the cooker, tucking it down into the liquid. Add the tomato, cover, and cook on low for 8 hours.

EVENING
Using a slotted spoon, remove the pork to a serving bowl. Add the rest of the can of coconut milk to the cooker and puree the sauce with an immersion blender. Taste and add salt, if needed. Return the pork to the cooker and serve.

Roasted squash and Scotch bonnet sauce

1 bunch fresh cilantro, including tender stems, chopped

Juice of 1 to 2 limes

About 2 teaspoons Thai black (sweet) soy sauce, or 2 teaspoons regular soy sauce plus 1 tablespoon honey

4 Scotch bonnet chiles

Salt

2 acorn squash

MORNING OR EVENING
Put the cilantro, lime juice, soy sauce, and ¼ cup (60 ml) water in a mini food processor. Wearing gloves, stem and seed the chiles. Snip them into the food processor. Process to a fine puree, taste, and add more lime juice and salt, if needed. Cover and refrigerate if making the sauce in the morning.

EVENING
Preheat the oven to 400°F (205°F). Cut the squash in half lengthwise and scrape out the seeds. Put the squash cut side down in one or two baking dishes, add water to just cover the bottom of the dish, and roast until tender, 30 to 45 minutes. Serve with the sauce.

Japanese Curry Rice

WITH *sweet apples with cayenne*

ALSO GOOD WITH *gingered Asian pear salad* (PAGE 150) OR *broccoli-sesame hash* (PAGE 145)

I'll admit the prep for this meal is a bit involved for a weekday morning, but if you make the curry roux and keep the remainder in the freezer, the next time you make this will be a breeze.

IN THE MORNING
Brown the pork and sauté the onion. If you have time, make the curry roux.

IN THE EVENING
Cook the rice and drain the liquid into a saucepan to make the sauce.

1 tablespoon vegetable oil

1½ pounds (680 g) pork shoulder or country-style ribs, cut into 1- to 2-inch (2.5- to 5-cm) pieces

Salt and freshly ground black pepper

1 onion, sliced

4 small carrots, cut into 1- to 1½-inch (2.5- to 5-cm) lengths

3 Yukon Gold potatoes (about 14 ounces/400 g total), cut into 1- to 2-inch (2.5- to 5-cm) pieces

For the curry roux:

4 tablespoons (½ stick/55 g) unsalted butter

6 tablespoons (35 g) all-purpose flour

2 tablespoons Madras (hot) curry powder

1 teaspoon garam masala

1½ cups (295 g) medium-grain rice, such as Calrose rice

MORNING

In a large skillet or sauté pan, heat the oil over medium-high heat. When it shimmers, add the pork and season it with salt and pepper. Cook, turning with a thin metal spatula, until the pieces are nicely browned on one or two sides, about 5 minutes, then transfer to the slow cooker.

Add the onion to the skillet and cook, stirring frequently, until tender and browned at the edges, about 5 minutes, then scrape into the cooker. Pour 1 cup (240 ml) water into the hot skillet, scraping up any browned bits, and pour the liquid into the cooker. Add the carrots and potatoes.

In a skillet or sauté pan, melt the butter over medium heat. Stir in the flour, curry powder, and garam masala and cook, stirring constantly with a heatproof spatula, for 2 minutes. Scrape into a bowl. Pour 1 cup (240 ml) water into the hot skillet, scraping up any browned bits, and pour the liquid into the cooker. Cover and cook on low for 8 hours. Cover the curry roux and set aside or refrigerate.

EVENING

Rinse the rice in a sieve under running water. Dump it into a 2-quart (2-L) saucepan and add 2 cups (480 ml) water and a pinch of salt. Bring to a boil, cover, and cook on the lowest heat until tender and all the water has been absorbed, about 15 minutes.

Holding the cooker lid askew, drain as much of the liquid as possible from the cooker into a saucepan. Bring to a boil over high heat. Whisk in half of the curry roux and simmer until just thickened. Return the sauce to the cooker and serve with the rice. Tightly wrap the remaining curry roux in plastic and freeze for up to 6 months.

Sweet apples with cayenne

2 crisp sweet apples
Juice of ½ lemon
Good pinch of ground cayenne
Pinch of salt

EVENING

Using a Thai green papaya/ mango shredder or the large holes of a box-type grater, grate the apples, including the peels—just hold the whole apple and grate one side until you reach the core, then turn the apple and grate the other sides. Toss in a bowl with the lemon juice, cayenne, and salt and serve.

Pork Mochimos

WITH *marinated bean and tomato salad*
ALSO GOOD WITH *chili garnishes* (PAGE 172) OR *quick-pickled vegetables* (PAGE 102)

Mochimos—salty pork (or often beef) cooked to fine shreds and tossed with fresh chiles and onion—are a new-to-me delight. It's a simple process, but it does require a bit of evening work at the stove, and some measure of kitchen confidence: The tender braised pork will stick to the skillet and turn golden as you stir and scrape it, and you have to trust that this is what should happen and that this is how the dish becomes something other and greater than plain sautéed meat. Embrace the Maillard reaction and the not-nonstick cookware that makes it work most efficiently.

If you have leftover mochimos (it freezes and reheats very well), it's great in burritos with soft beans or just pinched into a simple fried rice. I often make mochimos with leftovers from the Basic "Roast" Pork recipe (page 129).

IN THE MORNING
Load up the cooker.

IN THE EVENING
Brown and shred the pork in a skillet (in two batches or in two skillets) and stir in the onion and chiles.

---

3 pounds (1.4 kg) pork shoulder, cut into 1-inch (2.5-cm) chunks

2 teaspoons ancho chile powder (optional)

½ teaspoon ground cayenne (optional)

1 teaspoon salt, or more to taste

1 to 2 serrano chiles

½ onion

Corn tortillas, warmed (see page 100)

MORNING
Put the pork in the slow cooker and toss it with the chile powder and cayenne, if using, and the salt. Pour in ½ cup (120 ml) water. Cover and cook on low for 8 hours.

MORNING OR EVENING
Thinly slice the chiles and onion. If doing this in the morning, put them in a container together and refrigerate.

EVENING
Place a large skillet or sauté pan over medium-high heat. Using a slotted spoon, transfer half of the pork to the hot skillet and cook—turning and shredding the meat, and scraping the pan when it sticks (which is okay)—until the meat is deeply browned and crisp and most of it is in fine threads, 10 to 12 minutes. Transfer to a large bowl and repeat with the remaining pork. Toss the chile and onion slices with the warm pork, sprinkle with more salt, if needed, and serve.

Marinated bean and tomato salad

- 1 (14- to 15-ounce/400- to 430-g) can black beans or small red beans, drained and rinsed, or about 1½ cups cooked and drained beans (page 246)

- 3 medium round tomatoes (about 10 ounces/280 g), chopped

- 1 small red bell pepper, or a large poblano or Hatch chile, if you'd like more heat, seeded and diced

- ¼ sweet onion, diced

- Juice of ½ lime

- 1 large sprig fresh basil, torn, or ¼ cup (10 g) chopped fresh cilantro

- Salt to taste

MORNING

Combine all the ingredients in a medium bowl. Cover and refrigerate until evening.

139

Pork with Pineapple and Chiles

WITH *all-purpose tomato salsa*

ALSO GOOD WITH *mini faux pupusas* (PAGE 72) OR *marinated bean and tomato salad* (PAGE 139)

Here's a hearty meal of spicy braised pork, with just a touch of sweet-and-sour action from the pineapple, which is pureed into a sauce.

IN THE MORNING
Brown the pork.

IN THE EVENING
Cook the rice and puree the sauce.

---

1 tablespoon ancho chile powder

1½ teaspoons salt

1 teaspoon ground cumin

2½ pounds (1.2 kg) pork country-style ribs

1 tablespoon vegetable oil

2 cups (330 g) cubed fresh pineapple

4 dried chiles de árbol

2 cups (370 g) long-grain white rice

MORNING

In a cup, stir together the chile powder, salt, and cumin. Put the pork in the slow cooker and toss it with the spice mixture to coat it. In a large skillet or sauté pan, heat the oil over medium-high heat. When it shimmers, add half of the pork and cook until just browned on the bottom, about 2 minutes, then turn and brown the other side. Return to the cooker and repeat with the remaining pork.

Pour ½ cup (120 ml) water into the hot skillet and scrape up any browned bits, then pour the liquid into the cooker. Pile the pineapple on top of the pork and tuck the chiles into the pineapple and pork. Cover and cook on low for 8 hours.

EVENING

Put the rice in a sieve and rinse very well under running water. Dump into a 2-quart (2-L) sauce-pan and add 2¼ cups (540 ml) water and a good pinch of salt. Bring to a boil over high heat, stir once to unstick any grains, then cover and cook over the lowest heat for 14 minutes, or until all the water is absorbed and the rice is tender. Let stand, covered, for 3 minutes, then fluff with a fork or spatula.

Using a slotted spoon, transfer the pork and half of the pineapple to a bowl. With an immersion blender, puree the sauce in the cooker. Season with more salt, if needed, return the pork and pineapple to the cooker, and serve with the rice.

All-purpose tomato salsa

4 scallions

1 to 2 jalapeño chiles

Juice of 1 lime

14 ounces (400 g) plum tomatoes (about 6)

Goya adobo seasoning (see Note, page 103) or a mixture of salt, onion powder, granulated garlic, and a tiny bit of dried oregano, to taste

MORNING OR EVENING

Thinly slice the scallions, mince the jalapeños (seed them if you'd like less heat, and wear gloves), and toss them in a medium bowl with the lime juice. Dice the tomatoes and lift them from the cutting board to the bowl with your hands, leaving the excess juices behind. Toss and season to taste. Cover and refrigerate if doing this in the morning, or serve right away at room temperature.

Pork with Turnips, Tomatillos, and Greens

WITH *broiled sweet onions*

ALSO GOOD WITH *corn muffins* (PAGE 153) OR *cumin-spiced millet* (PAGE 231)

This recipe is loosely based on one by Rick Bayless that my parents make with big chunks of pork shoulder their butcher calls "pork cushions"; I've never seen that terminology used myself, but it feels appropriate. Bayless's process is of course a bit more complicated, and he uses potatoes and wild greens instead of turnips, but I really love the bite and faint bitterness of turnips and their greens (which mellow considerably over the course of a day in the slow cooker).

IN THE MORNING
Blend the sauce
and load up the cooker.
If you have time,
chop and wash the greens.

IN THE EVENING
Fold in the greens.

---

1 pound (455 g) tomatillos, husked and rinsed, chopped

1 large bunch fresh cilantro with stems, chopped

2 jalapeño or serrano chiles, chopped

2 cloves garlic, chopped

¾ teaspoon ground cumin

Salt and freshly ground black pepper

2½ pounds (1.2 kg) pork shoulder or loin, cut into big (3-inch/7.5-cm) chunks

12 ounces (340 g) turnips, peeled and cut into ¾-inch (2-cm) cubes

1 bunch (about 8 ounces/ 225 g) turnip greens

MORNING

Put the tomatillos, cilantro, chiles, garlic, cumin, 1½ teaspoons salt, and several grindings of pepper in the slow cooker. With an immersion blender, puree the sauce (or put everything in a blender, puree, and transfer to the cooker). Add the pork and turnips. Cover and cook on low for 8 hours.

MORNING OR EVENING

Chop the turnip greens and submerge them in a large bowl of water, swishing to remove any sand. Lift them into a colander and repeat the rinse with clean water until no more sand remains. Drain the greens well and set aside in the fridge if doing this in the morning.

EVENING

Turn the cooker to high. Gently fold the greens into the pork and sauce in the cooker, cover, and cook until the greens are wilted and just tender, 10 to 15 minutes. Season with more salt, if needed, and serve.

Broiled sweet onions

2 large sweet onions

Olive oil

Salt and freshly ground black pepper

EVENING

Preheat the broiler to high and set a rack about 6 inches (15 cm) from the heat source.

Cut the onions into rounds ¼ inch (6 mm) thick and arrange them in a single layer on a baking sheet. Brush on both sides with oil and sprinkle with salt and pepper. Broil until blackened in spots and tender, about 10 minutes, then turn with a spatula and cook on the other side for a few minutes. Serve hot.

Pork Adobo

WITH *iceberg and cucumber chunks*
ALSO GOOD WITH *gingered Asian pear salad* (PAGE 150) OR *sweet apples with cayenne* (PAGE 137)

Confession: I'd never had Filipino adobo before I made it myself. Before developing this recipe, I spent at least two weeks (evenings only, granted) reading about it in books and online and being led down Filipino-food-culture rabbit holes, and I think what I've come up with based on that research is a classic, bare-bones adobong baboy (pork adobo); it features the traditional key flavoring elements of most adobo: vinegar, soy sauce, black peppercorns, and bay leaves. It is one of the most extraordinary dishes I've ever made, and yet it may very well be unlike any other adobo you've had.

I began the process of learning about this dish, which had long been a simmering fascination for me, feeling sheepish and a bit mortified, worried I'd get something wrong or offend a huge number of readers because my vinegar-to-soy proportion was not what their grandmothers and their grandmothers' neighbors and all their neighbors' ancestors had insisted on. But in all my recent reading about Filipino food, one thing that struck me is how open and accommodating Filipino writers are when describing their food and recipes, particularly when it comes to this dish called "adobo," which it seems could be *just about anything* as long as it contains vinegar. This welcoming, anything-goes approach to traditional foods—certainly a function of the island food culture's many, widely diverse historical influences—was so refreshing to me, and I hope you'll read this pork adobo recipe and indeed all of the recipes in this book with the same level of informality.

IN THE MORNING
Brown the pork.

IN THE EVENING
Cook the rice and reduce
the sauce a bit.

RECIPE CONTINUES...

3 pounds (1.4 kg) boneless pork shoulder, cut into 1½-inch (4-cm) chunks, very large areas of fat trimmed off

1½ teaspoons salt

1 tablespoon vegetable oil

½ cup (120 ml) white wine vinegar (see Note)

¼ cup (60 ml) soy sauce

¼ cup (55 g) brown sugar

2 stalks lemongrass, lower 5 inches (12 cm) or so only (optional)

3 cloves garlic, crushed

2 inches (5 cm) fresh ginger, peeled and cut into thin matchsticks

1 teaspoon whole black peppercorns, some of them crushed lightly

4 bay leaves

2 cups (370 g) long-grain white rice

MORNING

Season the pork with the salt. In a large skillet or sauté pan, heat a little of the oil over medium-high heat. When it shimmers, add about one third of the pork in a single layer and cook, turning occasionally, until the pieces are nicely browned on two or more sides, about 5 minutes. Transfer to the slow cooker and repeat with the remaining pork in two more batches. Pour ½ cup (120 ml) water into the hot skillet, scraping up any browned bits, then pour the liquid into the cooker.

Pour the vinegar and soy sauce over the meat and stir in the brown sugar. Add the lemongrass, if using, garlic, ginger, peppercorns, and bay leaves. Cover and cook on low for 8 hours.

EVENING

Put the rice in a sieve and rinse very well under running water. Dump into a 2-quart (2-L) saucepan and add 2¼ cups (540 ml) water and a good pinch of salt. Bring to a boil over high heat, stir once to unstick any grains from the bottom of the pan, then cover and cook over the lowest heat for 14 minutes, or until all the water is absorbed and the rice is tender. Let stand, covered, for 3 minutes, then fluff with a fork or spatula.

If there's a lot of clear fat on the surface of the pork cooking liquid, use a large spoon to skim it off. Holding the cooker lid askew, drain as much of the liquid as possible from the cooker into a skillet (the one from browning the pork is fine) or a wide saucepan. Bring to a boil over high heat and cook until the liquid is reduced a bit, about 5 minutes. Pour it back into the cooker, turn the pork to coat, and serve with the rice (picking out the bay leaves and lemongrass stalks, if using, and making sure to spoon up some of the peppercorns as you serve—they sink to the bottom).

NOTE: You could use Filipino coconut vinegar here. It's less acidic than most wine vinegars, but I find it to be too sharp and overpowering.

Iceberg and cucumber chunks

Spoon some of the vinegary adobo sauce from the pork over the lettuce and cucumbers as a dressing. If you're serving this with another dish, you might wish to squeeze a little lime or sprinkle some rice vinegar over them—or leave them plain as a refreshing counterpoint to a rich or spicy dish.

1 small head iceberg lettuce, chilled

2 Persian, Asian, or any other crisp, crunchy cucumbers, chilled

EVENING

Cut the head of lettuce and the cucumbers into 1-inch (2.5-cm) chunks. Arrange in a serving bowl or on individual plates and serve. Really, that's it.

Honey-Braised Ribs

WITH *broccoli-sesame hash*
ALSO GOOD WITH *pan-seared green beans* (PAGE 89)
OR *baby kale salad with dates and pistachios* (PAGE 42)

It might seem like this is an awful lot of honey and that the ribs would be cloying, but the honey, which not only sweetens but also helps to keep the ribs moist as they cook all day, is tempered by the spices.

IN THE MORNING
Cut the slab into ribs and load up the cooker.

IN THE EVENING
Serve.

3½ pounds (1.6 kg) baby back ribs (1 smallish rack)

¾ cup (180 ml) honey

1½ teaspoons paprika

1 teaspoon ground cinnamon

1 teaspoon ground cumin

1 teaspoon salt

MORNING
Cut the rack of ribs between the bones into individual ribs and put them in the slow cooker. Drizzle in the honey. In a cup, combine the paprika, cinnamon, cumin, and salt and sprinkle the mixture over the ribs, turning them with your hand to coat them with the honey and spices. Cover and cook on low for 8 hours.

EVENING
Using tongs or a slotted spoon, transfer the ribs to a platter. Spoon some of the cooking liquid over them and serve.

Broccoli-sesame hash

For more texture, add ¼ cup (25 g) sliced almonds with the sesame seeds.

1 pound (455 g) broccoli with stalks

1 tablespoon olive oil

2 tablespoons sesame seeds

Salt and freshly ground black pepper

2 teaspoons fresh lemon juice

MORNING OR EVENING
Trim the bottoms of the broccoli stalks and scrape the stalks with a vegetable peeler to remove the tough peel. Coarsely chop the broccoli and, working in batches if necessary, pulse in a food processor until finely chopped and the largest bits are smaller than a chickpea. Cover and refrigerate if doing this in the morning.

EVENING
In a large skillet or sauté pan, heat the oil over medium-high heat. When it shimmers, add the sesame seeds and stir for 15 to 30 seconds, until golden and fragrant. Add the broccoli, a good pinch of salt, and several grindings of pepper and cook, stirring and turning with a spatula, until the broccoli starts to crisp and brown a bit, about 5 minutes. Add the lemon juice and about 3 tablespoons water, scraping up any browned bits, and cook, stirring, until the largest broccoli bits are just tender, 1 to 2 minutes longer. Season with more salt and pepper, if needed, and serve.

Garlicky Pork Ribs Soup with Tamarind and Greens

WITH *pandan water*

ALSO GOOD WITH *sweet corn curry cakes* (PAGE 204),
scallion pancakes (PAGE 233), OR *lemongrass rice* (PAGE 211)

This is a loose adaptation of the jaw phak kat in Andy Ricker's phenomenal book of (mostly northern) Thai recipes, *Pok Pok*. As soon as his long-awaited book arrived in the mail a couple of years ago, I flipped through it and then ran around to every Asian grocery store in Lincoln, Nebraska, where we lived at the time, hunting down ingredients. The sour, salty, murky (read: flavorful!) soup was the first dish I made, and it was truly extraordinary. This weekday slow cooker–friendly version is a bit simpler and more pork-forward than Ricker's, but I think just as good.

IN THE MORNING
Make a seasoning paste and load up the cooker. In the morning or evening, fry the sliced shallot and dried chiles.

IN THE EVENING
Sauté the greens and stir them into the soup.

---

8 cloves garlic

8 dried red chiles, preferably Thai, stemmed, four of them broken into pieces

2 large shallots, one chopped and one thinly sliced

Salt and freshly ground black pepper

2 to 3 pounds (910 g to 1.4 kg) meaty pork ribs, or 2 pounds (910 g) country-style ribs

1 tablespoon fish sauce, or more to taste

1 tablespoon miso paste

1 tablespoon tamarind concentrate, such as Tamicon brand

About 5 tablespoons (75 ml) vegetable oil

1 pound (455 g) sturdy greens, such as yu choy or Chinese broccoli, cut into 2-inch (5-cm) lengths

MORNING

Using a mortar and pestle, smash the garlic, the broken-up dried chiles, the chopped shallot, and a good pinch of salt to a paste. Put the paste in the slow cooker with the pork ribs, 6 cups (1.4 L) water, several grindings of pepper, the fish sauce, miso paste, and tamarind. Cover and cook on low for 8 hours.

MORNING OR EVENING

In a large skillet or sauté pan, heat 4 tablespoons (60 ml) of the oil over medium-high heat. When it shimmers, add the sliced shallot and cook, stirring with a slotted spoon, until deeply browned, 5 to 6 minutes. Remove to a paper towel to drain. Return the oil to medium-high heat, add the whole dried chiles, and cook for 30 seconds, until just darkened a shade. Remove to the paper towel to drain. Set aside at room temperature; keep the skillet handy (no need to wash it yet).

EVENING

Place the skillet with any remaining oil (add a little oil, if needed) over medium-high heat. Add the greens and stir until just wilted, then cover and cook until the thickest stems are tender, about 10 minutes, stirring occasionally and adding about ½ cup (60 ml) water if they start to stick to the pan. Gently fold the greens into the soup in the cooker (the ribs will be falling-off-the-bone tender; fish out and discard the bones, if you'd like), season with more salt or fish sauce, if needed, and serve with the fried shallot and chiles on the side for topping.

RECIPE CONTINUES...

Pandan water

2 quarts or liters fresh cold water

**1 strip fresh or frozen thawed
pandan leaf**

MORNING

Put the water and pandan leaf in
a pitcher and refrigerate for at least
6 hours to infuse, then serve cold.

Shredded Pork and Sour Kimchi Soup

WITH *gingered Asian pear salad*
ALSO GOOD WITH *fried bean thread noodles* (PAGE 75) OR *coconut oil sticky rice* (PAGE 163)

A great way to use kimchi that's been in the refrigerator awhile and is perhaps too sour to eat on its own, this soup could not be simpler. If you'd like, use less pork and stir a diced block of firm tofu into the soup in the evening.

IN THE MORNING
Load up the cooker.

IN THE EVENING
Shred the pork and season the broth.

2 pounds (910 g) well-trimmed boneless pork shoulder or country-style ribs, cut into large chunks

About 2½ cups (375 g) kimchi, the more sour the better

6 cups (1.4 L) vegetable stock (page 240) or chicken or turkey stock (page 240)

About 3 tablespoons Chinese light soy sauce

1 to 2 tablespoons rice vinegar

Gochujang to taste (see Note)

MORNING

Put the pork, kimchi, and stock in the slow cooker. Cover and cook on low for 8 hours.

EVENING

Turn the cooker to high. Using a slotted spoon, transfer the pork to a bowl (it's fine if some kimchi comes along). With two forks, shred the pork, then return it to the cooker to reheat. Season the soup with soy sauce, vinegar, and gochujang (push the pepper paste through the holes in the slotted spoon to speed its distribution) and serve.

NOTE: Gochujang, Korean hot pepper paste, is available in good grocery stores now, in the Asian foods section. It comes in a plastic tub and can be refrigerated for weeks or months after you open it. Often you'll have a choice between hot and mild—which one you choose is up to you; the heat of the finished soup will also depend on how spicy your kimchi is. With a store-bought, fairly mild kimchi, I've found that 1 tablespoon of the hot gochujang is just right.

Gingered Asian pear salad

2 Asian pears

3 thin coins fresh peeled ginger, cut into thin slivers

Grated zest of ½ orange

3 teaspoons rice vinegar

1 teaspoon Chinese light soy sauce

1 tablespoon sesame seeds, toasted

Green tops of 1 scallion, thinly sliced on the bias

EVENING

Using a mandoline, a Thai green mango/papaya shredder, or a good knife and knife skills, cut the pears into fine matchstick strips, discarding the cores. Put in a bowl and toss with the ginger, orange zest, vinegar, and soy sauce. Top with the sesame seeds and scallion and serve immediately.

Small-Batch Burgoo

WITH *corn muffins*
ALSO GOOD WITH *tangy potato salad* (PAGE 36)
OR *sautéed green tomatoes with bread crumb topping* (PAGE 47)

This actually makes a pretty full pot of stew, but because Kentucky's approximately third-most-famous dish is so often made for huge gatherings, in pots whose volume is measured in gallons, I thought I should clarify up front that this is an immediate-family-size version. Usually it's made with all sorts of meats, whatever wild game or spare parts have been lingering in the freezer a tad too long, so feel free to take that approach here.

IN THE MORNING
Load up the cooker.

IN THE EVENING
Shred the meat and season to taste.

---

2 pounds (910 g) pork (shoulder, country-style ribs, or boneless) and/or chicken (boneless, skinless thighs or breasts), cut into large chunks

1 (28-ounce/794-g) can crushed tomatoes

1 small rib celery, diced

1 small carrot, diced

½ onion, diced

1½ cups (210 g) fresh or frozen sweet corn kernels

1½ cups (265 g) frozen lima beans, preferably Fordhooks

1 large russet potato, peeled and diced

1 bay leaf

1 cup (240 ml) beef stock (page 243) or chicken or turkey stock (page 240)

Salt and freshly ground black pepper

Worcestershire sauce

Ground cayenne

MORNING

Put the meat, tomatoes, celery, carrot, onion, corn, beans, potato, bay leaf, stock, 1 teaspoon salt, and several grindings of pepper in the slow cooker. Cover and cook on low for 8 hours.

EVENING

Using two forks, shred the meat. (If it's easier, fish out the chunks of meat with tongs, shred them in a bowl, then return them to the cooker.) Season the stew with more salt and pepper, if needed, about 2 teaspoons Worcestershire sauce, and at least ¼ teaspoon cayenne. It should be tangy, peppery, and just a little spicy. Serve.

I know, I know: Rachael Ray? But I swear this will make a difference in how efficiently you can prep ingredients. Have a spare bowl near your cutting board, and put all trimmings, peels, cores, eggshells, meat bones and trimmed-off fat, ingredient packaging, and basically anything you're going to throw away in the bowl. Then dump everything in the trash at once. (If you keep a compost pile, obviously don't put the meat trimmings or packaging in the bowl.) Unless your kitchen is set up superefficiently and your garbage can is directly under your work surface, this will save you tons of time, even considering that you then have an extra bowl to wash.

Corn muffins

As with any quick bread, you can mix the dry ingredients in the morning and leave the bowl on the counter; mix the wet ingredients, cover, and refrigerate until evening. Then when you're ready to bake in the evening, just stir the wet ingredients a bit to break up the solidified butter and dump into the dry ingredients to make the batter.

- 2½ cups (320 g) fine cornmeal, preferably stone-ground, white or yellow
- 4 teaspoons baking powder
- 1 teaspoon salt
- ½ cup (1 stick/115 g) unsalted butter
- 1½ cups (360 ml) milk
- 1 large egg
- 1 cup (140 g) fresh or frozen sweet corn kernels

EVENING

Preheat the oven to 425°F (220°C). Butter a 12-cup muffin tin or spray with cooking oil spray.

In a large bowl, whisk together the cornmeal, baking powder, and salt. Melt the butter, then add the milk and egg and whisk to combine. Pour the milk mixture into the cornmeal mixture and stir with a spatula until just incorporated; fold in the corn kernels. Pour into the muffin tin, filling the wells almost to the top. Bake until golden brown at the edges, 15 to 20 minutes. Let cool in the pan for 5 minutes, then loosen the edges of the muffins with a thin knife and pop them from the pan. Serve warm or at room temperature.

Pork and Apple Cider Stew

WITH *crusty rolls*

ALSO GOOD WITH *seared radicchio* (PAGE 56) OR *herb salad* (PAGE 31)

A little bit sweet with cider and chunks of apple, this thick and hearty stew makes a truly comforting one-dish fall meal.

IN THE MORNING
Brown the pork and onion.

IN THE EVENING
Reduce the sauce.

---

2 pounds (910 g) pork shoulder or boneless country-style ribs, cut into 1½-inch (4-cm) pieces

Salt and freshly ground black pepper

2 tablespoons all-purpose flour

2 tablespoons olive or vegetable oil

½ onion, chopped

2 cups (480 ml) apple cider

3 small carrots, cut into 1-inch (2.5-cm) lengths

8 ounces (225 g) tiny waxy-type potatoes, or larger potatoes cut into 1-inch (2.5-cm) pieces

1 apple, cored and cut into 1-inch (2.5-cm) pieces

1 bay leaf

MORNING

Season the pork with salt and pepper and toss the pieces in the flour to coat. In a large skillet or sauté pan, heat 1 tablespoon of the oil over medium-high heat. Add half of the pork and cook until the pieces are browned on two or more sides, about 5 minutes total. Transfer to the slow cooker and repeat with the remaining pork, in the oil left in the skillet.

Heat the remaining 1 tablespoon oil in the skillet and add the onion and a pinch of salt; cook, stirring frequently, for 2 to 3 minutes, until softened and wilted a bit, then scrape the onion into the cooker. Pour a little of the cider into the hot skillet, scraping up any browned bits, then pour the liquid into the cooker and add the remaining cider, the carrots, potatoes, apple, and bay leaf. Sprinkle with 1 teaspoon salt and several grindings of pepper. Cover and cook on low for 8 hours.

EVENING

Holding the cooker lid askew, drain as much of the liquid as possible from the cooker into a skillet (the one used for browning is fine) or wide saucepan. Bring to a boil over high heat and cook, stirring occasionally, until the sauce is reduced a bit, about 5 minutes; pour the sauce back into the cooker. Season with more salt and pepper, if needed, and serve.

Crusty rolls

If you don't have a long morning available, start these yeast-risen rolls the night before—just shape them and let them rise slowly in the fridge.

4 cups (510 g) all-purpose flour (or half white whole wheat flour), or more, if needed

1½ cups (360 ml) warm water

2 teaspoons instant yeast

Pinch of sugar

2 teaspoons salt

1 tablespoon unsalted butter, melted, plus more for the baking dish

MORNING OR EVENING BEFORE

Put the flour in the bowl of a stand mixer (or a large bowl), make a well in the center, and add the water, yeast, and sugar to the well. Mix with the dough hook (or by hand), adding the salt as you mix. Knead in the mixer on low speed (or by hand on a work surface) for 5 (or 10) minutes, until smooth, adding a little more flour, if needed. Cover the dough with an overturned bowl and let rise until doubled, 1 to 2 hours.

Divide into 8 portions and roll into balls. Generously butter a pie dish or similar baking dish and arrange the balls in the dish; they should almost touch one another. (I put one in the center, and the rest in a circle surrounding it.) Drizzle the butter over the balls and gently rub with your fingers (or use a brush) to coat them. Cover the dish with plastic and either let rise for 30 minutes or refrigerate until ready to bake.

EVENING

Preheat the oven to 400°F (205°C). If the dough balls were refrigerated, bring them to room temperature while you preheat the oven. Uncover the dish and bake until nicely browned, 30 to 35 minutes (spread a little more butter over the tops for the last few minutes, if you'd like). Serve warm.

Fragrant Braised Pork Belly Sandwiches

WITH *green apple rojak*

ALSO GOOD WITH *quick-pickled vegetables* (PAGE 102) OR *quickie cilantro-lime topping* (PAGE 81)

This is my shortcut version of rou jia mo, or "Chinese hamburgers." English muffins make a very fine substitute for the chewy, holey flatbreads, but I'd encourage you to try the homemade version sometime—it's easy and fun!

IN THE MORNING
Load up the cooker and, if you have time, slice the scallion greens and fresh peppers.

IN THE EVENING
Trim the pork belly, chop it, and reheat in a skillet with the scallions and peppers. Toast the English muffins.

2 pieces star anise

5 dried red chiles

5 green cardamom pods, cracked

1 cinnamon stick

1 teaspoon coriander seeds

½ teaspoon cumin seeds

½ teaspoon Sichuan peppercorns

2 pounds (910 g) pork belly, cut into four pieces

¼ cup (60 ml) Chinese light soy sauce (not "lite")

¼ cup (60 ml) Shaoxing wine

3 scallions

3 coins fresh ginger

1 wide strip orange zest

2 tablespoons brown sugar

2 green long hot peppers

Fresh cilantro and/or mint sprigs

English muffins or homemade mo (recipe follows)

MORNING
Put the star anise, dried chiles, cardamom, cinnamon, coriander seeds, cumin seeds, and Sichuan peppercorns in a muslin spice bag or enclose in a double layer of cheesecloth. Put the bag in the slow cooker, along with the pork belly, soy sauce, wine, the white parts of the scallions, the ginger, orange zest, brown sugar, and 1 cup (240 ml) water. Cover and cook on low for 8 hours.

MORNING OR EVENING
Thinly slice the scallion greens and the fresh peppers on the bias. If doing this in the morning, cover and refrigerate.

EVENING
Using a slotted spoon, transfer the pork to a cutting board. Trim off the skin and as much of the underlying layer of fat as you'd like, then finely chop the meat and the remaining fat. Transfer to a large skillet or sauté pan. Holding a sieve over the skillet, ladle in about 1 cup (240 ml) of the liquid from the cooker. Place over medium heat and reheat the pork, stirring frequently.

RECIPE CONTINUES...

Add the sliced scallions and fresh peppers and toss to combine and heat through (the scallions and pepper should remain crunchy-crisp).

Toast the English muffins and spoon in the pork, along with a few sprigs of cilantro per sandwich.

Green apple rojak

⅓ cup (50 g) salted shelled peanuts

4 dried red chiles, preferably Thai, stemmed

1 tablespoon tamarind concentrate, such as Tamicon brand

2 tablespoons jaggery or brown sugar

2 Granny Smith or other tart green apples

MORNING OR EVENING

In a large mortar and pestle, pound the peanuts until they're finely crushed but not paste-like. Set aside half of them to use as garnish.

In a small skillet or sauté pan, toast the chiles over medium heat until they're darkened on both sides, about 3 minutes. Break them into pieces and add them to the mortar. Pound the chiles and peanuts together until they form a paste and the chile pieces are mere flakes. Stir in the tamarind, brown sugar, and 2 tablespoons water. Set aside at room temperature until evening.

EVENING

Core the apples and cut them into ¾-inch (2-cm) chunks. Put them in a bowl. Add the peanut sauce and toss to coat. Transfer to a serving dish, sprinkle with the reserved peanuts, and serve.

Mo (Xi'an-style flatbreads)

Makes about 6

3 cups (375 g) all-purpose flour, plus more for rolling out

½ teaspoon salt

1 cup (240 ml) warm water

1 teaspoon instant yeast

MORNING OR EVENING

In a large bowl, stir all the ingredients together to make a smooth dough. Knead on the countertop for 5 minutes. If doing this in the morning, put the ball of dough back in the cleaned bowl, cover with plastic wrap, and refrigerate. If doing this in the evening, cover the dough on the counter with the bowl and let rest for 15 to 20 minutes.

EVENING

Preheat the oven to 350°F (175°C). Divide the dough into golf-ball-size pieces (about six) and use a floured small rolling pin to flatten each into a round 4 to 5 inches (10 to 12 cm) in diameter and ¼ inch (6 mm) thick.

Heat a well-seasoned wok or a large griddle over medium heat. When a drop of water on the surface evaporates immediately, it's hot enough. Working in batches, put the dough rounds on the wok (no oil is needed) and cook until the bottom is flecked with brown, 2 to 3 minutes, then flip and brown the other side and transfer to a baking sheet. Repeat with the remaining dough rounds. Transfer to the oven and bake for 5 to 10 minutes. Let cool for a few minutes, then split in half to serve.

Cabbage and Beer Brats

WITH *quark and caraway mash*
ALSO GOOD WITH *butter-roasted mixed potatoes* (PAGE 120) OR *two peas with marjoram* (PAGE 97)

The sausages become very tender over eight hours, and infuse the lightly sweetened cabbage with the juices they exude in the process.

IN THE MORNING
Brown the sausages.

IN THE EVENING
Serve.

1 small head (about 1½ pounds/680 g) green or red cabbage, cored and cut into large chunks

1½ tablespoons brown sugar

1 teaspoon salt

1 tablespoon vegetable oil

6 beer bratwursts

½ onion, sliced ½ inch (12 mm) thick

1 (12-ounce/360-ml) bottle of beer, or most of it

MORNING

Put the cabbage in the slow cooker and sprinkle with the brown sugar and salt.

In a large skillet or sauté pan, heat the oil over medium-high heat. When it shimmers, add the sausages and cook until browned, about 2 minutes on each side. Arrange the sausages over the cabbage in the cooker. Add the onion to the skillet over medium heat and cook for 1 minute, then pour in the beer, stirring to scrape up any browned bits; pour the liquid into the cooker. Cover and cook on low for 8 hours.

EVENING

Using tongs or a slotted spoon, transfer the sausages, onion, and cabbage to a platter and serve, spooning some of the cooking liquid over the sausages and vegetables.

Quark and caraway mash

If you don't have quark on hand, use plain Greek yogurt or labneh.

3 russet potatoes, peeled, if desired, and cut into chunks

1 teaspoon caraway seeds

Salt and freshly ground black pepper

⅔ cup (165 ml) quark (page 253)

2 tablespoons unsalted butter

EVENING

Put the potatoes, caraway, and 1 teaspoon salt in a large saucepan and cover with water. Bring to a boil, then lower the heat and simmer until the potatoes are very tender, 10 to 15 minutes. Drain in a colander (some of the caraway will be washed away, but that's fine), return to the pan, and mash in the quark and butter. Season with salt and pepper to taste and serve.

Red Beans and Rice

WITH *quick-cooked shredded collards*

ALSO GOOD WITH *fried okra* (PAGE 86) OR *chayote with garlic buttered bread crumbs* (PAGE 83)

Kidney beans need to be boiled to neutralize a toxin they contain—if you're confident that your particular slow cooker will bring the liquid to a full boil for at least 10 minutes, you can skip the preboiling step.

IN THE MORNING
Boil the beans for
10 minutes.

IN THE EVENING
Cook the rice and ladle
excess liquid from the
beans. If you'd like, sear
the andouille and add it
to the beans.

---

1 pound (455 g) dried kidney
beans

1 large green bell pepper

2 ribs celery

½ onion

3 cloves garlic

1 smoked ham hock

1 bay leaf

2 cups long-grain rice

Salt and freshly ground
black pepper

3 tablespoons all-purpose
flour, if needed

1 to 2 links (7 to 14
ounces/200 to 400 g)
andouille sausage, cut into
rounds ¼ inch (6 mm) thick
(optional)

Cajun seasoning mix or
ground cayenne (optional)

MORNING

Rinse the beans in a sieve under running water. Dump into a saucepan and add water to cover by 2 inches (5 cm). Bring to a boil, then lower the heat but keep it at a boil, and cook for 10 minutes.

Meanwhile, cut the bell pepper and celery into 1-inch (2.5-cm) pieces, dice the onion, and chop the garlic. Put them in the slow cooker. Drain the beans and add them to the cooker, along with the ham hock, bay leaf, and 6 cups (1.4 L) water. Cover and cook on low for 8 hours.

EVENING

Put the rice in a sieve and rinse very well under running water. Dump into a 2-quart (2-L) saucepan and add 2¼ cups (540 ml) water and a good pinch of salt. Bring to a boil over high heat, stir once to unstick any grains from the bottom of the pan, then cover and cook over the lowest heat for 14 minutes, or until all the water is absorbed and the rice is tender. Let stand, covered, for 3 minutes, then fluff with a fork or spatula.

While the rice is cooking, turn the cooker to high. Using tongs, transfer the ham hock to a bowl. Ladle as much of the excess liquid from the cooker as you can and discard it. Pull the meat from the ham hock in bite-size pieces and return them to the cooker, discarding the bone and any large pieces of fat. If the beans are still quite liquid, mash some of them with a wooden spoon, hit them with an immersion blender for a few seconds, or ladle out some liquid into a small bowl, whisk in the flour, and stir the mixture back into the beans and let cook, uncovered, for 10 to 15 more minutes.

If using the andouille, place a skillet or sauté pan over high heat. Add the sausage and cook until the slices are nicely browned on one side, 2 to 3 minutes, then turn and brown them on the other side. Transfer to the beans and gently stir.

Season the beans with salt, plenty of black pepper, and Cajun seasoning, if desired. Serve with the rice.

Quick-cooked shredded collards

1 large bunch collard greens (about 1 pound/455 g)

2 tablespoons olive oil or schmaltz (page 251)

2 cloves garlic, chopped

3 or 4 chiles de árbol

Salt

Vinegar-based hot sauce

MORNING OR EVENING

Wash the collards and pull out the tough center ribs (anything thicker than a pencil). Stack the leaves, roll them up, and cut the roll crosswise into ½-inch (12-mm) strips. Put in a bag and refrigerate if doing this in the morning.

EVENING

In a Dutch oven, heat the oil over medium heat. When it shimmers, add the garlic and chiles. Cook, stirring, until the garlic is golden, about 3 minutes. Pile in the collards and toss with tongs for 2 to 3 minutes. Add a good pinch of salt and 1 cup (240 ml) water, cover, and simmer until the collards are almost tender, about 5 minutes. Uncover and simmer for another 3 to 5 minutes. Serve with the hot sauce on the side.

Balinese-Style Banana Leaf–Wrapped Pork Chops

WITH *coconut oil sticky rice*
ALSO GOOD WITH *basic coconut rice* (PAGE 107) OR *bok choy brown basmati rice* (PAGE 111)

On a whim a few years ago I bought a three-author cookbook published in the UK with the glorious title *Best-Ever Cooking of Malaysia, Singapore, Indonesia & the Philippines: Ingredients, Techniques, Traditions, & All the Popular Local Dishes*. And they aren't kidding. It's an absolutely insane book: step-by-step photographs of every single dish (all 340 of them—how'd they do that?), no-holds-barred ingredients lists (terasi and belacan, milkfish and mutton, sour carambola greens), and extensive tips and notes on every page. This recipe was inspired by one for a spice paste–rubbed and leaf-wrapped whole roast duck (which I swear I'm going to try one of these days).

IN THE MORNING
Make the seasoning paste and load up the banana leaf–lined cooker.

IN THE EVENING
Open the banana leaf and remove and slice the pork.

3 large shallots, chopped

5 cloves garlic, chopped

2 thumb-size pieces fresh turmeric, peeled and chopped

2-inch (5-cm) piece of fresh ginger, peeled and chopped

2 jalapeño or serrano chiles, chopped

4 fresh kaffir lime leaves, minced

2 stalks lemongrass, tops and tough outer leaves removed, chopped

3 tablespoons grated unsweetened coconut

1 tablespoon fish sauce

½ teaspoon salt

Freshly ground black pepper

1 large piece of banana leaf, rinsed, thawed if frozen

4 thick-cut bone-in pork chops

Lime wedges

MORNING

In a mini food processor or a good blender, combine the shallots, garlic, turmeric, ginger, chiles, lime leaves, lemongrass, coconut, fish sauce, salt, and several grindings of black pepper. Pulse to make a very smooth paste, scraping down the sides of the bowl as needed.

Cut a piece of banana leaf to line the whole bottom of the pot and come up and over the long edges. Season the chops lightly with salt on both sides. Pat the shallot paste on both sides of each pork chop and arrange the chops like falling dominoes in the banana leaf–lined cooker. Fold the edges of the leaf over the top of the chops to enclose them. Cover and cook on low for 8 hours.

Open the banana leaf package and use tongs or a metal spatula to remove the chops to a carving board or serving platter. Serve one chop per person, or slice the meat off the bone to serve, spooning juices from the cooker over the meat. It'll be messy, but delicious, either way. Put lime wedges on the table for people to squeeze over the pork.

Coconut oil sticky rice

- **2 cups (400 g) glutinous rice**
- **2 tablespoons coconut oil, melted**
- **Banana leaves, rinsed and cut to fit two bamboo steamer levels 8 inches (20 cm) in diameter**

Put the rice in a bowl and add cold water to cover by several inches. Set aside to soak until evening.

Drain the rice in a sieve and rinse well under running water. Return it to the bowl and drizzle with the oil, tossing to coat well. Divide the rice between two 8-inch (20-cm) bamboo steamer levels lined with banana leaf circles, spreading it evenly in the trays. Bring a pot of water or about 1 ½ inches (4 cm) water in the bottom of a wok to a boil, place the stacked steamer on top, covered (the water should not touch the steamer), and steam for 20 minutes, or until the rice is tender. Serve hot.

Smoked Sausage, White Bean, and Spinach Soup

WITH *retro garlic bread*
ALSO GOOD WITH *crusty rolls* (PAGE 155) OR *romaine salad with creamy herb dressing* (PAGE 175)

If your ham hock is very meaty (or if you use two hocks), you might not even need to add the sausage, which really is just gilding the lily.

IN THE MORNING
Load up the cooker.

IN THE EVENING
Pull the meat off the ham hock and sear
the sausage.
Fold in the spinach.

1 smoked ham hock

2 cups (365 g) dried Great Northern beans

4 ounces (115 g) baby spinach

12 ounces (340 g) smoked sausage, such as kielbasa, cut into rounds ¼ inch (6 mm) thick

Salt and freshly ground black pepper

MORNING
Put the ham hock in the slow cooker and add the beans and 8 cups (2 L) water. Cover and cook on low for 8 hours.

EVENING
Turn the cooker to high. Using tongs or a slotted spoon, transfer the ham hock to a bowl; when cool enough to handle, pull the meat off the bone, discarding any large pieces of fat, and return the meat to the cooker. Fold in the spinach.

Place a large skillet or sauté pan over high heat. Add the sausage and cook until the slices are nicely browned on one side, 2 to 3 minutes, then turn and brown them on the other side. Transfer to the soup and gently stir. Season with salt and pepper and serve.

Retro garlic bread

4 tablespoons (55 g) unsalted butter, softened (20 seconds in a microwave oven will do the job)

1 teaspoon granulated garlic

¾ teaspoon salt

8 large, thick slices Italian-style bread

MORNING OR EVENING
Stir together the butter, garlic, and salt. Spread it on both sides of the bread slices and place them on a baking sheet; set aside.

EVENING
Preheat the broiler to high and set the rack about 6 inches (15 cm) from the heat source. Broil the bread, watching it closely, until golden brown and bubbly, 2 to 3 minutes. Flip the slices over and broil the other side until browned. Serve hot.

Classic Split Pea Soup

WITH *carrot-top pesto*
ALSO GOOD WITH *almond-lemon pistou* (PAGE 49) OR *baby kale salad with dates and pistachios* (PAGE 42)

There is no need to get fancy when it comes to split pea soup. It's one of the world's most perfect foods.

IN THE MORNING
Load up the cooker.

IN THE EVENING
Pull the meat from
the ham hock.

---

1 pound (455 g) dried green split peas

1 smoked ham hock

1 bunch carrots (about 7 small), cut into ½-inch (12-mm) pieces, tops removed and reserved for pesto (below), if desired

1 large russet potato, peeled and cut into ½-inch (12-mm) pieces

Salt and freshly ground black pepper

MORNING
Rinse the split peas in a sieve under running water. Dump into the slow cooker and add 6 cups (1.4 L) water. Add the ham hock, carrots, and potato. Cover and cook on low for 8 hours.

EVENING
Using tongs, transfer the ham hock to a bowl. Pull the meat from the bone in bite-size pieces and return them to the soup, discarding the bone and any large pieces of fat. Season the soup with salt and plenty of pepper. If you'd like it thicker, hit it with an immersion blender for a few seconds to break up some of the split peas and vegetables. Serve.

Carrot-top pesto

I like this pesto-type dollop to be quite lemony, the better to brighten long-cooked dishes, but if you're not as big a lemon fan, add the juice and zest a little at a time, tasting as you go.

1 bunch carrot tops

¼ cup (30 g) chopped walnuts

1 clove garlic, chopped

2 tablespoons olive oil

Grated zest and juice of ½ lemon

½ teaspoon salt

Freshly ground black pepper

MORNING OR EVENING
Wash the carrot tops and spin them dry. Chop them and put in a mini food processor with the walnuts, garlic, oil, lemon zest and juice, salt, and a few grindings of pepper. Pulse until finely chopped and combined, scraping the side of the bowl as needed. Transfer to a container, and cover and refrigerate if doing this in the morning. Let come to room temperature before serving.

CHAPTER 4

Beef

Your Basic Chili

WITH *fresh-corn cheddar cornbread*
ALSO GOOD WITH *chili garnishes* (PAGE 172) OR *sautéed fresh poblanos and corn* (PAGE 39)

I'm no purist when it comes to chili. (If you are, turn to the dried chile–based one on page 172.) I appreciate just about any long-cooked stew with a protein and cumin and chiles—with or without tomatoes, beans, even fresh chiles and corn; it's all fair game as far as I'm concerned. Here is a very simple chili, which I hope you'll see as a template for tweaking: Add more tomatoes, if you'd like, or different varieties of chile powder (and some cayenne for more heat), add some corn kernels or diced sweet peppers at the end, substitute a few chopped fresh or canned tomatillos for some of the tomatoes, try soy sauce or a splash of fish sauce instead of Worcestershire—make it your own.

IN THE MORNING
Brown the beef and onion and load up the cooker.

IN THE EVENING
Serve.

3 pounds (1.4 kg) ground beef (chuck is good)

1 onion, diced

1 tablespoon ground cumin

1 tablespoon ancho chile powder, or more to taste

2 teaspoons salt, or more to taste

1 (28-ounce/794-g) can crushed tomatoes

1 (14.5-ounce/411-g) can diced tomatoes

1 (14- to 15-ounce/400- to 430-g) can kidney beans, drained and rinsed, or about 1½ cups cooked and drained kidney beans (page 246)

2 teaspoons Worcestershire sauce

MORNING
Heat a large skillet or sauté pan over high heat and add one third of the beef. Cook, breaking it up and stirring with a spatula or spoon, until almost all the pink is gone, about 5 minutes, then drain off any liquid and transfer the meat to the slow cooker. Repeat with the remaining beef in two batches. Add the onion, cumin, chile powder, salt, crushed and diced tomatoes, beans, and Worcestershire sauce to the cooker. Cover and cook on low for 8 hours.

EVENING
Season with more salt and/or chile powder, if needed, then serve.

Fresh-corn cheddar cornbread

If you'd like to save time in the evening, mix the dry ingredients in the morning and leave them on the counter, and mix the wet ingredients and cover and refrigerate. In the evening just dump the wet into dry, stir, pour into the hot skillet, and bake.

2 cups (360) fine cornmeal, preferably stone-ground, white or yellow

½ cup (65 g) all-purpose flour

2½ teaspoons baking powder

½ teaspoon salt

1½ cups (360 ml) buttermilk

1 cup (115 g) shredded cheddar cheese

1 cup (135 to 145 g) fresh or frozen sweet corn kernels (from about 1 ear)

2 jalapeño or serrano chiles, seeded and minced (optional)

2 tablespoons minced fresh cilantro

¼ cup (60 ml) vegetable oil, plus more for the skillet

EVENING

Preheat the oven to 450°F (230°C). Oil a 10-inch (25-cm) cast-iron skillet and put it in the oven as it heats up.

In a large bowl, whisk together the cornmeal, flour, baking powder, and salt. In another large bowl, whisk together the buttermilk, cheese, corn, chiles, if using, cilantro, and oil. Pour the buttermilk mixture into the cornmeal mixture and stir with a rubber spatula until just incorporated. Scrape the batter into the hot skillet and bake until a toothpick inserted in the center comes out clean, about 25 minutes. Slice into wedges and serve straight from the skillet (keep a pot holder on the handle to avoid mistakenly grabbing on to the hot pan).

Chile Chili

WITH *chili garnishes*

ALSO GOOD WITH *chilled radish chips* (PAGE 134) OR *avocado-lime topping* (PAGE 76)

Instead of rehydrating the chiles and tomatoes, blending, and straining, you can use 3 cups (720 ml) chili base (page 244) and skip to the beef browning step.

IN THE MORNING
Simmer the dried chiles to make the chili base. Brown the beef.

IN THE EVENING
Whisk in the masa harina to thicken the stew.

---

4 ounces (115 g) guajillo and/or New Mexico chiles (about 16), stemmed and snipped into pieces with scissors

3 to 6 dried chiles de árbol, stemmed, or more, if you'd like more heat

1 ancho chile, stemmed and seeded (optional)

½ cup (30 g) sun-dried tomatoes, or 2 plum tomatoes, chopped

4 cups (960 ml) boiling water

3 pounds (1.4 kg) beef for stew

3 tablespoons vegetable oil

1 (12-ounce/360-ml) bottle of beer

1 tablespoon chili powder (see Note)

2 morilla chiles (smoke-dried red jalapeños) (optional)

6 tablespoons (45 g) masa harina, or more, if needed

MORNING

Shake out as many of the guajillo seeds as possible (but don't lose your mind over it). Put the guajillo chiles, chiles de árbol, ancho chile, if using, and tomatoes in a blender and pour the boiling water over them. Let soak for at least 10 minutes, until the chiles are softened. Puree until very smooth. Set a fine-mesh sieve over the slow cooker and pour in the chile puree, pushing the puree and liquid through with a spatula; discard the bits of skin and seeds in the sieve.

In a large skillet or sauté pan, heat 1 tablespoon of the oil over high heat. When it shimmers, add one-third of the beef and cook until browned on one or more sides, 3 to 5 minutes total, then scrape into the cooker and repeat with the remaining oil and beef. Return the skillet to high heat and pour in the beer, scraping up any browned bits. Boil the beer until reduced by half, about 5 minutes, then pour into the cooker. Add the chili powder, morilla chiles, if using, and 1 teaspoon salt. Cover and cook on low for 8 hours.

EVENING

Ladle a bit of the liquid into a small bowl and whisk in the masa harina, then stir the mixture back into the chili. If you'd like a thicker stew, repeat with more masa harina. Season with more salt, if needed. Serve, removing and discarding the morilla chiles, if you'd like.

NOTE: For the chili powder, you can combine 2 teaspoons ancho chile powder, 1 teaspoon ground cumin, 1 teaspoon garlic powder, 1 teaspoon onion powder, and a pinch of dried oregano.

Chili garnishes

Sliced avocados

Lime wedges

Sliced radishes

Chopped fresh cilantro

Sour cream, quark (page 253), or plain Greek yogurt

Diced onion

Corn tortillas, warmed (see page 100)

EVENING

Arrange all the garnishes on a platter and in bowls and serve.

No-Ketchup Sloppy Joes

WITH *smothered butter beans*

ALSO GOOD WITH *two peas with marjoram* (PAGE 97) OR *tangy potato salad* (PAGE 36)

Sloppy Joes fall into the same category of food nostalgia for me as s'mores: loved them as a kid, and appreciate the concept in general, but now find the original versions so cloying as to be (almost) inedible. Following is my correction to the usual oversweet, sticky Sloppy Joe, no ketchup needed. To my adult palate it tastes exactly as I remember it tasting as a kid—and my daughter probably has no idea that this messy sandwich she likes so much is usually a whole lot sweeter.

IN THE MORNING
Brown the beef.

IN THE EVENING
Toast the buns.

1 tablespoon vegetable oil

3 pounds (1.4 kg) ground beef (chuck is best here)

1 small red bell pepper, diced

1 (14.5-ounce/411-g) can crushed tomatoes

4 heaping tablespoons (85 g) tomato paste

2 teaspoons onion powder

½ teaspoon dry mustard powder

1 tablespoon Worcestershire sauce

Juice of 1 lemon

¼ cup brown sugar, or more to taste

Salt and freshly ground black pepper

Soft buns, split

MORNING

In a large skillet or sauté pan, heat the oil over high heat. When it shimmers, add the beef and cook, stirring and breaking it up, until no pink remains, 8 to 10 minutes. Drain off excess liquid, then dump the beef into the slow cooker. Stir in the bell pepper, tomatoes, tomato paste, onion powder, mustard powder, Worcestershire sauce, lemon juice, brown sugar, 1 teaspoon salt, and several grindings of black pepper. Cover and cook on low for 8 hours.

EVENING

Toast the buns in a toaster or on a baking sheet under the broiler. Season the beef with more salt, pepper, and brown sugar, if needed, then serve on the buns.

Smothered butter beans

If you make this with frozen home-cooked limas (page 246), they'll need only 10 minutes of simmering.

1 tablespoon unsalted butter

1 shallot, thinly sliced

1 pint (10 ounces/280 g) cherry or grape tomatoes, halved, or quartered if large

12 ounces (340 g) frozen baby lima beans, rinsed and drained

Salt and freshly ground black pepper

EVENING

In a large skillet or sauté pan, melt the butter over medium-high heat. Add the shallot and cook, stirring, until golden, about 1½ minutes. Add the tomatoes and lima beans; season with salt and pepper. Add 1 cup (240 ml) water, cover, and cook for 15 to 20 minutes longer, until the lima beans are tender, tossing occasionally and adding a little more water if the pan seems dry. Serve.

Cincinnati-Style Chili

WITH *romaine salad with creamy herb dressing*
ALSO GOOD WITH *Parmesan roasted broccoli spears* (PAGE 182) OR *herb salad* (PAGE 31)

I've been refining this recipe for at least eleven years, and I'm pretty sure this is how I'll make Cincinnati chili (a favorite of my husband Derek's) from here out, with just a hint of sweet spice and a square of chocolate melted in at the end. How you want to serve it is up to you: Go for the traditional interpretation with spaghetti, beans, and a snowy mound of finely shredded orange cheddar, or just serve it on its own.

IN THE MORNING
Puree the tomatoes and aromatics. Sauté the ground beef, drain, and load the cooker.

IN THE EVENING
Stir in the chocolate.

---

1 (28-ounce/794-g) can whole or crushed tomatoes

1 small onion, chopped

1 clove garlic, chopped

1 teaspoon ground cumin

¼ teaspoon ground cloves

¼ teaspoon ground allspice

¼ teaspoon ground cayenne, or more to taste

Salt and freshly ground black pepper

1 tablespoon vegetable oil

2½ pounds (1.2 kg) ground beef

2 cinnamon sticks

1 ounce (28 g) unsweetened chocolate

Accompaniments (optional):

1 pound (455 g) dried spaghetti

2 (14- to 15-ounce/400- to 430-g) cans kidney or other red beans, drained and rinsed, or about 3 cups cooked and drained beans (page 246)

8 ounces (225 g) sharp cheddar cheese

MORNING

Put the tomatoes, onion, garlic, cumin, cloves, allspice, cayenne, a large pinch of salt, and several grindings of black pepper in the slow cooker and use an immersion blender to puree it (tilt the cooker if necessary to keep the blender head submerged).

In a large skillet or sauté pan, heat the oil over medium-high heat until it shimmers. Add the beef and cook, turning frequently with a metal spatula and breaking up the pieces, until no longer pink, 8 to 10 minutes. Drain in a colander (or put a lid over the pan and pour off the excess liquid and fat). Scrape the beef into the slow cooker and add the cinnamon sticks. Cover and cook on low for 8 hours.

EVENING

Stir the chocolate into the chili and let it melt, then season with salt to taste. Put the lid back on and reheat for a few minutes or as long as it takes to set the table and/or prepare any accompaniments.

Make the accompaniments, if you'd like: Bring a large pot of water to a boil and add several pinches of salt. Add the spaghetti and cook according to the package instructions, until al dente. While the spaghetti cooks, put the beans in a sieve and dip them into the boiling water for a few seconds to heat; transfer to a small bowl. Drain the spaghetti and put in a bowl. Into another bowl or onto a piece of waxed paper, very finely grate the cheese—you can use the small holes on a box grater or, for even snowier results, a Microplane zester. Tong a nest of spaghetti into shallow bowls, top with the beans, then a huge pile of cheese.

Romaine salad with creamy herb dressing

1 cup (240 ml) quark (page 253) or plain thick Greek yogurt (preferably full-fat) or labneh

1 cup (50 g) chopped fresh parsley

2 tablespoons chopped fresh basil

2 tablespoons fresh lemon juice

1 teaspoon salt, or to taste

Freshly ground black pepper

3 to 4 romaine hearts

MORNING OR EVENING

In a mini food processor or blender, combine the quark, parsley, basil, lemon juice, salt, and several grindings of pepper, pulsing until the herbs are finely minced. Add water a tablespoon at a time, until the dressing is thick but just pourable, 2 to 3 tablespoons. Add more salt and pepper, if needed.

Cut off the bottoms of the lettuce heads, coarsely chop the leaves, and wash and spin dry. Cover and refrigerate if doing this in the morning (right in the salad spinner, or in a resealable plastic bag).

EVENING

Toss the lettuce with dressing to just coat the leaves. Serve immediately.

Unconstructed Cabbage Rolls

WITH *dilled cucumbers*

ALSO GOOD WITH *pan-seared green beans* (PAGE 89) OR *two peas with marjoram* (PAGE 97)

This stew has all the flavors of cabbage rolls—right down to the citric acid and ginger snap cookies used by my western-Pennsylvania grandmother—but none of the fuss associated with steaming a head of cabbage, removing the leaves, and forming the actual rolls.

IN THE MORNING
Brown the beef
and cook the onion.

IN THE EVENING
Cook the rice.

2½ pounds (1.2 kg) ground beef

1 (28-ounce/794-g) can crushed tomatoes

½ teaspoon citric acid

Salt and freshly ground black pepper

1 tablespoon olive oil

½ onion, diced

8 ginger snap cookies

½ head green cabbage, cored and cut into 1½-inch (4-cm) chunks

2 cups (370 g) long-grain white rice

MORNING

In a large skillet or sauté pan, cook the beef over medium-high heat, stirring to break it up, until most of the pink is gone, 5 to 8 minutes. Pour off any liquid and transfer the beef to the slow cooker; stir in the tomatoes, citric acid, 1½ teaspoons salt, and plenty of pepper.

Return the skillet to medium heat and add the oil, onion, and a pinch of salt and cook, stirring, until just tender, 2 to 3 minutes. Pour in ½ cup (120 ml) water and scrape up any browned bits, then stir the onion and liquid into the beef mixture. Add the cookies, put the cabbage on top, and sprinkle with salt and pepper. Cover and cook on low for 8 hours.

EVENING

Put the rice in a sieve and rinse very well under running water. Dump into a 2-quart (2-L) saucepan and add 2¼ cups (540 ml) water and a good pinch of salt. Bring to a boil over high heat, stir once to unstick any grains from the bottom of the pan, then cover and cook over the lowest heat for 14 minutes, or until all the water is absorbed and the rice is tender. Let stand, covered, for 3 minutes, then fluff with a fork or spatula.

Stir the cabbage and beef mixture, season with more salt and pepper, if needed, and serve over the rice.

Dilled cucumbers

1 English cucumber
   (about 15 ounces/430 g)

1 teaspoon salt

2 teaspoons chopped
   fresh dill

1 tablespoon white wine
   vinegar

Two pinches of sugar

MORNING

Very thinly slice the cucumber into rounds (a mandoline is best for this). Put them in a bowl and sprinkle with the salt and dill, then toss to distribute the salt and dill evenly. Press a piece of plastic wrap directly over the cucumbers and flatten them in the bowl (or stack another bowl on top of the first to press the cucumbers down). Put weights (cans of tomatoes, for example) on the cucumbers and refrigerate until evening.

EVENING

Remove the weights and plastic and drain the cucumbers well, squeezing them to remove excess liquid. Sprinkle with the vinegar and sugar, toss well, and refrigerate until ready to serve.

Sugo

WITH *chicken pâté toasts*

ALSO GOOD WITH *grizzled asparagus* (PAGE 201) OR *herb salad* (PAGE 31)

I wanted to include both the familiar cream-enriched ragù (page 183) and this more unusual meat sauce for pasta, because I think there's a place for each of them in the home cook's repertoire. The contrasting additions of bright lemon zest and funky quick-sautéed chicken livers just before serving make this sauce company-worthy. Both this sugo and the ragù make excellent weekend slow cooking projects—make a bunch and freeze it for even easier meals later.

IN THE MORNING
Rehydrate the porcini, and sauté the onion, garlic, and beef.

IN THE EVENING
Cook the pasta and chicken livers, if using, and stir the lemon zest and parsley into the sauce.

½ ounce (14 g) dried porcini mushrooms

1½ cups (360 ml) hot water

1 or 2 tablespoons olive oil

½ onion, diced

Salt and freshly ground black pepper

2 cloves garlic, chopped

1 pound (455 g) lean ground beef

¼ cup (60 ml) red wine

1 carrot, peeled and finely diced

1 rib celery, finely diced

1 (28-ounce/794-g) can crushed tomatoes, or 1 (24-ounce/680-g) jar passata di pomodoro (strained tomatoes)

Fresh or dried long pasta

2 large chicken livers (about 3½ ounces/100 g total), finely chopped (optional)

Grated zest of 1 lemon

2 tablespoons chopped fresh parsley

MORNING

Put the mushrooms in a bowl and cover with the hot water; set aside to soak.

In a skillet or sauté pan, heat 1 tablespoon oil over medium-high heat. When it shimmers, add the onion and a pinch of salt and cook, stirring, until translucent, about 5 minutes. Add the garlic and stir for 1 minute, then add the beef and cook, stirring, until most of the pink is gone. Pour in the wine and scrape up any browned bits, then scrape the mixture into the slow cooker. Add the carrot, celery, and tomatoes.

Lift the mushrooms from the soaking liquid, agitating them gently to make sure no sand remains lodged in them. Mince the mushrooms and add them to the cooker. Strain the soaking liquid through a fine-mesh sieve into the cooker, discarding any grit in the bottom of the bowl. Stir in 1 teaspoon salt. Cover and cook on low for 8 hours.

Bring a large pot of salted water to a boil. Add the pasta and cook until al dente; drain.

If you're using the chicken livers, in a skillet or sauté pan, heat 1 tablespoon oil. When it shimmers, add the livers and cook, stirring, until cooked through and a little crisp in spots, 4 to 5 minutes. Scrape into the sauce in the cooker. Stir in the lemon zest and parsley, season with salt and pepper, and serve with the pasta.

Chicken pâté toasts

If you're using chicken livers in the sauce, just use whatever's left of the pound here. Otherwise use the full pound.

1 tablespoon olive oil

¼ cup (40 g) minced shallot (about 1 large)

¼ cup (60 ml) brandy or red wine

Scant 1 pound (455 g) chicken livers, chopped

Salt and freshly ground black pepper

2 teaspoons minced fresh sage, plus more for garnish

2 teaspoons drained capers (optional)

About 6 thin slices crusty bread, toasted

In a small saucepan, heat the oil over medium heat. When it shimmers, add the shallot and cook, stirring, until it's just starting to brown at the edges, about 3 minutes. Add the brandy, increase the heat to medium-high, and boil for 1 minute. Add the livers, ¾ teaspoon salt, several grindings of pepper, and a splash of water and cook, stirring frequently, until the livers are just cooked through, 5 to 7 minutes—cut into a thick piece to check: They should have just a bit of pink in the center. Using a slotted spoon, transfer to a mini food processor and pour in most of the liquid. Add the sage and pulse until the mixture is quite smooth. Stir in the capers, if using. If doing this in the morning, transfer to a sealable container and refrigerate. If doing this in the evening, let the pâté cool to just warm before serving.

Spread the pâté (either cold or still warm) onto slices of toast, top each with a sage leaf, and serve.

Meatballs in Marinara

WITH *Parmesan roasted broccoli spears*
ALSO GOOD WITH *basil zucchini* (PAGE 191) OR *spinach-Gruyère toasts* (PAGE 194)

If you have a bit of space in your freezer, it almost always makes sense to mix up extra meatballs and freeze them for another meal, as the amount of prep work involved in making double the quantity is only negligibly greater.

IN THE MORNING
Shape the meatballs and put half of them in the freezer for next time. Briefly brown the meatballs and load up the cooker.

IN THE EVENING
Puree the sauce.

1 (28-ounce/794-g) can whole tomatoes

2 carrots, chopped

1 clove garlic, chopped

Salt and freshly ground black pepper

½ cup (120 ml) milk

1 cup (100 g) fine dry bread crumbs

2 large eggs

½ cup (50 g) grated Parmesan cheese

¼ cup (13 g) chopped fresh parsley

3½ pounds (1.6 kg) lean ground beef, or 1 pound (455 g) ground turkey and 2½ pounds (1.2 kg) ground beef

1 tablespoon olive oil

Dried spaghetti or other long pasta

MORNING

Put the tomatoes, carrots, garlic, a good pinch of salt, a grinding of pepper, and 1 cup (240 ml) water in the slow cooker.

In a large bowl, combine the milk, bread crumbs, eggs, cheese, 1 teaspoon salt, several grindings of pepper, and the parsley and stir well. Add the beef and use your hands or a stiff spatula to combine it with the milk mixture. Shape into 2-inch (5-cm) balls and put half of them on a waxed paper–lined tray in the freezer (when they're firm, transfer to a freezer bag and keep in the freezer for up to 3 months; thaw in the refrigerator overnight, then brown and slow-cook as below).

In a large skillet or sauté pan, heat the oil over medium-high heat. Add the unfrozen meatballs in a single layer (work in batches, if necessary, with a little oil for each batch) and cook, turning with a thin metal spatula, until lightly browned on two or more sides, 4 to 5 minutes total—they don't have to be completely browned all over or cooked through. Transfer to the cooker, nestling them into the sauce. Cover and cook on low for 8 hours.

EVENING

Bring a large pot of salted water to a boil. Add the pasta and cook until al dente; drain.

Using a slotted spoon or tongs, transfer the meatballs to a bowl. With an immersion blender, puree the sauce. Season with more salt and pepper, if needed, then return the meatballs to the sauce. Serve with the pasta.

RECIPE CONTINUES...

Parmesan roasted broccoli spears

- **2 heads broccoli with long stalks (about 1¼ pounds/ 570 g)**
- **2 tablespoons olive oil**
- **⅓ cup (30 g) grated Parmesan cheese**
- **Salt and freshly ground black pepper**

MORNING OR EVENING

Trim the bottom ⅛ inch (3 mm) off the broccoli stalks and use a knife or a vegetable peeler to scrape the tough outer layer of the stalks. Cut the broccoli heads into rough spears—a small floret at the top, with as much of the long stalk as possible attached to each. (If you have time, and if you prefer softer broccoli, blanch it for 1 to 2 minutes in a pot of boiling water, drain in a colander, and cool under running water.) If doing this in the morning, put in a baking dish or bowl, cover, and refrigerate.

EVENING

Preheat the oven to 400°F (205°C). Put a large not-nonstick baking sheet in the oven to heat.

Drizzle the broccoli with the oil and rub it in well with your hands to thoroughly coat the spears. Sprinkle with the cheese, a couple of good pinches of salt, and a few grindings of pepper. Toss well. Spread the broccoli on the hot baking sheet in a single layer (it should be hot enough that the broccoli sizzles immediately), scraping any cheese and oil left in the baking dish over the spears. Roast until the broccoli is tender and the cheese bits are nicely browned, about 20 minutes. Use a thin metal spatula to remove the broccoli (and any browned bits of cheese) from the baking sheet to a serving dish or platter and serve.

Ragù Bolognese

WITH *celery, spinach, and Parmesan salad*
ALSO GOOD WITH *garlic braised broccoli rabe* (PAGE 193) OR *grizzled asparagus* (PAGE 201)

This and the sugo recipe on page 178 are adaptations of somewhat more complicated recipes by Giuliano Bugialli. His are the only ragù recipes I've seen that call for snipping the meat into the pot with shears—a technique well worth trying out in this case, as it yields a pleasant nubby-shredded consistency that you wouldn't get if using ground meat or by shredding larger pieces after cooking.

IN THE MORNING
Sauté the onion and prosciutto, snip the meat with kitchen shears, and load up the cooker.

IN THE EVENING
Stir in the cream and cook the pasta.

2 tablespoons unsalted butter

2 slices prosciutto, diced

½ onion, diced

1 carrot, peeled and finely diced

1 rib celery, finely diced

1 (28-ounce/794-g) can crushed tomatoes, or 1 (24-ounce/680-g) bottle passata di pomodoro

1½ pounds (680 g) beef sirloin or half sirloin and half pork loin

½ cup (120 ml) white wine

Salt and freshly ground black pepper

Fresh or dried tagliatelle or fettucine pasta

¼ cup (60 ml) heavy cream

MORNING

In a large skillet or sauté pan, melt the butter over medium heat. Add the prosciutto and onion and cook, stirring, until the onion is very soft and golden, 8 to 10 minutes.

Meanwhile, put the carrot, celery, and tomatoes in the slow cooker. Using kitchen shears, snip the beef sirloin into tiny pieces into the cooker (or use a knife and finely mince on a cutting board and transfer to the cooker).

To the skillet with the onion, add the wine, scraping up any browned bits, and cook for 3 to 5 minutes to reduce slightly. Stir into the tomato mixture in the slow cooker, along with 1 teaspoon salt and several grindings of pepper. Cover and cook on low for 8 hours.

EVENING

Bring a large pot of salted water to a boil. Add the pasta and cook until al dente; drain.

Stir the cream into the ragù. Season with more salt, if needed, and serve with the pasta.

RECIPE CONTINUES...

Celery, spinach, and Parmesan salad

2 tablespoons fresh lemon
   juice

½ teaspoon salt

Freshly ground black pepper

2 tablespoons olive oil

4 ribs celery

6 ounces (170 g) baby
   spinach

About 1½ ounces (40 g)
   Parmesan cheese

EVENING

In a salad bowl using a fork,
whisk the lemon juice, salt, and
several grindings of pepper to
dissolve the salt, then gradually
whisk in the oil.

Trim and very thinly
slice the celery on the bias and
toss it with the dressing. Add
the spinach and toss. Using a
vegetable peeler, shave the cheese
over the top. Serve.

Spinach Meatloaf

WITH *honey-lemon raw red pepper relish*
ALSO GOOD WITH *braised cabbage* (PAGE 225) OR *ginger-butter carrots* (PAGE 209)

Meatloaf is one of those comfort foods I fall back on every couple of months; the only problem with it is that a decent-size one (hello, leftovers) takes *forever* to bake in the oven—always longer than I expect, which doesn't work very well for weekdays, exactly when I tend to want comforting meals. I'll admit I was surprised to discover only recently that an excellent old-school meatloaf can be made in a slow cooker. The top doesn't get as browned and crusty as it does in the oven, but that's fixed here with a toasted bread crumb topping that's added just before serving.

IN THE MORNING
Shape the meatloaf and put it in the cooker. Dry out the bread crusts.

IN THE EVENING
Toast the crust crumbs.

---

2 slices soft bread, crusts removed and reserved, torn into pieces (about 1 cup/60 g)

½ cup (120 ml) milk

2 large eggs

2 teaspoons salt

Freshly ground black pepper

½ teaspoon ground fennel (optional)

1 (10-ounce/283-g) package frozen chopped spinach, thawed and squeezed dry

¼ cup (13 g) chopped fresh parsley

1 large carrot, peeled and cut into ⅛-inch (3-mm) cubes

2 pounds (910 g) ground meat (I like half lean beef, a quarter pork, and a quarter turkey)

4 sticks celery, cut to the width of your cooker

1 tablespoon olive oil

In a large bowl, combine the torn bread and the milk, then add the eggs, salt, several grindings of pepper, and the fennel, if using, and stir well. Stir in the spinach, parsley, and carrot, then add the ground meat and mix with your hands to thoroughly incorporate them into the spinach mixture. Shape into a loaf in the bowl.

Arrange the celery sticks crosswise in the bottom of the slow cooker pot (to hold the meatloaf up over the liquid it will release), then drape a large sheet of aluminum foil crosswise in the cooker over the celery and up and over the sides of the pot. Turn the meatloaf out of the bowl and onto the foil in the cooker. Cover the cooker (catching the foil under the lid) and cook on low for 8 hours. If you're cooking for less than 8 hours, check the internal temperature of the meatloaf with an instant-read thermometer; it should be at least 160°F (70°C).

Tear the reserved bread crusts into small crumbs and spread on a baking sheet in the oven to dry out until evening.

Drizzle the crumbs with the oil and season with salt and pepper. Preheat the oven to 350°F (175°C). Bake until the crumbs are golden.

Carefully use the foil to lift the meatloaf out of the cooker and transfer it to a platter. Top with the toasted crumbs and serve.

Honey-lemon raw red pepper relish

1 red bell pepper, diced

½ sweet red onion, diced

Juice of 1 lemon

2 teaspoons honey

Salt

Put the red pepper, onion, lemon, honey, and a good pinch of salt in a mini food processor and pulse until just combined and minced (or mince the vegetables with a knife, transfer to a bowl, and whisk in the remaining ingredients). Cover and refrigerate until ready to serve.

Brisket with Carrots and Prunes

WITH *skillet potatoes*
ALSO GOOD WITH *quark and caraway mash* (PAGE 159) OR *creamed cauliflower* (PAGE 221)

This is fine straight out of the slow cooker, but best if you have time in the evening to cook down the braising liquid to make a sweet-sour glaze for the tender beef (and any vegetables you'd like to serve alongside it).

IN THE MORNING
Brown the brisket.

IN THE EVENING
Slice the brisket and reduce the sauce.

1 (3- to 4-pound/1.4- to 1.8-kg) beef brisket (flat)

Salt and freshly ground black pepper

1 tablespoon vegetable oil

1 cup (240 ml) cider vinegar

½ cup (110 g) brown sugar

5 small carrots, peeled

½ cup (80 g) pitted prunes

MORNING

Season the beef all over with about 2 teaspoons salt and several grindings of pepper. In a large skillet or sauté pan, heat the oil over medium-high heat. When it shimmers, add the brisket and cook until nicely browned, turning once with tongs, about 5 minutes per side. Transfer to the cooker.

Pour ½ cup (120 ml) water into the skillet, scraping up any browned bits, then pour the liquid into the cooker. Pour in the vinegar and sprinkle with the brown sugar. Tuck the carrots into the liquid around the brisket. Cover and cook on low for 8 hours.

EVENING

Using tongs or two sturdy spatulas, transfer the brisket and carrots to a carving board. Pour the liquid from the cooker into a wide saucepan or sauté pan, place over high heat, and bring to a boil. Boil until the sauce is reduced a bit and slightly thickened, 10 to 15 minutes, adding the prunes in the last 5 minutes to plump.

Thickly slice the meat and transfer it with the carrots to a serving platter. Pour the sauce and prunes over and serve.

RECIPE CONTINUES…

Skillet potatoes

- **1¾ pounds (800 g) potatoes (russets and 1 sweet potato)**
- **2 tablespoons ghee (page 254)**
- **Salt and freshly ground black pepper**

EVENING

Using a mandoline (or a sharp chef's knife and mad knife skills), slice the potatoes ⅛ inch (3 mm) thick.

In a 10-inch (25-cm) skillet or sauté pan, heat 1 tablespoon of the ghee over medium-high heat. When it shimmers, quickly and carefully add the potato slices in fairly even layers, sprinkling each layer with a pinch of salt and a grinding of pepper. Cover the skillet, lower the heat to medium, and cook the potatoes without disturbing them for 10 minutes. Lift the lid and slide a thin metal spatula underneath to check the level of browning; if the potatoes on the bottom are deeply browned, lower the heat to medium-low, cover, and cook for 10 minutes longer, or until the potatoes on the top layer are tender. (If the potatoes are not yet deeply browned, cook for 5 more minutes on medium, then lower the heat and cook for 5 minutes.)

Using the spatula, lift big sections of the potatoes and turn them over so the browned potatoes are on top. Dollop the remaining 1 tablespoon ghee in between the sections, shaking the pan to get it underneath. Raise the heat to medium-high and cook, uncovered, for about 5 minutes longer, until the bottom layer is nicely browned. Serve.

Weekday Sunday Gravy

WITH *basil zucchini*

ALSO GOOD WITH *grizzled asparagus* (PAGE 201) OR *Parmesan roasted broccoli spears* (PAGE 181)

There's truly no better way to make "gravy" than in a slow cooker. I like the lean round roast here—it's what my boss at the Italian restaurant always used, ending up with a pot of deeply flavorful marinara and a softball-size hunk of beef that would almost crumble as you sliced it—but a thick chuck roast would be good too.

IN THE MORNING
Brown the roast and the onion and garlic.

IN THE EVENING
Slice the roast and puree the sauce.

---

1 (3-pound/1.4-kg) beef round roast

Salt and freshly ground black pepper

2 tablespoons olive oil

½ sweet onion, diced

2 cloves garlic, chopped

1 (28-ounce/794-g) can crushed tomatoes

2 tablespoons tomato paste

1 large sprig fresh basil

Dried pasta

MORNING

Season the roast all over with salt and pepper. In a large skillet or sauté pan, heat 1 tablespoon of the oil over medium-high heat. When it shimmers, add the roast and cook, turning with tongs, until browned on most of the sides, about 7 minutes total. Transfer to the slow cooker.

Return the skillet to medium heat and add the remaining 1 tablespoon oil, the onion, and garlic; cook, stirring, until the onion is translucent, 5 to 7 minutes, then pour in ½ cup (120 ml) water and stir to scrape up any browned bits. Pour the liquid over the roast and add the tomatoes, tomato paste, and basil sprig. Cover and cook on low for 8 hours.

EVENING

Bring a large pot of salted water to a boil. Add the pasta and cook until al dente; drain.

Transfer the roast to a carving board and slice it against the grain or pull it apart. Season the sauce with salt and pepper. If you'd like, puree the sauce with an immersion blender. Return the meat to the sauce, or serve the meat on its own and toss the pasta with sauce to coat.

Basil zucchini

3 zucchini

1 clove garlic

1 tablespoon olive oil

Salt and freshly ground black pepper

2 large sprigs fresh basil

MORNING OR EVENING

Cut the zucchini into rounds ⅛ inch (3 mm) thick and mince the garlic. If doing this in the morning, put both in a bowl, cover, and refrigerate.

EVENING

In a large skillet or sauté pan, heat the oil over medium-high heat. When it shimmers, add the zucchini and garlic and spread out in the pan. Sprinkle lightly with salt and pepper and cook, undisturbed, for 3 minutes. Flip and cook for 3 minutes, then flip again and cook for 3 more minutes, or until the zucchini is nicely browned and just tender. Tear in the basil and serve.

Simple Pot Roast with Dried Porcini

WITH *garlic braised broccoli rabe*

ALSO GOOD WITH *skillet potatoes* (PAGE 190) OR *quark and caraway mash* (PAGE 159)

Dried mushrooms give this basic pot roast even more deep, roasty flavor; you can substitute dried shiitakes, if you'd like, or leave them out altogether and add a good beef stock (page 243) to the slow cooker instead of the soaking water.

IN THE MORNING
Soak the porcini and sear the roast.

IN THE EVENING
Slice the roast.

½ ounce (14 g) dried porcini mushrooms

2½ pounds (1.2 kg) chuck roast

Salt and freshly ground black pepper

1 tablespoon olive oil

½ cup (120 ml) red wine

MORNING

In a small bowl, cover the porcini with hot water and let soak for 15 minutes.

Meanwhile, season the roast with about 1½ teaspoons salt and pepper to taste. In a large skillet or sauté pan, heat the oil over medium-high heat. When it shimmers, add the roast and cook for about 5 minutes on each side; transfer the roast to the slow cooker.

Pour the wine into the skillet and stir to scrape up any browned bits, bring to a boil, and cook for 2 minutes; pour the liquid into the cooker. Agitate the porcini a bit to remove any sand, then lift them out of the soaking liquid and add them to the cooker. Strain the soaking liquid through a fine-mesh sieve into the cooker, leaving any sand in the bottom of the bowl. Cover and cook on low for 8 hours.

EVENING

Using tongs or a slotted spoon, transfer the roast to a carving board. Thickly slice or pull apart into serving-size pieces and serve, spooning the porcini and some of the cooking liquid over the meat.

Garlic braised broccoli rabe

1 bunch broccoli rabe (about 14 ounces/400 g)

3 cloves garlic

2 tablespoons olive oil

1 cup (240 ml) stock

Salt

Pinch of crushed red pepper

MORNING OR EVENING

Wash the broccoli rabe and trim the bottoms of the stems. If you'd like, cut the bunch crosswise into 2-inch (5-cm) lengths; or leave the leaves and stalks whole. Crush and peel the garlic cloves but keep them mostly whole.

EVENING

Put the garlic cloves and oil in a large deep skillet or sauté pan. Place over medium heat and cook slowly, turning the garlic with tongs, until the garlic is golden and softened, about 5 minutes. Add the broccoli rabe, stock, a good pinch of salt (less if your stock is salted), and the crushed red pepper. Cover and cook over medium heat until the broccoli rabe stems are tender but not mushy, about 10 minutes, turning the greens in the pan half-way through so they braise evenly. Serve.

LEFTOVER BRAISED MEAT?

Make medieval runzas: Bake these filled buns on a Sunday afternoon and tuck them into lunchboxes throughout the week, or assemble them one evening, stash them in the fridge, and bake them the next day for supper. If you'd like, add a few slivers of Manchego or other cheese as you fill each bun.

1 sweet potato, peeled and diced

3 cups (320 g) minced (food-processored) green cabbage

½ cup (75 g) raisins

1 heaping cup (280 g) pureed pot roast (meat and porcini)

½ teaspoon ground cumin

¼ teaspoon ground cinnamon

¼ teaspoon freshly grated nutmeg

⅛ teaspoon ground mace (optional)

Salt and freshly ground black pepper

Dough from 1 recipe crusty rolls (page 155), risen until doubled

Put the sweet potato in a pot and cover with water. Bring to a boil, add the cabbage and raisins, cover, and cook for 5 minutes. Drain well in a sieve, then transfer to a large bowl and stir in the meat, cumin, cinnamon, nutmeg, mace (if using), salt, and pepper.

Cut the dough into sixteen portions and roll each out on a floured surface to a circle about 6 inches (15 cm) in diameter. Put ¼ cup (about 40 g) filling in the center of each, gather the edges of the dough over the filling, and pinch to seal. Arrange seam side down on a parchment-lined baking sheet, cover with plastic wrap, and let rise in a warm spot for 30 minutes to 1 hour (or refrigerate for up to 1 day, then bring to room temperature).

Preheat the oven to 400°F (205°C). Uncover the buns and bake until nicely browned, 30 to 35 minutes.

Sweet-Dark Onion Soup

WITH *spinach-Gruyère toasts*
ALSO GOOD WITH *seared halloumi and chile mince* (PAGE 60)
OR *baby kale salad with dates and pistachios* (PAGE 42)

The slow cooker is a wonderful tool for effortlessly cooking onions to a deep brown color and silky tenderness.

IN THE MORNING
Load up the cooker.

IN THE EVENING
Serve.

2 pounds (910 g) onions

Salt and freshly ground black pepper

4 cups (960 ml) good-quality beef stock (page 243)

1 tablespoon tomato paste

1 tablespoon miso paste

1 bay leaf

MORNING

Cut the onions into quarters, then slice the quarters crosswise ½ inch (6 mm) thick. Put them in the slow cooker and toss with 1 teaspoon salt and several grindings of pepper. Add the stock, tomato paste, miso paste, bay leaf, and 1 cup (240 ml) water. Cover and cook on low for 8 hours.

EVENING

Season with more salt or pepper, if needed, then serve.

Spinach-Gruyère toasts

½ cup (85 g) packed cooked spinach, squeezed dry and chopped

4 ounces (115 g) Gruyère cheese, chopped

¼ cup (60 g) cream cheese

½ teaspoon dry mustard powder, such as Coleman's

Pinch of freshly grated nutmeg

6 to 8 diagonal slices of baguette

MORNING OR EVENING

Put the spinach, Gruyère, cream cheese, mustard powder, and nutmeg in a mini food processor and pulse to combine well, scraping the sides of the bowl as needed. Cover and refrigerate if doing this in the morning.

EVENING

Preheat the broiler to high and set a rack about 6 inches (15 cm) from the heat source. Arrange the bread slices on a baking sheet and broil until golden, about 2 minutes. Flip the slices and spread them with the spinach-cheese mixture. Return to the oven and broil until the cheese is melted and the edges are beginning to brown, 2 to 3 minutes. Let cool for a few minutes, then serve.

Beef and Butternut Squash Tagine

WITH *almond couscous*

ALSO GOOD WITH *cumin spiced millet* (PAGE 231) OR *fancy saffron-butter basmati rice* (PAGE 117)

This is a most basic tagine recipe, and you should feel free to experiment with it: Try different spice combinations (keep cumin and cinnamon in the mix, but tinker away with the rest—cardamom and ground ginger would be good additions); add some browned onion and garlic and deglaze the skillet with the water; use lamb or goat instead of beef, or replace some of the meat with cooked and drained chickpeas (page 246); use different dried fruits.

IN THE MORNING
Load up the cooker.

IN THE EVENING
Stir in the raisins.

2½ pounds (1.2 kg) beef stew meat

2 teaspoons paprika

1 teaspoon fennel seeds, crushed

1 teaspoon ground cumin

½ teaspoon ground cinnamon

Salt and freshly ground black pepper

1 pound (455 g) butternut squash (about ½ small), peeled and cut into 1-inch (2.5-cm) pieces

1 cup (240 ml) crushed tomatoes

⅓ cup (50 g) raisins

MORNING

Put the beef in the slow cooker and toss with the paprika, fennel, cumin, cinnamon, 1½ teaspoons salt, and several grindings of pepper. Pile the squash on top of the beef and pour the tomatoes and ½ cup (120 ml) water over the top. Cover and cook on low for 8 hours.

EVENING

Season with more salt, if needed. Stir in the raisins. When they've softened a bit, serve.

Almond couscous

1 tablespoon olive oil

¼ cup (25 g) sliced almonds

1½ cups (290 g) instant couscous, preferably whole wheat

¾ teaspoon salt

2 tablespoons chopped fresh cilantro

EVENING

In a 2-quart (2-L) saucepan, heat the oil over medium heat. When it shimmers, add the almonds and cook, stirring, until golden, about 2 minutes. Add the couscous and stir for a few seconds to coat with the oil, then add 1¼ cups (300 ml) water and the salt. Bring to a boil, then cover and turn off the heat. Let stand for 10 minutes, then fluff with a fork or spatula, fold in the cilantro, and serve.

Beef with Winter Savory and Cipollini

WITH *roasted Brussels sprouts and shiitakes*
ALSO GOOD WITH *garlic sautéed dandelion greens* (PAGE 58) OR *skillet potatoes* (PAGE 190)

Winter savory is my mom's pet herb: She's been encouraging me to experiment with it more for years, and keeps sending dried savory from her huge kitchen garden in Washington State. Its flavor is distinctive and not easily described, like a combination of woody herbs (rosemary, oregano, thyme...) plus grassy mountain mint. If you don't have any on hand, you can use a sprig of fresh rosemary or a teaspoon of crumbled dried rosemary in its place, but you should definitely seek it out, if you can, for this pot roast. It's also great with roasted vegetables and in bean-based soups.

IN THE MORNING
Brown the beef and blanch and peel the cipollini.

IN THE EVENING
Serve.

3 pounds (1.4 kg) beef chuck roast or steaks, trimmed and cut into small fist-size chunks

Salt and freshly ground black pepper

1 tablespoon olive oil, or more, if needed

½ cup (120 ml) red wine

1 cup (240 ml) beef stock (page 243) or water

8 ounces (225 g) cipollini onions

1 heaping teaspoon crushed dried winter savory

MORNING

Season the beef with salt and pepper. In a large skillet or sauté pan, heat 1 tablespoon oil over medium-high heat. When it shimmers, add half of the beef and cook, turning, until the chunks are nicely browned on two or more sides, about 5 minutes total; transfer to the slow cooker. Brown the remaining beef in the oil remaining in the skillet (add a little oil, if needed); transfer to the cooker. Pour the wine into the hot skillet, scraping up any browned bits, then pour into the cooker, along with the stock.

Bring a pot of water to a boil, add the cipollini, and blanch for 30 seconds, then drain in a colander and cool under running water. Trim off the roots and tops and slip off the peels, then add the cipollini to the cooker, tucking them in around the beef. Sprinkle in the savory. Cover and cook on low for 8 hours.

EVENING

Using a slotted spoon, transfer the beef and cipollini to a platter. Spoon some of the liquid from the cooker over everything and serve.

Roasted Brussels sprouts and shiitakes

You'll need two baking sheets for this—the vegetables take up a lot of space at first, and shrink as they roast, their flavor becoming more concentrated.

2 pounds (910 g) Brussels sprouts

10 ounces (280 g/about 4 cups) sliced shiitake mushroom caps

6 tablespoons (90 ml) olive oil

1 teaspoon salt

Freshly ground black pepper

MORNING OR EVENING

Trim the Brussels sprouts bottoms, remove any discolored leaves, and cut lengthwise into quarters if large, halves if small. Cover and refrigerate if doing this in the morning.

EVENING

Preheat the oven to 400°F (205°C) and put two rimmed baking sheets in the oven to heat.

In a large bowl, toss the Brussels sprouts, mushrooms, oil, salt, and several grindings of pepper together well. Spread evenly on the hot baking sheet. Roast until nicely browned, tender, and the edges of the vegetables are crisp, 25 to 30 minutes. Serve hot.

Brisket Soup with Rice Noodles

WITH *soy-steamed broccoli*
ALSO GOOD WITH *collard slaw* (PAGE 115) OR *sweet chile-garlic sauce* (PAGE 80)

You can use chuck roast instead of the brisket flat here; even a leaner-looking cut will work fine. Be sure to use a good stock, if you can: The broth, full of heady aromatics, is the real star of this dish.

IN THE MORNING
Brown the beef.

IN THE EVENING
Add the scallions and sauté the garlic and ginger. Cook the noodles.

1½ pounds (680 g) beef brisket (flat only), cut into 2-inch (5-cm) pieces

Salt and freshly ground black pepper

2 tablespoons vegetable oil

7 cups (1.7 L) good-quality beef stock (page 243)

2 pieces star anise

1 cinnamon stick

½ teaspoon fennel seeds

4 whole cloves

3 green cardamom pods, cracked

2 scallions, cut into 1-inch (2.5-cm) lengths

Salt or Chinese light soy sauce, if needed

4 cloves garlic, minced

5 coins fresh ginger, minced

Medium-wide rice noodles

MORNING

Season the beef with salt and pepper. In a large skillet or sauté pan, heat 1 tablespoon of the oil over high heat. When it shimmers, add the beef and cook, turning occasionally, until the pieces are browned on two or three sides, about 5 minutes total. Transfer to the slow cooker. Pour ½ cup (120 ml) water into the hot skillet and scrape up any browned bits, then pour the liquid into the cooker, along with the stock. Put the spices in a muslin spice bag or enclose in a double layer of cheesecloth and submerge it in the stock. Cover and cook on low for 8 hours.

EVENING

Skim any foam or excess fat from the surface of the broth and remove and discard the spices. Add the scallions to the soup, season with salt or soy sauce, and cover.

In a skillet or sauté pan, heat the remaining 1 tablespoon oil over medium heat. When it shimmers, add the garlic and ginger and stir until golden. Add to the soup.

Cook the noodles until just al dente (about 5 minutes in boiling water). Drain and divide among individual serving bowls. Ladle the soup over the noodles and serve.

Soy-steamed broccoli

1 pound (455 g) broccoli

1 clove garlic, minced

2 coins fresh peeled ginger, minced

1 tablespoon vegetable oil

Good pinch of crushed red pepper

1 teaspoon Chinese light soy sauce, or more to taste

Pinch of sugar

MORNING OR EVENING

Cut off the broccoli stalks and save them for another use (fried rice is a good one, or cut them into sticks for dipping into hummus or other dips). Cut into small florets, chopping the stems into roughly ½-inch (12-mm) pieces. Put the garlic and ginger in a large skillet or sauté pan and add the oil.

EVENING

Place the skillet over medium-high heat and cook, stirring, until the garlic and ginger are golden, about 2 minutes. Add the broccoli and crushed red pepper, ½ cup (120 ml) water, and the soy sauce, and sprinkle with the sugar. Cover and cook, stirring occasionally, until the broccoli is just tender, about 5 minutes. Add more soy sauce, if needed, then serve.

Creamed Beef with Whole Wheat Pastry Crisps

WITH *grizzled asparagus*
ALSO GOOD WITH *herb salad* (PAGE 31) OR *pan-seared green beans* (PAGE 89)

Not a light meal, by any means, but so satisfying and comforting. Lots of sliced onions simmer to golden tenderness underneath browned slabs of chuck, which is then easily shredded and stirred together with the onions and a cream sauce made from the cooking liquid. If you don't have time to make the pastry crisps, you could bake some squares of thawed frozen puff pastry to serve under or over the creamed beef, or just toast some good bread.

IN THE MORNING
Brown the beef and load up the cooker.
Make the pastry dough if you have time.

IN THE EVENING
Drain the liquid and make it into a cream sauce.
Roll out and bake the pastry crisps.

3½ cups (14 ounces/400 g) sliced onions (4 small or 2 large)

2 pounds (910 g) well-trimmed chuck steaks or roast

Salt and freshly ground black pepper

1 tablespoon olive or vegetable oil

½ cup (120 ml) beef stock (page 243) or water

2 cups (250 g) plus 1 tablespoon white whole wheat or all-purpose flour

7 tablespoons (100 g) unsalted butter

1 large egg, lightly beaten

Ice water

⅔ cup (165 ml) heavy cream

MORNING
Put the onions in the slow cooker.

Season the beef all over with salt (about 1½ teaspoons) and pepper. In a large skillet, heat the oil over high heat. When it shimmers, add the beef and cook until browned on both sides, about 5 minutes total. Transfer to the cooker, setting the beef on top of the onions. Pour the stock into the hot skillet and scrape up any browned bits, then scrape the liquid into the cooker. Cover and cook on low for 8 hours.

In a medium bowl, combine the 2 cups (250 g) flour and a pinch of salt, then cut in 6 tablespoons (85 g) of the butter with a pastry blender (or two knives held together) until the butter is in pieces no larger than ragged peas. Add half of the beaten egg and toss with a spatula to distribute it throughout the flour mixture. Sprinkle in ice water, a couple of tablespoons at a time, tossing and stirring to combine, until the dough holds together and can be shaped into a ball. If doing this in the morning, wrap the ball of dough in plastic wrap and refrigerate.

EVENING

Preheat the oven to 450°F (230°C). Line a baking sheet with parchment paper. Unwrap the dough and roll it out between two sheets of plastic to about ⅛ inch (3 mm) thick. Cut the dough into rough squares, strips, triangles, or whatever shapes you'd like and transfer to the baking sheet. Brush with the remaining beaten egg and bake until crisp and golden, 15 to 20 minutes.

Meanwhile, holding the lid of the cooker slightly askew and using pot holders, drain as much liquid as possible from the cooker into a saucepan. Return the pot to the cooker and keep covered.

To the liquid in the saucepan, add the cream and bring to a boil over high heat. Mash the flour into the butter with a fork, then whisk the mixture bit by bit into the cream mixture and cook until the liquid thickens slightly. Pour it back into the cooker and use two forks to shred the beef and combine it with the onions and cream sauce. Season with more salt and pepper, if needed, and serve with the pastry crisps.

Grizzled asparagus

1 bunch asparagus, tough bottoms snapped off

1 tablespoon olive oil

Salt and freshly ground black pepper

EVENING

Preheat the oven to 450°F (230°C). Put a rimmed baking sheet in the oven to heat. Remove the hot pan from the oven and quickly spread the asparagus out on the pan, drizzle with the oil, and season with salt and pepper. Shake the pan to roll the asparagus and coat it with the oil, then bake until the tips are crisp and the stalks are wrinkled, 10 to 12 minutes. Serve.

Jungle Curry Stew

WITH *sweet corn curry cakes*

ALSO GOOD WITH *coconut oil sticky rice* (PAGE 163) OR *pandan water* (PAGE 149)

The beef in this brothy, spicy dish—no coconut milk here—will be quite tender and almost falling apart after eight hours, and completely infused with flavor. If you can find tiny green eggplants, use a big handful of those instead of the diced regular eggplant—their bitterness plays well with the slightly sweet broth.

IN THE MORNING
Load up the cooker.

IN THE EVENING
Sauté the vegetables and season the stew.

3 tablespoons red curry paste

1 tablespoon grated palm sugar or brown sugar

1½ pounds (680 g) beef stew meat

3 kaffir lime leaves

2 or more fresh Thai chiles, split but left whole

1 tablespoon vegetable or coconut oil

1 thin Asian eggplant, or ½ small globe eggplant, diced

3 ounces (85 g) green beans, trimmed and cut in half crosswise

Salt

6 sprigs jarred green peppercorns in brine, drained and rinsed (optional)

½ cup (20 g) fresh Thai basil sprigs

2 tablespoons fish sauce, or more to taste

Juice of 1 or more limes

MORNING

Pour 3 cups (720 ml) water into the slow cooker and stir in the curry paste and palm sugar. Add the beef, lime leaves, and Thai chiles. Cover and cook on low for 8 hours.

EVENING

In a large skillet or sauté pan, heat the oil over medium-high heat. When it shimmers, add the eggplant and green beans and a pinch of salt. Cook, stirring frequently, until the eggplant is golden and the vegetables are just tender, 5 to 7 minutes. Add the vegetables to the cooker along with the peppercorn sprigs, if using, the basil and the fish sauce. Add lime juice and more fish sauce to taste. Serve.

RECIPE CONTINUES...

Sweet corn curry cakes

These can be either baked on an oiled baking sheet or shallow-fried in a skillet in batches—the results are almost identical, so use whichever method makes the most sense for you.

- **3 cups (435 g) fresh sweet corn kernels (from 3 to 4 ears)**
- **½ cup (20 g) chopped fresh cilantro with tender stems**
- **2 small scallions, thinly sliced**
- **2 kaffir lime leaves, center ribs removed, thinly sliced**
- **2 large eggs**
- **¾ cup (90 g) rice flour**
- **2 teaspoons Madras (hot) curry powder**
- **1 teaspoon salt**
- **Vegetable or coconut oil**

MORNING OR EVENING

In a large bowl, combine the corn, cilantro, scallions, and lime leaves. Beat the eggs together in a small bowl, then stir them into the vegetables with a fork. Sift in the rice flour, curry powder, and salt and stir until no more dry flour is visible. Cover and refrigerate if doing this in the morning; stir well before proceeding.

EVENING

If baking, preheat the oven to 425°F (220°C) and generously oil a baking sheet. Drop ¼-cup (60-ml) mounds of the corn mixture onto the baking sheet (about 12) and spread them into rounds about 3 inches (7.5 cm) in diameter. Bake for 10 minutes, then use a thin metal spatula to flip them and bake for 10 more minutes, until nicely browned. Serve hot.

If shallow-frying, in a large skillet or sauté pan, heat 3 tablespoons oil over medium-high heat. When it shimmers, working in batches of three or four, carefully drop ¼-cup (60-ml) mounds of the corn mixture into the skillet and spread them into rounds about 3 inches (7.5 cm) in diameter. Cook for 2 to 3 minutes, until nicely browned on the bottom, then use a thin metal spatula to flip them and cook for another 2 to 3 minutes. Remove to paper towels to drain and repeat with the remaining corn mixture, adding a little more oil to the skillet as needed. Serve hot.

Garlicky Short Ribs

WITH *basic soft polenta*

ALSO GOOD WITH *cranberry-orange wild rice* (PAGE 114) OR *creamed cauliflower* (PAGE 221)

This might seem like a lot of garlic, but it mellows considerably and sweetens a bit in the slow cooker. The bite of raw garlic in the thyme gremolata topping contrasts well with the unctuous, almost sticky short ribs.

IN THE MORNING
Brown the ribs and sauté the garlic. If you have time, make the gremolata.

IN THE EVENING
Skim the fat and serve.

2 to 3 pounds (910 g to 1.4 kg) meaty beef short ribs

Salt and freshly ground black pepper

5 cloves garlic, minced

½ cup (120 ml) red wine

½ cup (120 ml) beef stock (page 243)

3 sprigs fresh thyme

For the gremolata:

Zest of 1 lemon, removed in strips with a vegetable peeler

¼ cup (13 g) chopped fresh parsley

2 tablespoons fresh thyme leaves

2 cloves garlic

Salt

MORNING

Season the short ribs with salt and pepper. In a large skillet or sauté pan over medium-high heat, working in batches if necessary, cook the ribs (with no oil), turning with tongs, until browned on at least two sides, 5 to 7 minutes total per batch. Using the tongs, transfer to the slow cooker. Drain off all but a tablespoon or so of the fat from the skillet and add the garlic. Cook, stirring, over medium heat for 1 to 2 minutes, until golden. Pour in the wine and boil until it has reduced by about half, then scrape into the cooker. Add the stock and tuck in the thyme sprigs. Cover and cook on low for 8 hours.

MORNING OR EVENING

Make the gremolata: Finely mince the lemon zest, along with the parsley, thyme, and garlic, and add a good pinch of salt. Put in a small container, cover, and refrigerate if doing this in the morning.

EVENING

With a large spoon or a turkey baster, skim the clear fat from the surface of the liquid in the cooker and discard. Transfer the short ribs to a platter, spoon some of the cooking liquid over them, and serve with the gremolata for topping.

Basic soft polenta

3 cups (720 ml) vegetable stock (page 240) or water

½ teaspoon salt, if needed

1 cup (120 g) polenta or coarse-ground cornmeal

In a heavy 2-quart (2-L) saucepan, bring the stock to a boil (add the salt if using water instead of stock) over high heat. Gradually whisk in the polenta and lower the heat to low. Cook, frequently whisking and stirring into the corners of the pan with a heatproof spatula or wooden spoon, until the individual grains of corn are tender and the polenta is thick, 10 to 25 minutes (different polentas cook at quite different rates). Serve hot.

Leftover short ribs?

Pull the meat off the bones and keep it in the fridge for up to several days, ready for the most glorious tacos you've ever made: Mince white onion and lots of fresh cilantro together on a cutting board or in a mini food processor. Heat the short rib meat in a skillet over medium-high heat, turning with a thin metal spatula, until crisp and deeply browned, about 2 minutes (it doesn't take long), adding a pinch or so of ground cumin and cayenne. Warm corn tortillas and fill them with crisp meat and the onion-cilantro mixture, with lime wedges for squeezing.

Beef Shanks with Lemon and Rosemary

WITH *ginger-butter carrots*

ALSO GOOD WITH *celery, spinach, and Parmesan salad* (PAGE 185) OR *basic soft polenta* (PAGE 206)

Beef shanks are well-marbled cross-section cuts from the leg, usually about an inch or so thick, and in my opinion are one of the most flavor-packed long-cooking cuts you can get. Their texture after braising is similar to that of oxtails and short ribs, but they're much meatier. Layered with lemon slices and fresh rosemary, these are braised simply in red wine. You could make a full-fledged gremolata for topping (see page 206), but I think they need nothing more than a grating of lemon zest and some fresh parsley. Some warmed bread would be welcome on the table for soaking up the braising liquid.

IN THE MORNING
Brown the shanks and layer them in the cooker.

IN THE EVENING
Garnish the shanks with lemon zest and parsley.

---

3 to 4 pounds (1.4 to 1.8 kg) bone-in beef shanks (4 to 6 pieces 1 inch/2.5 cm thick)

Salt and freshly ground black pepper

2 tablespoons olive oil

2 lemons, one thinly sliced, seeds picked out, the other for zesting

2 sprigs fresh rosemary, broken into a few pieces each

1 cup (240 ml) red wine

¼ cup (13 g) chopped fresh parsley

MORNING

Season the shanks on both sides with salt and pepper. In a large skillet or sauté pan, heat 1 tablespoon of the oil over medium-high heat. When it shimmers, add half of the shanks, in one layer, and cook until lightly browned on both sides, about 5 minutes total. Transfer them to the slow cooker, tucking them down into the bottom of the pot in one layer, and top with half of the lemon slices and rosemary. Brown the remaining shanks (no need to add more oil to the skillet) and put them atop the first layer, and top with the remaining lemon slices and rosemary. Pour the wine into the hot skillet, scraping up any browned bits, then pour the liquid into the cooker. Cover and cook on low for 8 hours.

EVENING

Using a slotted spoon, gently transfer the shanks to a serving platter; they'll fall apart a bit, but that's fine—charming, even. Season the cooking liquid with salt and pepper, if needed, then spoon some of it over the shanks. Grate the zest of the remaining lemon over the top, sprinkle with the parsley, and serve.

Ginger-butter carrots

1 pound (455 g) carrots

3 thin coins fresh peeled ginger

1 tablespoon unsalted butter

Rounded ¼ teaspoon salt

MORNING OR EVENING

Cut the carrots into sticks or coins ¼ inch (6 mm) thick. Thinly slice the ginger coins into slivers. If doing this in the morning, put the carrots, ginger, and knob of butter in a container together, cover, and refrigerate.

EVENING

Put the carrots, ginger, butter, salt, and 1 cup (240 ml) water in a large skillet or sauté pan. Bring to a boil and cook, turning the carrots once or twice with a spoon or tongs, until most of the water has evaporated and the carrots are tender, about 8 minutes; you'll notice the sound in the skillet change from bubbling to sizzling, and that's when it's ready. Serve.

Rendang Pedang

WITH *lemongrass rice*
ALSO GOOD WITH *corn on the cob, basic coconut rice* (PAGE 107),
OR *gingered Asian pear salad* (PAGE 150)

Rendang is one of my all-time favorite foods, partly for sentimental reasons (on our first not-date, six or so years before we got married, Derek and I had Indonesian food) and partly because it hits all my favorite notes: spicy (chiles fresh and ground), herby (lemongrass, and lots of it), and tart (tamarind).

IN THE MORNING
Puree the sauce and load up the cooker.

IN THE EVENING
If necessary, reduce the sauce on the stovetop.

1 red bell pepper, chopped

1 serrano chile, chopped

4 cloves garlic, chopped

2-inch (5-cm) piece fresh ginger, peeled and chopped

2 teaspoons ground cumin

1 teaspoon ground coriander

1 teaspoon hot paprika

½ teaspoon turmeric

½ (13.5-ounce/400-ml) can coconut milk

2 large stalks lemongrass, chopped, tough tops and outer leaves trimmed off and reserved for lemongrass rice (opposite)

1 tablespoon tamarind concentrate, such as Tamicon brand

½ tablespoon jaggery or brown sugar

1 teaspoon salt, or more to taste

2 pounds (910 g) beef stew meat

MORNING

In a good blender or mini food processor, combine the bell pepper, serrano chile, garlic, ginger, cumin, coriander, hot paprika, turmeric, coconut milk, chopped lemongrass, tamarind, jaggery, and salt. Puree until very smooth, then scrape into the slow cooker. Add the beef and turn to coat it with the sauce. Cover and cook on low for 8 hours.

EVENING

If the sauce is very thin, ladle as much of it as possible from the cooker into a wide saucepan (leaving the beef in the cooker pot). Bring the sauce to a boil over high heat, then lower the heat a bit and boil, stirring frequently, until the sauce is reduced and thickened somewhat. Season with more salt, if needed, then return the sauce to the cooker with the beef and serve.

Lemongrass rice

2 cups (360 g) basmati rice

Salt

Lemongrass tops, tied together in a half-knot

EVENING

Put the rice in a sieve and rinse very well under running water. Dump into a 2-quart (2-L) saucepan and add 2 ¼ cups (540 ml) water, a good pinch of salt, and the knotted lemongrass. Bring to a boil over high heat, stir once to unstick any grains from the bottom of the pan, then cover and cook over the lowest heat for 14 minutes, or until all the water is absorbed and the rice is tender. Let stand, covered, for 3 minutes, then fluff with a fork or spatula.

Ropa Vieja

WITH *fried plantains*
ALSO GOOD WITH *faux mini pupusas* (PAGE 72) OR *warmed corn tortillas* (SEE PAGE 100)

Use long-grained flank steak (cut to fit your skillet and slow cooker, if necessary) and you'll achieve the most beautiful mess of "old rags" you've ever seen, but a thick chuck roast or any other lesser cut of meat will work fine too.

This is a dish in which browning the meat isn't strictly necessary, but if you have a bit of extra time in the morning it'll add another level of flavor: Season the flank steak and brown it in a skillet in a little oil for about 5 minutes total, put it in the slow cooker, and deglaze the skillet with the wine, scraping up any browned bits and pouring the liquid over the steak.

IN THE MORNING
Load up the cooker. If you have time, sauté the bell pepper and carrot.

IN THE EVENING
Shred the steak and stir in the vegetables.

1 (2- to 2½-pound/910 g- to 1.2-kg) flank steak

1 teaspoon ground achiote (annatto), or 1 teaspoon sweet paprika plus ¼ teaspoon ground turmeric

½ teaspoon ground cumin

½ teaspoon ground cinnamon

Salt and freshly ground black pepper

1 small onion, thinly sliced

4 cloves garlic, crushed

¼ cup (60 ml) wine (red or white) or water

1 (14.5-ounce/411-g) can whole tomatoes

1 tablespoon tomato paste

1 tablespoon vegetable oil

1 carrot, cut into sticks ¼ inch (6 mm) thick

1 green bell pepper, seeded and cut into strips ½ inch (12 mm) wide

2 tablespoons drained capers in brine, or ¼ cup (30 g) drained pickled jalapeño chile slices

RECIPE CONTINUES...

Put the steak in the slow cooker, sprinkle it all over with the achiote, cumin, cinnamon, 1 teaspoon salt, and several grindings of black pepper, and nestle it into the bottom of the pot, folding it over on itself if necessary.

Add the onion and garlic, the wine, tomatoes and their juices, tomato paste, and a good pinch of salt, cover, and cook on low for 8 hours.

MORNING OR EVENING

Put the oil in a sauté pan and heat over medium-high heat until it shimmers. Add the carrot and bell pepper and a pinch of salt and cook, stirring frequently, until just tender, about 5 minutes. Transfer to a bowl, cover, and refrigerate if doing this in the morning.

EVENING

Turn the cooker to high. Using tongs, remove the steak from the cooking liquid and put it in a baking dish. Shred the meat into long strands by holding the far end with the tongs and drawing a fork toward you along the meat with the grain to tear it; repeat until it looks like a mass of torn rags. Return it to the slow cooker, along with the sautéed bell pepper and carrot, season with salt to taste, and heat through. Sprinkle the capers over the shredded steak and sauce. Serve.

Fried plantains

Starchy semi-ripe plantains, which are available in most supermarket produce sections and look like over-size bananas, make a crisp, comforting accompaniment—my daughter likes swishing them into pooling sauce on her plate.

Vegetable oil

¼ cup (30 g) rice flour

2 large plantains, yellow with some black spots

Salt

MORNING OR EVENING

Get everything ready for plantain frying: Put a large sauté pan on the stove and add enough oil to cover the bottom by about ⅛ inch (3 mm). Line a cutting board and a plate with paper towels or brown paper and set them near the sauté pan. Find a heavy object (such as a sturdy drinking glass or canning jar) that you can use to flatten the plantain rounds. Put the rice flour in a bowl.

EVENING

Cut a slit in the peel of each plantain all the way down the length of the fruit, then cut the fruit crosswise into rounds ¾ inch (2 cm) thick and peel off the peel from each round (this is easier than peeling the whole thing at once, banana-style). Put the rounds in the rice flour and toss to coat. Heat the oil in the sauté pan over medium heat until it shimmers. Put the rounds in the oil and cook until nicely browned, about 3 minutes per side. Using tongs, transfer the plantains to the paper-lined cutting board, then use the heavy object to smash each plantain round to about ¼ inch (6 mm) thick. Return them to the hot oil briefly to brown again over medium heat, then transfer to the paper-lined plate, sprinkle with salt, and serve.

Leftover ropa?

It's even better the next day, in tacos.
Put it in a saucepan and reheat, adding
a little cayenne and more ground cumin,
if you'd like. Set out little bowls of
toppings: crumbled cotija or feta cheese,
sprigs of fresh cilantro, sliced fresh
serrano chiles, pickled onions (see page
102), lime wedges, shredded cabbage.
Warm corn tortillas in a hot, dry heavy
skillet, flipping each one twice with your
fingers or tongs; wrap them in a clean tea
towel or cloth napkin as you warm them.

Wintry Borscht

WITH *dark bread, eggplant quark, and pickled beet stems*
ALSO GOOD WITH *crusty rolls* (PAGE 155) OR *spinach-Gruyère toasts* (PAGE 194)

In eight hours, not only will the beef have become meltingly tender but the beets will have turned a beautiful pale blush and given much of their original color to the intensely flavorful broth.

IN THE MORNING
Brown the beef and onion and stash the beet greens in the fridge.

IN THE EVENING
Add the greens and let them cook for 15 minutes or so.

1½ pounds (680 g) beef stew meat, in 1-inch (2.5-cm) pieces

Salt and freshly ground black pepper

1 tablespoon olive oil

½ onion, diced

3 beets about 3½ inches (9 cm) in diameter, with tops

1 large Yukon Gold potato

2 large carrots

4 cups (960 ml) beef stock (page 243) or water, or a combination

1 bay leaf

About ¼ cup (13 g) chopped fresh dill

MORNING

Season the beef with salt and pepper. In a large skillet or sauté pan, heat the oil over medium-high heat. When it shimmers, add the beef in one layer (or close to it). Cook, turning occasionally, until the pieces are nicely browned on one or two sides, about 5 minutes total. Transfer to the slow cooker.

To the skillet, add the onion and a pinch of salt and cook, stirring frequently, until just softened, about 3 minutes. Pour in ½ cup (120 ml) water, scraping up any browned bits, then pour the onion and liquid into the cooker.

Cut the tops from the beets and wash the greens well. Cut the stems away from the leaves and save them for pickled beet stems (page 218), if you'd like. Cut the leaves crosswise into ½-inch (12-mm) ribbons and put them in the refrigerator. Peel the beets and cut them into quarters, then into ½-inch (12-mm) slices. Cut the potato the same way, and cut the carrots into ¾-inch (2-cm) pieces.

Add the beets, potato, carrots, stock, and bay leaf to the cooker. Cover and cook on low for 8 hours.

EVENING

Turn the cooker to high. Fold the beet greens into the borscht and season the broth with salt and pepper, if needed. Cover and cook until the greens are just tender, 15 to 30 minutes. Serve, with the dill for sprinkling.

RECIPE CONTINUES...

Dark bread, eggplant quark, and pickled beet stems

If you're not up for making the eggplant quark, just spread the bread slices with plain quark, soft goat cheese, very thick labneh, or feta pureed in a food processor.

For the pickled beet stems:

- Stems from 1 bunch (about 3) beets
- 1 cup (240 ml) white wine vinegar
- 1 teaspoon honey
- ½ teaspoon salt
- ½ teaspoon whole allspice berries

For the eggplant quark:

- 1 large Italian eggplant (about 1 pound 5 ounces/600 g), or 3 or 4 long Asian eggplants
- 1 tablespoon olive oil
- Salt and freshly ground black pepper
- ½ cup (120 ml) quark (page 253) or plain Greek yogurt (preferably full-fat) or labneh
- Grated zest and juice of 1 small lemon

To serve:

- About 6 thin slices of dark bread, such as good pumpernickel or whole wheat

Make the pickled beet stems: Put the beet stems in a heatproof nonreactive container (such as a canning jar or glass storage container, or a bowl). In a small saucepan or in a glass measuring cup in a microwave oven, bring the vinegar, honey, salt, and allspice to a boil and stir to dissolve the salt and honey. Pour the liquid over the beet stems. Let cool for a few minutes, then cover and refrigerate.

Make the eggplant quark: Preheat the broiler to high and set a rack about 6 inches (15 cm) from the heat source.

Cut a large eggplant lengthwise into eighths, or small ones in half. Put them cut sides up on a baking sheet, drizzle with the oil, and sprinkle with salt and a few grindings of pepper. Broil until the eggplants are very soft and deeply browned, 15 to 20 minutes. Let cool for a few minutes, then scrape the flesh onto a cutting board and discard the peel and stem. Finely chop the flesh and scrape it into a bowl. Add the quark and stir it in vigorously with a fork. Add the lemon zest and juice, and season with more salt (about ½ teaspoon) and pepper, if needed.

EVENING

Spread the bread with the eggplant quark, top with the beet stems (chop them first for easier eating, or leave them whole for dramatic effect), and serve.

Oxtails with Allspice, Thyme, and Habaneros

WITH *creamed cauliflower*

ALSO GOOD WITH *brown rice and peas* (PAGE 235) OR *quick-cooked shredded collards* (PAGE 161)

You can substitute beef short ribs for the oxtails—they'll be only slightly less sticky-unctuous.

IN THE MORNING

Brown the oxtails and sauté the garlic. If you have time, make the habanero sauce.

IN THE EVENING

Skim the fat and serve.

---

2 to 3 pounds (910 g to 1.4 kg) oxtails, cut by the butcher into 1- to 2-inch/2.5- to 5-cm sections

2 teaspoons whole allspice, finely ground

Salt and freshly ground black pepper

1 teaspoon olive oil

5 cloves garlic, minced

2 tablespoons rum

⅔ cup (165 ml) beef stock (page 243)

5 large sprigs fresh thyme

For the habanero sauce:

2 habanero or Scotch bonnet chiles

1 tablespoon fresh thyme leaves

Grated zest and juice of ½ orange

Juice of ½ lime

1 teaspoon brown sugar

Salt

MORNING

Season the oxtails with the allspice and salt and pepper. In a large skillet or sauté pan over medium-high heat, working in batches if necessary, cook the oxtails (with no oil), turning with tongs, until browned on at least two sides, 5 to 7 minutes total per batch. Using the tongs, transfer to the slow cooker. Drain off the fat from the skillet and add the oil. Add the garlic and stir over medium heat for 1 to 2 minutes, until golden. Pour in the rum and boil until it has reduced almost completely, then scrape into the cooker. Add the stock and tuck in the thyme sprigs. Cover and cook on low for 8 hours.

MORNING OR EVENING

Make the habanero sauce: Wearing gloves, seed and mince the chiles, then stir in the thyme, orange zest and juice, lime juice, brown sugar, and salt to taste. If doing this in the morning, cover and refrigerate.

EVENING

With a large spoon or a turkey baster, skim the clear fat from the surface of the liquid in the cooker and discard. Transfer the oxtails to a platter, spoon some of the garlic cooking liquid over them, and serve with the habanero sauce for drizzling on top.

Creamed cauliflower

1 head cauliflower, trimmed and coarsely chopped

½ teaspoon salt, or to taste

⅓ cup (75 ml) heavy cream

4 cloves roasted garlic (page 251)

EVENING

Put the cauliflower in a large saucepan and add enough water to come up about two-thirds of the way (about 3 cups/720 ml). Add the salt, cover, and bring to a boil over high heat, then lower the heat and simmer until very tender, about 15 minutes. Add the cream and garlic. With an immersion blender, puree until smooth. Stir in more salt, if needed, then serve.

CHAPTER 5

Lamb
and Goat

Feta Moussaka

WITH *simple garlic spinach*

ALSO GOOD WITH *grizzled asparagus* (PAGE 201) OR *dilled cucumbers* (PAGE 177)

It may be a little sloppy, and not as compact as a baked moussaka held together with béchamel, but this one has all the right flavors and (most of the) classic textures of tender layered potato slices and mint-scented lamb sauce. I've also made versions in which the feta is sprinkled atop each potato layer, but this method, with feta simply spread on top at the end of cooking, is simpler.

IN THE MORNING
Sear the eggplant, brown the lamb and onion and garlic, and layer the ingredients in the cooker.

IN THE EVENING
Sprinkle with feta and serve.

Olive oil

1 eggplant (about 1¼ pounds/570 g), peeled and cut into slabs ¼ inch (6 mm) thick

Salt and freshly ground black pepper

1 onion, diced

2 cloves garlic, chopped

1 pound (455 g) ground lamb

1½ teaspoons dried mint

½ teaspoon dried marjoram or oregano

1 (14.5-ounce/411-g) can crushed tomatoes

1 (6-ounce/170-g) can tomato paste

2 small russet potatoes, peeled and thinly sliced

4 ounces (115 g) feta cheese, crumbled

MORNING

In a large skillet or sauté pan, heat a thin film of oil over medium-high heat. Add a couple of slabs of eggplant and sprinkle with salt and pepper. Cook until seared, about 1 minute per side, and remove to a plate. Repeat with the remaining eggplant.

In the same skillet, swirl 1 tablespoon oil. Add the onion, garlic, and a pinch of salt and cook, stirring, until the onion is translucent, about 5 minutes. Add the lamb and cook, stirring, until most of the pink has disappeared, 3 to 5 minutes; drain and add the mint, marjoram, 1 teaspoon salt, several grindings of pepper, the tomatoes, and tomato paste.

In the slow cooker, make layers, lightly sprinkling the potato layers with salt and pepper: eggplant slices, lamb sauce, potatoes—repeating until the ingredients are used up and ending with sauce. Cover, inserting a heavy-duty paper towel underneath the lid to collect condensation, and cook on low for 8 hours.

EVENING

Sprinkle the feta over the top and let stand until the cheese has softened a bit and the casserole has settled. Use a thin metal spatula to cut down through the layers and lift out servings.

Simple garlic spinach

1 tablespoon olive oil

2 cloves garlic, minced

Pinch of crushed red pepper

8 ounces (255 g) spinach

Salt

EVENING

In a large deep skillet or sauté pan, or a Dutch oven, heat the oil over medium-high heat. When it shimmers, add the garlic and stir with tongs until it's just golden, about 1½ to 2 minutes. Add the crushed red pepper and pile in the spinach; sprinkle lightly with salt, then toss with the tongs until the spinach is just wilted and starting to stick to the pan, about 2 minutes. Taste and add more salt, if needed (I use a scant ½ teaspoon total). Lift the spinach to a serving bowl and serve.

Scotch Broth

WITH *braised cabbage*

ALSO GOOD WITH *quick-cooked shredded collards* (PAGE 161) OR *lemon kale* (PAGE 124)

If you're new to using lamb in your home cooking, this would be a fine recipe to start with—a rib-sticking stew with the friendliest winter vegetables, bulked up with nutty whole-grain barley.

IN THE MORNING
Brown the lamb.

IN THE EVENING
Add the parsley.

12 ounces (340 g) boneless lamb stew meat, in 1- to 2-inch (2.5- to 5-cm) pieces

Salt and freshly ground black pepper

1 tablespoon olive oil

¾ cup (150 g) pot (not pearled) barley

1 leek (white and light green parts), halved lengthwise, washed, then sliced crosswise ¼ inch (6 mm) thick

2 carrots, peeled and cut into 1-inch (2.5-cm) pieces

2 ribs celery, cut into 1-inch (2.5-cm) pieces

1 russet potato, peeled and cut into 1-inch (2.5-cm) pieces

1 tablespoon chopped fresh parsley

MORNING

Season the lamb with salt and pepper. In a large skillet or sauté pan, heat the oil over high heat. When it shimmers, add the lamb and cook, turning with a thin metal spatula, until the pieces are browned on at least two sides, about 5 minutes total. Transfer to the slow cooker. Pour ½ cup (120 ml) water into the hot skillet and scrape up any browned bits, then pour the liquid into the cooker.

Rinse the barley in a sieve under running water, then add it to the cooker, along with the leek, carrots, celery, potato, and 6 cups (1.4 L) water. Cover and cook on low for 8 hours.

EVENING

Stir in the parsley and add more salt and pepper, if needed. Serve.

Braised cabbage

1 tablespoon olive oil

½ onion, diced

Salt and freshly ground black pepper

½ small head green cabbage, cored and thinly sliced

In a deep skillet or sauté pan, heat the oil over medium-high heat. When it shimmers, add the onion and a pinch of salt and cook, stirring frequently, until softened, about 3 minutes. Add the cabbage, a good pinch of salt, several grindings of pepper, and 1 cup (240 ml) water. Cover and cook for 10 minutes, then uncover and cook, turning the cabbage occasionally, until very tender, 5 to 10 minutes longer. Season with more salt and pepper, if needed, then serve hot.

Lamb Harira

WITH *beghrir and honey water*
ALSO GOOD WITH *baby kale salad with dates and pistachios* (PAGE 42) OR *herb salad* (PAGE 31)

Harira is a widely variable stew that's often served in Morocco for late-night meals during Ramadan; the only real constants among the many recipes I've seen are lentils and chickpeas. This version features just a bit of tender lamb, which is mostly for flavoring the lentils (you could reasonably use even less than the amount I suggest here). It's traditionally served with dates and lemon wedges, and beghrir, holey pancakes dipped in warm diluted honey.

IN THE MORNING
Brown the lamb and load up the cooker.

IN THE EVENING
Stir in the cilantro.

- 1 tablespoon ghee (page 254) or olive oil
- 12 ounces (340 g) lamb stew meat, cut into small pieces
- 1 pound (455 g) brown or red lentils
- 1 (14- to 15-ounce/400- to 430-g) can chickpeas, drained and rinsed, or about 1½ cups cooked and drained chickpeas
- 1 (14.5-ounce/411-g) can crushed tomatoes
- 2 teaspoons paprika
- ½ teaspoon ground cinnamon
- ½ teaspoon ground ginger
- Salt and freshly ground black pepper
- ¼ cup (10 g) chopped fresh cilantro
- Lemon wedges
- Pitted dates (optional)

MORNING

In a large skillet or sauté pan, heat the ghee over medium-high heat. When it shimmers, add the lamb and cook, turning with a metal spatula, until the pieces are lightly browned on one or two sides, about 5 minutes total. Transfer to the slow cooker. Pour 1 cup (240 ml) water into the hot skillet, scraping up any browned bits, then pour the liquid into the cooker.

Rinse the lentils in a sieve under running water. Dump into the cooker and add the chickpeas, tomatoes, paprika, cinnamon, ginger, and 5 cups (1.2 L) water. Cover and cook on low for 8 hours.

EVENING

Season with salt (about 2 teaspoons) and several grindings of pepper. Stir in the cilantro. If you'd like, hit the lentils with an immersion blender for a couple of seconds (it's fine if some of the lamb gets blended) to break them up and thicken the stew. Serve in bowls or on plates if the stew is very thick, with lemon wedges and dates, if desired, on the side.

RECIPE CONTINUES...

Beghrir and honey water

**Makes about 30 (4-inch/
10-cm) pancakes**

**2¼ cups (380 g) semolina
flour**

**1 cup (125 g) all-purpose
flour**

2 teaspoons instant yeast

**1½ teaspoons baking
powder**

**1 tablespoon honey, plus ¼
cup (60 ml) or more
for serving**

**3½ cups (840 ml) warm
water**

1 teaspoon salt

MORNING OR EVENING

Put all the ingredients (add the salt last) in a blender and blend until just combined. Let stand until very bubbly and risen slightly, about 30 minutes, or, if you're doing this in the morning, put the batter in the refrigerator until evening.

EVENING

If the batter is in the fridge, take it out and let it sit at room temperature for 15 to 30 minutes. Stir the batter gently if it has separated. It should be very bubbly and light. Heat a large well--seasoned cast-iron or nonstick griddle (or use a skillet and make just one or two at a time) until a drop of water on the surface evaporates immediately. Ladle ¼-cup (60-ml) spoonfuls of batter onto the griddle and cook until the bottoms are deep golden and the tops are fully dry and riddled with holes, about 2 minutes; don't flip them—cook on one side only. Use a thin metal spatula to transfer the beghrir to a platter in a single layer and repeat to make more. If there aren't many holes in the surface, let the batter stand for a bit longer before making more.

In a small saucepan or microwave-safe cup, warm equal parts honey and water until they can easily be stirred together. Serve with the beghrir for dipping or drizzling.

Lamb with Turnips and Yogurt

WITH *lemony seared okra*

ALSO GOOD WITH *Mom's naan* (PAGE 109) OR *lightly spiced basmati rice* (PAGE 69)

My friend Regan made a lamb and turnip curry dish similar to this for one of the many inspiring dinners she made for us and other friends years ago. The bitterness of the turnips is offset by the creamy yogurt.

IN THE MORNING
Sauté the onion, garlic, and ginger and set aside until evening.
Brown the lamb.

IN THE EVENING
Puree the sauce with the yogurt.

---

2 tablespoons vegetable oil or ghee (page 254)

½ large onion, thinly sliced

1 clove garlic, chopped

1 teaspoon minced fresh ginger

Salt

12 to 14 ounces (340 to 400 g) boneless lamb stew meat in 1½-inch (4-cm) pieces

1 teaspoon ground coriander

½ teaspoon turmeric

¼ teaspoon ground cayenne

12 to 14 ounces (340 to 400 g) small turnips (about 3), peeled and cut into quarters

½ cup (120 ml) plain Greek yogurt (preferably full-fat)

½ teaspoon garam masala

MORNING

In a large skillet or sauté pan, heat 1 tablespoon of the oil over medium heat. Add the onion, garlic, ginger, and a pinch of salt and cook, stirring until golden, 5 to 7 minutes. Scrape into a bowl and set aside until evening (refrigerate and reheat, if you'd like).

In the same skillet, heat the remaining 1 tablespoon oil over medium-high heat. When it shimmers, add the lamb and sprinkle it with the coriander, turmeric, cayenne, and 1 teaspoon salt. Cook, turning occasionally with a thin metal spatula, until the lamb is browned and crusty on one or two sides, 3 to 5 minutes. Transfer to the slow cooker and pour ½ cup (120 ml) water into the pan and stir to scrape up any browned bits; pour the liquid over the lamb. Pile the turnips on top. Cover and cook on low for 8 hours.

EVENING

Using a slotted spoon, transfer the lamb and turnips to a bowl. With an immersion blender, blend in the yogurt a little at a time, then the garam masala. Season with more salt, if needed. Return the lamb and turnips to the sauce and serve topped with the onion mixture.

Lemony seared okra

2 tablespoons vegetable oil or ghee (page 254)

1 large shallot, thinly sliced

8 ounces (225 g) okra, stems trimmed, cut in half lengthwise

½ teaspoon salt

½ lemon, cut into wedges and seeded

EVENING

In a large skillet or sauté pan, heat 1 tablespoon of the oil over medium-high heat. When it shimmers, add the shallot and cook, stirring, until nicely browned, 1 to 2 minutes. Add the okra and salt and shake the pan to distribute the halves evenly in the pan. Cook, pressing down with a spatula so they get maximum hot-surface contact, for 1 minute, then toss, shake them into an even layer again, and cook, pressing, for another 1 minute. Continue doing this until the okra is bright green, tender, and blackened in spots, about 7 minutes total; the shallot will get very dark brown or black—and that's what you want. Squeeze the lemon wedges over the okra, toss in the squeezed lemon, and serve.

Lamb, Rhubarb, and Parsley Khoresh

WITH *cumin-spiced millet*
ALSO GOOD WITH *fancy saffron-butter basmati rice* (PAGE 117) OR *almond couscous* (PAGE 195)

My mom suggested I make a "spring lamb stew," and this is what I came up with. Probably not what she meant, but I honestly could not have come up with anything more springlike than this beautifully pink and green, delightfully tart Persian-inspired khoresh.

IN THE MORNING
Brown the lamb and sauté the onion.

IN THE EVENING
Sauté the remaining rhubarb and fold it and the herbs into the stew.

1½ pounds (680 g) boneless lamb stew meat, in 1- to 2-inch (2.5- to 5-cm) pieces

Salt and freshly ground black pepper

3 tablespoons olive oil

1 small onion, diced

½ teaspoon turmeric

2 large bunches fresh parsley (about 7 ounces/200 g total)

1 pound (455 g) rhubarb

1 bunch fresh mint, stemmed

1 teaspoon sugar, or more to taste

Season the lamb with 1 teaspoon salt and several grindings of pepper. In a large skillet or sauté pan, heat 1 tablespoon of the oil over high heat. When it shimmers, add the lamb and cook, turning with a thin metal spatula, until the pieces are browned on at least two sides, about 5 minutes total. Transfer to the slow cooker.

Return the skillet to medium heat and add 1 tablespoon oil, the onion, and a pinch of salt. Cook, stirring, for 3 minutes, add the turmeric and stir for 30 seconds, then pour in ½ cup (120 ml) water and scrape up any browned bits. Scrape the onion mixture into the cooker.

Finely chop the thickest parsley stems from the bunches and add them to the cooker. Slice half of the rhubarb cross-wise ½ inch (12 mm) thick and add the slices to the cooker. Cover and cook on low for 8 hours.

Finely chop the remaining parsley and the mint leaves together. Slice the remaining rhubarb on the bias ¼ inch (6 mm) thick. If doing this in the morning, put the herbs and rhubarb in containers and refrigerate.

In a skillet or sauté pan, heat the remaining 1 tablespoon oil over medium-high heat. When it shimmers, add the rhubarb and a pinch of salt and cook, stirring frequently, until just tender, about 5 minutes, adding the sugar in the last minute. Gently fold the rhubarb and the parsley and mint into the stew. Season with more salt and sugar, if needed, then serve.

Cumin-spiced millet

1½ cups (300 g) millet

1½ tablespoons olive oil

1 teaspoon cumin seeds

1 teaspoon salt

Rinse the millet in a sieve under running water. Put the oil and cumin seeds in a 2-quart (2-L) saucepan, place over medium-high heat, and cook, stirring frequently, until fragrant and darkened a shade, 1½ to 2 minutes. Add the millet and cook, stirring frequently, until you can just smell the millet (it smells a bit like cornmeal), about 3 minutes. Stir in the salt and 2½ cups (600 ml) water (carefully, as it will sputter a bit), bring to a boil over high heat, then lower the heat to low, cover, and cook until all the water is absorbed and the grains are tender, 20 to 25 minutes. Fluff and serve.

Sichuan Lamb Shanks

WITH *scallion pancakes*
ALSO GOOD WITH *cumin-spiced millet* (PAGE 231)

A while back, I saw a reference to a roast lamb shank dish served at Supernormal, a pan-Asian restaurant in Melbourne, Australia, and immediately ordered Andrew McConnell's book from overseas, hoping the recipe for the dish would be in it. (It was.) Having never tried the original dish, I don't know if this slow cooker version is even remotely similar—I've simplified the seasonings and technique a great deal here—but it's delicious. The sauce, while not nearly as complicated as the original recipe (and lacking any very hard to find ingredients), is layered and complex: salty and fragrant, tangy and just barely sweet. The shanks are fancy enough for a dinner party—if you'd like, allow one shank for every two people, and remove the meat from the bones before serving. Or do as I would and just have people pull the meat off the bone with tongs as they serve themselves from a platter.

Four lamb shanks will just barely fit in an oval 3½- or 4-quart (3.5-L) slow cooker (I don't think a round pot would hold them). You could increase the quantities by half (six shanks, etc.) and use a larger cooker if you'd like each person to have his or her own shank—a very generous serving.

IN THE MORNING
Brown the lamb and sauté the garlic and ginger. If you have time, toast and grind the Sichuan peppercorns.

IN THE EVENING
Puree the sauce.

1 tablespoon freshly ground toasted cumin

1 tablespoon hot paprika

½ teaspoon Chinese five-spice powder

Salt

4 lamb shanks

2 tablespoons vegetable oil

6 cloves garlic, chopped

3 coins fresh ginger, chopped

¼ cup (60 ml) Shaoxing wine

3 tablespoons yellow soybean paste, or 2 tablespoons miso paste

¼ cup (60 ml) oyster sauce

1 (14.5-ounce) can crushed tomatoes

1 tablespoon Sichuan peppercorns

In a cup, combine the cumin, paprika, five-spice, and 1 teaspoon salt. Rub the mixture into the lamb shanks. In a large skillet or sauté pan, heat 1 tablespoon of the oil over medium-high heat. Add two of the shanks and cook, turning with tongs, until browned on all sides, about 5 minutes total. Transfer to the slow cooker and brown the remaining shanks in the oil left in the skillet.

Wipe out the skillet with a paper towel if there are lots of dark spice bits, then add the remaining 1 tablespoon oil, the garlic, and ginger and cook over medium heat for 1 minute. Pour in the wine, scraping up any browned bits, then remove from the heat and stir in the soybean paste, oyster sauce, and tomatoes. Pour the mixture over the lamb in the cooker and turn to coat the shanks with the sauce. The sauce won't cover the shanks completely, but try to nestle the shanks in as snugly as possible. Cover and cook on low for 8 hours.

In a small skillet or sauté pan over medium heat, toast the Sichuan peppercorns, stirring frequently, until fragrant and darkened a shade, about 3 minutes. Let cool, then coarsely grind with a mortar and pestle or spice grinder. Set aside in a small serving bowl.

Using tongs, transfer the lamb shanks to a large platter. With an immersion blender, puree the sauce in the cooker, season with salt, if needed, then spoon it over and around the lamb. Serve, with the Sichuan peppercorns on the side for sprinkling.

Scallion pancakes

Makes 12

This recipe is closely based on one in Corinne Trang's Essentials of Asian Cuisine—*it always works perfectly. You can stack the rolled-out pancakes between layers of waxed paper, cover with plastic wrap, and refrigerate them for up to a day or freeze for several weeks before pan-frying (no need to defrost first).*

- **2 cups (255 g) all-purpose flour**
- **1 teaspoon baking powder**
- **2 tablespoons vegetable oil, plus more for pan-frying**
- **Sesame oil for brushing**
- **Salt**
- **1 bunch scallions, very thinly sliced**

In a medium bowl, whisk together the flour and baking powder, then drizzle in the 2 tablespoons vegetable oil and toss. Stir in about 1 cup (240 ml) water to make a soft dough. Transfer the dough to a work surface and knead until it's smooth and elastic, about 5 minutes; it shouldn't be stiff. If it's difficult to knead, set it aside to rest for a few minutes before trying again. Cover with the overturned bowl and let the dough rest for 30 minutes.

Shape into a log and cut into twelve equal portions. Use a small rolling pin to roll each portion into a thin rectangle about 12 inches (30.5 cm) long. Brush lightly with sesame oil, sprinkle lightly with a pinch of salt and scallions, then roll up the rectangle from one long side to enclose the scallions. Shape the roll into a flat spiral and pinch the end to the spiral to secure it. Using the rolling pin, lightly floured, roll the spiral out as thin and flat as possible (the scallions will poke through the dough, and that's fine), then set aside and repeat to make the remaining pancakes. Put them on a plate in a single layer, or with waxed paper between the layers, cover with plastic wrap, and refrigerate.

In a large skillet or sauté pan, heat about ⅛ inch (3 mm) vegetable oil over medium-high heat. When it shimmers, add two or three pancakes and cook until nicely browned on each side, 4 to 5 minutes total. Remove to paper towels to drain. Repeat with the remaining pancakes and more oil, if needed, then serve.

Curry Goat and Potatoes

WITH *brown rice and peas*

ALSO GOOD WITH *basic coconut rice* (PAGE 107) OR *garlic sautéed dandelion greens* (PAGE 58)

Hot curry powder plus two Scotch bonnet or habanero chiles will make a sinus-clearingly spicy curry (which is just right for me, but may be a bit much for others). Use a Jamaican or mild curry powder and/or just one chile to dial it back.

IN THE MORNING
Brown the goat and onion and garlic.

IN THE EVENING
Puree the sauce.

2 pounds (910 g) well-trimmed boneless goat stew meat, in 1-inch (2.5-cm) pieces

3 tablespoons Madras (hot) or Jamaican curry powder (see Note)

½ teaspoon ground allspice

½ teaspoon turmeric

Salt

2 tablespoons olive oil

½ sweet onion, chopped

3 cloves garlic, chopped

1 (13.5-ounce/400-ml) can coconut milk

1½ teaspoons fresh thyme

2 Yukon Gold or peeled russet potatoes (about 14 ounces/400 g), cut into ¾-inch (2-cm) pieces

1 large tomato, peeled, seeded, and torn

1 or 2 Scotch bonnet or habanero chiles, slit in a few places

1 scallion, thinly sliced

MORNING

Put the goat in the slow cooker and toss the pieces in the curry powder, allspice, turmeric, and 1½ teaspoons salt to coat. In a large skillet or sauté pan, heat 1 tablespoon of the oil over medium-high heat. Add half of the goat and cook until the pieces are browned on two or more sides, about 5 minutes total. Transfer to a bowl and repeat with the remaining oil and goat (it's okay if some of the spices remain in the cooker). Return all the goat and any accumulated juices to the slow cooker.

To the skillet over medium heat, add the onion and garlic and cook until softened a bit, about 3 minutes. Pour in ½ cup (120 ml) water, scraping up any browned bits, then scrape into the cooker. Stir in the coconut milk, thyme, potatoes, and tomato, and tuck in the Scotch bonnet chiles. Cover and cook on low for 8 hours.

EVENING

Turn the cooker to high. Remove and discard the chiles. Gently stir the curry a bit to loosen it up, then use a slotted spoon to transfer the goat, potatoes, and most of the tomatoes and other solids to a bowl. With an immersion blender, puree the sauce, tilting the cooker so the blender head is submerged. Return the goat and vegetables to the cooker and season with more salt, if needed. Serve, with the scallion sprinkled on top.

NOTE: I prefer Madras curry powder here; it's much more flavorful and complex than the Jamaican variety, which is more turmeric-dominated and often includes salt and granulated garlic (and a little allspice). Use the Jamaican, though, if you're after a dish that's truer to its Caribbean roots.

Brown rice and peas

- 1 tablespoon olive oil
- 2 scallions, thinly sliced, white and green parts kept separate
- 2 cloves garlic, minced
- ¼ teaspoon ground allspice
- 1½ cups (270 g) long-grain brown rice
- 1 small (5.6-ounce/165-ml) can coconut milk
- Salt and freshly ground black pepper
- 1½ cups (400 g) cooked and drained Central American small red beans (page 246), or 1 (14- to 15-ounce/400- to 430-g) can kidney beans, drained and rinsed

EVENING

In a wide 3-quart (3-L) saucepan, heat the oil over medium-high heat. When it shimmers, add the scallion whites and garlic and cook, stirring, for 2 minutes. Add the allspice and rice and stir for 30 seconds. Stir in the coconut milk, 2 ½ cups (600 ml) water, ½ teaspoon salt, and several grindings of pepper. Bring to a boil, then lower the heat and simmer, stirring occasionally, until most of the liquid is evaporated and absorbed, about 25 minutes.

Pile the beans and scallion greens on top, drizzle in another ½ cup (120 ml) water, cover, and cook until the rice is tender and almost all the liquid is absorbed, about 10 minutes. Stir gently to fold in the beans, season with more salt, if needed, and serve.

235

Nash's Tomato Goat Curry

WITH *coconut chutney*
ALSO GOOD WITH ***cardamom roasted sweet potatoes*** (PAGE 45) OR ***spiced chopped vegetables*** (PAGE 43)

My friends Nash Patel and Leda Scheintaub have a very popular food truck in Brattleboro, Vermont, called Dosa Kitchen, and they're currently at work on a cookbook of truly masterful dosa recipes and the curries and chutneys and everything else that goes with dosas. Nash graciously sent a recipe for an intensely fragrant goat curry (probably the best aroma that's ever emanated from my kitchen), which I've adapted for the slow cooker and streamlined a bit for weekday home cooking.

IN THE MORNING
Make the spice paste and sauté the aromatics.

IN THE EVENING
Cook the rice.

2 pounds (910 g) boneless goat stew meat, in 1- to 1½-inch (2.5- to 4-cm) pieces

1 teaspoon turmeric

3 tablespoons dried grated unsweetened coconut

1 cinnamon stick, broken

1½ teaspoons coriander seeds

1½ teaspoons cumin seeds

1 teaspoon fennel seeds

½ teaspoon whole black peppercorns

4 whole cloves

Seeds from 8 green cardamom pods

1 (14.5-ounce/411-g) can crushed tomatoes

Salt

2 tablespoons coconut oil

10 to 15 fresh curry leaves (see Notes)

1 large red onion, diced

2 tablespoons ginger-garlic paste (see Notes)

1 teaspoon paprika or Kashmiri chile powder, or more to taste

2 cups (360 g) basmati rice, or dosas made with store-bought batter

MORNING

Put the goat in the slow cooker and toss with the turmeric.

In a skillet or sauté pan, combine the coconut, cinnamon, coriander seeds, cumin seeds, fennel seeds, peppercorns, cloves, and cardamom. Place over medium heat and toast, stirring frequently, until fragrant and the coconut is golden, 4 to 5 minutes. Scrape into a spice grinder and let cool for a few minutes. Grind very fine and add to the cooker, along with the tomatoes and 1 ½ teaspoons salt.

In the skillet or sauté pan, heat the coconut oil over medium-high heat. When it shimmers, add the curry leaves, onion, and a pinch of salt and cook, stirring frequently, until the onion is translucent and golden at the edges, 5 to 7 minutes. Add the ginger-garlic paste and paprika and cook, stirring, for 2 minutes. Scrape into the cooker and stir well. Pour 1 cup (240 ml) water into the hot skillet, scraping up any browned bits, and pour the liquid into the cooker. Cover and cook on low for 8 hours.

EVENING

Put the rice in a sieve and rinse very well under running water. Dump into a 2-quart (2-L) saucepan and add 2 ¼ cups (540 ml) water and a good pinch of salt. Bring to a boil over high heat, stir once to unstick any grains from the bottom of the pan, then cover and cook over the lowest heat for 14 minutes, or until all the water is absorbed and the rice is tender. Let stand, covered, for 3 minutes, then fluff with a fork or spatula.

Season the goat with more salt or paprika, if needed, and serve with the rice.

NOTES: Look for curry leaves in Indian, Middle Eastern, or Asian grocery stores and get a bunch of them if you find good-looking— glossy, bright green—sprigs. They'll keep, in a tightly sealed bag in the refrigerator crisper drawer, for weeks, and are wonderful in dal (see pages 43, 45, and 46 for examples) and any roasted vegetables (see the sweet potatoes on page 45).

To make ginger-garlic paste for the refrigerator or freezer: In a mini food processor, pulse two parts chopped ginger and one part garlic cloves until very finely minced, adding a little water, if needed, to get the paste moving in the processor. Spoon 1-tablespoon portions into an ice cube tray and freeze, putting the cubes in a freezer bag when they're solid; or cover and refrigerate for up to 1 week.

Coconut chutney

- 1 cup (85 g) dried grated unsweetened coconut
- ¼ teaspoon salt, or more to taste
- 1 cup (240 ml) hot water
- 1 tablespoon coconut oil
- 5 fresh curry leaves (see Notes at left)
- 1 tablespoon urad dal (skinned split black gram, optional)
- ½ teaspoon brown mustard seeds
- 1 small serrano chile, seeded and minced
- 1 teaspoon ginger-garlic paste (see Notes at left)

MORNING

Put the coconut, salt, and hot water in a blender or mini food processor and set aside to soak for 5 minutes.

In a small skillet or sauté pan, heat the coconut oil over medium-high heat. Add the curry leaves, urad dal, if using, mustard seeds, serrano chile, and ginger-garlic paste; stir for 30 seconds, then remove from the heat.

Blend or process the coconut and water until smooth, then transfer to a bowl and stir in the oil and seasonings. Add more salt, if needed. Cover and refrigerate until evening.

Weekend Slow Cooking

Lagniappe

Vegetable Stock

Makes about 2 quarts (2 L)
in a large slow cooker

About 8 ounces (225 g) tomato
trimmings (peels, cores, seeds)

Handful of dried mushrooms, or
stems trimmed from 2 pounds
(910 g) fresh mushrooms,
washed well

Green tops from 2 leeks, washed well
and chopped

½ onion, peeled and cut in half

3 carrots, chopped

Stems from 1 large bunch fresh
parsley

Heel of 1 head celery, or 3 ribs,
chopped

1 teaspoon whole black peppercorns

2 bay leaves

Put all the ingredients in a large (6- to 8-quart/6-
to 8-L) slow cooker and pour in 2 quarts (2 L)
water. Cover and cook on high for 8 hours.

Set a fine-mesh sieve over a large bowl or pot
and pour in the stock, pressing on the vegetables
to extract as much of the stock as possible; discard
the solids in the sieve. Let the stock cool to almost
room temperature (you can set the bowl in a
larger pan of ice water to speed the cooling), then
refrigerate for up to 5 days or freeze for up to 6
months.

Chicken or Turkey Stock

Makes about 2 quarts (2 L)
in a large slow cooker

2½ to 3 pounds (1.2 to 1.4 kg) chicken
bones (wing tips, backs, necks, or
from deboned parts) or a whole
turkey breast carcass

½ onion, peeled and cut in half

3 carrots, chopped

Stems from 1 large bunch fresh
parsley

Heel of 1 head celery, or 3 ribs,
chopped

Green top from 1 leek, washed well
and chopped

1 teaspoon whole black peppercorns

2 bay leaves

Put all the ingredients in a large (6- to 8-quart/6-
to 8-L) slow cooker and pour in 2 quarts (2 L)
water. Cover and cook on low for 10 to 14 hours.

Set a fine-mesh sieve over a large bowl or pot
and pour in the stock, pressing on the solids to
extract as much of the stock as possible; discard
the solids in the sieve. Let the stock cool to almost
room temperature (you can set the bowl in a
larger pan of ice water to speed the cooling), then
refrigerate overnight. Skim off the solidified fat.
Keep the stock in the refrigerator for up to 5 days
or freeze for up to 6 months.

Lemongrass Beef Bone Stock

Makes about 2½ quarts (2.4 L) in a 6-quart (6.5-L) OR *larger slow cooker*

I do not make any claims about bone broth being revivifying or especially healthful, but I do know that warming a little cup of this rich stock and loading it with lime, herbs, and spicy things is a fine thing to do for yourself on a cold winter afternoon.

4 pounds (1.8 kg) raw beef bones

Tops of 3 stalks lemongrass, chopped or crushed

2 thumb-size pieces galangal or ginger, chopped

4 kaffir lime leaves

To serve: Fresh lime juice, torn fresh cilantro, hot sauce, soy sauce or tamari, snipped Thai chiles

Put the bones, lemongrass, galangal, lime leaves, and about 2½ quarts (2.4 L) water in a large slow cooker. Cover and cook on high for 12 to 24 hours—as long as you can! You should be able to almost crush a smaller bone with tongs.

Strain through a fine-mesh sieve into a large bowl, let cool, then refrigerate; skim off the solidified fat, if you'd like, then transfer the stock to smaller containers to refrigerate or freeze (half-pint/240-ml jars with at least ½ inch/12 mm of headspace are easy to thaw when you need a single serving). Reheat to serve, and season to taste—I like it very lime-y and sinus-clearingly spicy.

Beef Stock

Makes about 2 quarts (2 L) in a large slow cooker

4 pounds (1.8 kg) beef bones

½ large onion, peeled and cut in half

3 carrots, chopped

Stems from 1 large bunch fresh parsley

Heel of 1 head celery, or 3 ribs, chopped

1 teaspoon whole black peppercorns

3 bay leaves

Preheat the oven to 450°F (230°C). Put the bones and onion on a rimmed baking sheet and roast until nicely browned and sizzling, about 30 minutes.

Using tongs, transfer to a large (6- to 8-quart/ 6- to 8-L) slow cooker, discarding the rendered fat on the baking sheet. Add the carrots, parsley, celery, peppercorns, and bay leaves and pour in 2 quarts (2 L) water. Cover and cook on high for 8 hours.

Remove and discard the bones. Set a fine-mesh sieve over a large bowl or pot and pour in the stock, pressing on the vegetables to extract as much of the stock as possible; discard the solids in the sieve. Let the stock cool to almost room temperature (you can set the bowl in a larger pan of ice water to speed the cooling), then refrigerate overnight. Skim off the solidified fat. Keep the stock in the refrigerator for up to 5 days or freeze for up to 6 months.

Chili Base

Makes about 6 cups (1.4 L), enough for two batches of chili (PAGE 172)
OR *four batches of posole* (PAGE 132)

8 ounces (225 g) dried guajillo and/or New Mexico chiles (about 32), stemmed and snipped into pieces with scissors

12 chiles de árbol, stemmed

1 cup (60 g) sun-dried tomatoes

Shake out as many of the guajillo seeds as possible (but don't lose your mind over it). Put the guajillo and árbol chiles and sun-dried tomatoes in the slow cooker and add 8 cups (2 L) water. Cover and cook on low for 6 to 8 hours.

Scoop the chiles and liquid (leave any sunken seeds behind) into a blender, working in batches if your blender is small, and let cool for a few minutes. Blend until very smooth. Set a fine-mesh sieve over a deep pot and pour in the chile puree, pushing the puree and liquid through with a spatula; discard the bits of skin and seeds in the sieve. Transfer the puree to freezer-safe containers in about 1½- or 3-cup (360- or 720-ml) portions and keep in the freezer for up to 6 months.

Dried Beans and Hominy

Yield varies from about 4½ to 7 cups (765 g to 1.2 kg)

I've cooked beans in many different ways over the years (stovetop, pressure cooking, with and without salt, presoaked and unsoaked, and so on), and this is by far the best method. It's a completely hassle-free process that results in tender, creamy-textured, perfectly salted beans that can be used for any purpose: Drain them and use them in soups or salads; freeze them and break off chunks to thaw and use as needed; spoon off excess cooking liquid, hit the soupy beans with an immersion blender for a few seconds or smash some with a spoon, and serve them as is; sauté onion and garlic in schmaltz or oil, add beans and seasoning, and mash them around in the skillet to make refried beans.

You'll notice I've left blank spaces for cooking times on page 248. That's because different beans, even of the same type, cook at surprisingly different rates. Older beans will take longer than fresher beans—and very old, stale beans may not even soften at all, which is why you should try to buy your beans from sources with lots of turnover. Beans from different producers and growers all cook up a bit differently. When you've found ones you like, note the cooking times and set your slow cooker accordingly the next time you use them. Or, of course, just check on them after about 6 hours and every hour or so afterward until they've reached the consistency you want.

If you prefer, soak the beans overnight in cold water to cover them by at least 2 inches (5 cm) and drain them before adding fresh water and cooking as below—but it's totally up to you. I've found that it doesn't make a huge difference in cooking times; in fact, side-by-side tests I did of soaked and unsoaked black beans resulted in no discernible difference at all in the cooking time or finished product. Soaking first sometimes (not always) results in beans that hold their shape a little more.

1 pound (455 g) dried beans (except kidney beans) or hominy

1 teaspoon dried epazote (optional, see Note, page 63)

Aromatics (all optional): ½ onion (diced or kept in one piece), 2 cloves garlic (chopped or kept whole), dried red chiles or a pinch of crushed red pepper, 1 bay leaf

2 teaspoons salt

Rinse the beans or hominy in a sieve under running water. Dump them into the cooker and add 6 cups (1.4 L) or, for chickpeas or hominy, 8 cups (2 L) cold water, and the epazote and aromatics, if using. Cover and cook on low for 6 to 12 hours for beans, or 4 to 5 hours for white or yellow hominy (fill in your times on the next page, if you'd like, for future reference), until the beans are as tender as you want them; hominy should be tender and just a little chewy.

Uncover, gently stir in the salt, and let cool in the liquid. Drain in a colander, rinse briefly, if you'd like (I prefer not to rinse hominy, because the liquid that remains after draining is nice and thick and flavorful), and pick out the chiles and bay leaf, if you used them. Spoon into containers or freezer bags and store in the refrigerator for up to 1 week or in the freezer for up to 6 months.

black beans	_____ hours
Great Northern beans	_____ hours
navy beans	_____ hours
cannellini beans	_____ hours
pinto beans	_____ hours
small red beans	_____ hours
lima beans	_____ hours
mayacoba beans:	_____ hours
chickpeas	_____ hours
hominy	_____ hours

Kidney beans

Kidney beans contain a toxin that can cause an upset stomach, so they have to be boiled for at least 10 minutes to kill it off. Hotter-running slow cookers will have them boiling by the end of the cooking time and that'll do the trick, but to be sure you should boil them first: Put the rinsed beans in a large saucepan, add cold water to cover them by at least 2 inches (5 cm), and bring to a boil on the stovetop over high heat. Boil for 10 minutes, then drain, put them in the slow cooker, and proceed with the recipe on page 247.

kidney beans: _____ **hours**

Black bean soup

A very refined and flavorful starter-weight (thinnish) soup can be made after your beans and aromatics have cooked. Drain the beans over a large saucepan to save the cooking liquid, then add just a couple of big spoonfuls of the cooked beans to the liquid, reheat, puree with an immersion blender, adjust the thickness by blending in a little water or more beans, if needed, and add a splash of sweet Spanish sherry and a pinch each of ground cumin and cayenne.

Brown Rice (or Whole-Grain Blend)

Makes about 7 cups (1.4 kg)

**2 cups (340 g) long-grain brown rice or a
blend of brown rice, wild rice, wheat
berries, and rye berries**

½ teaspoon salt

Rinse the rice in a sieve under running water, then
dump into the slow cooker. Add the salt and 5 cups
(1.2 L) water. Cover and cook on low for 3 to 4 hours,
until tender, checking it occasionally to make sure
it doesn't overcook. Drain in a sieve and rinse under
running water to cool. Store covered in the refrigerator for up to 5 days or in the freezer for up to 6
months.

Hearty Whole Grains

*Yield varies from about 5 to 6 cups
(760 g to 1 kg)*

**1 pound (455 g) hearty whole grains:
hard wheat berries, rye berries, spelt,
or pot barley**

1½ teaspoons salt (optional)

Rinse the grains in a sieve under running water, then
dump into the slow cooker. Add 6 cups (1.4 L) water.
Cover and cook on low for 3 to 4 hours, until tender,
checking them occasionally to make sure they don't
overcook. Stir in the salt, if using, in the last 30
minutes or so. Drain in a sieve. Store covered in the
refrigerator for up to 5 days or in the freezer for up to
6 months.

OVERCOOKED GRAINS?

I don't know why I so often forget about the whole grains in the slow cooker, or put them in one of my cookers
that lacks an automatic keep-warm switch. Maybe because I am secretly hoping for a congee-style savory
porridge or an oatmeal-like sweet hot breakfast.Make a spicy porridge bowl: In a saucepan, add about 1 cup
(240 ml) stock or water to every 2 cups (375 g) overcooked grains. Bring to a simmer and cook, stirring, until
heated through and creamy, about 5 minutes. Scoop into bowls and drizzle with soy sauce or tamari to taste.
Top with garlic chips (thinly sliced garlic cooked in a small sauté pan in olive oil until golden and drained
on a paper towel), chile paste (sambal oelek) or sriracha, chopped fresh cilantro, and, if you'd like, chopped
or shredded cooked meat (the roast pork on page 129, for example). Or use them as a hearty breakfast
porridge: Reheat the grains with some milk (or buttermilk), sweeten with maple syrup, and top with fresh
fruit, toasted coconut, sliced almonds, and sesame seeds.

Schmaltz

Makes about 1 cup (240 ml)

Schmaltz is traditionally made by slowly cooking chicken fat and skin bits with diced onion (the crisped-up solids are gribenes, and are served separately). I don't really have time to snip up the skin and cook it carefully on the stovetop, but I do love using chicken fat for cooking, so this is my compromise. Incidentally, I've tried adding diced onion to the cooker along with the chicken trimmings, and I wouldn't recommend it: The onion burns too easily.

Several of my slow cooker recipes here call for chicken pieces still on the bone but without the skin (which turns rubbery and unappealing in the slow cooker), or for well-trimmed boneless, skinless thighs; save up the skin and fat trimmings in a bag in the freezer, and when you have a pound or two collected, dump them in the cooker for the day.

1 pound (455 g) chicken skin and fat

Put the skin and fat in the slow cooker. Cover and cook on low, stirring every couple of hours, for 6 to 8 hours, until the skin is golden and crisp. Pour through a fine-mesh sieve into a heatproof container and let cool, then cover and keep in the refrigerator for up to several weeks or in the freezer for up to 6 months.

Quark

Makes about 2 cups (480 ml), a smidge more if using full-fat buttermilk, a little less if using low-fat

I became obsessed with quark, a soft fresh cheese that's used like thick yogurt or cream cheese, while testing a few of the recipes in Luisa Weiss's *Classic German Baking*. She makes it in a 150°F (66°C) oven, and her method is foolproof, but I've been using slow cookers on the lowest warm or keep-warm setting with great success too. Slow cookers' warm functions vary greatly, and ideally you'll want to make this in a cooker with a very low warm temperature: If the buttermilk is heated in a relatively hot cooker, it will solidify quickly (in about 2 hours), but the resulting quark is firmer and sometimes less smooth. A lower warm setting will take longer, up to 8 hours, but will result in a somewhat creamier quark. The first time you make this, check it at 2 hours and then every hour afterward until it's done, and make a note of your time below for future reference.

Quark is incredibly versatile and easy and cheap to make, and could very well become a staple in your refrigerator. Save the drained whey, refrigerate it separately from the quark, and use it in smoothies or bread doughs or just drink it plain—it's tart and refreshing.

½ gallon (2 L) cultured buttermilk, full-fat or low-fat

Pour the buttermilk into the slow cooker. Cover and turn the cooker to the warm or keep-warm setting (or the yogurt setting at "normal" on an Instant Pot). The buttermilk will separate into a creamy top layer about the thickness of Greek yogurt (but fluffier in texture) and a watery bottom layer and will be firm and just warm to the touch in the center. This will take 2 to 8 hours, depending on your cooker.

Put a sieve or colander over a bowl and line it with four layers of rinsed and squeezed cheesecloth and use a slotted spoon or skimmer to gently spoon the creamy top layer in, leaving the watery whey behind. Let drain at room temperature for 2 to 4 hours, then transfer to a sealable container and refrigerate for up to 1 week.

OVERCOOKED QUARK?

It's still perfectly usable in all the recipes that include it here, but if you want to enjoy it plain you might wish to blend it in a blender or food processor to smooth it out a bit and stir in a little plain buttermilk or cream or half-and-half. Or drain it until very thick and add fine salt to taste—you'll have something similar to goat cheese.

Ghee

Makes about 5 cups (1.2 L)

If you want to increase the batch size, use a larger cooker—don't fill the cooker more than halfway with butter, as it sometimes plops and bubbles as it cooks.

3 pounds (1.4 kg) unsalted butter

Cut the butter into chunks and put them in a 3 ½-quart (3.3-L) or larger slow cooker. Put the lid on slightly askew or propped above the rim of the insert with chopsticks and cook on high for 4 to 5 hours; there will be a layer of crunchy-looking foam on the top that will be golden at the edges, and the layer of solids in the bottom of the pot will have turned from white to caramel colored. Try not to jostle the cooker as the butter cooks, as that can cause it to sputter and plop.

Let the butter cool a bit, then use a large spoon to skim off the foam (discard it or save it for spreading on bread and sandwiches). Without disturbing the solids at the bottom, ladle the clear, golden ghee into clean, dry containers—glass canning jars are ideal. Discard the solids. Let the ghee cool completely, then put the lids on and store in a cool spot or in the refrigerator for up to several months.

Dulce de Leche

Makes about 2 1/2 cups (600 ml), OR *3 scant half-pint (240-ml) jars*

Dulce de leche is a thick caramelized milk "jam," and you should probably have some on hand for impromptu treats. You can warm it up and spoon it over cinnamon ice cream, spread a layer in the bottom of an apple pie before you bake it or drizzle it over a freeform galette just out of the oven, or just slather it still cold onto a toasted store-bought hot dog bun (no judgment here). It makes a great hostess gift, too, and will keep for quite a while in the refrigerator.

Method 1:

½ gallon (2 L) whole milk

2 cups (400 g) sugar

½ vanilla bean, split and scraped, or 1 small cinnamon stick (optional)

Put the milk, sugar, and vanilla bean, if using, in the slow cooker. Put the lid on slightly askew and cook on high for 12 to 20 hours (it really depends on your cooker), stirring occasionally, especially at the beginning (to dissolve the sugar as the milk heats) and the end (as it darkens on the bottom and edges). If using the vanilla bean or cinnamon, remove it when the milk has enough of its flavor for your taste (cinnamon especially can overwhelm the dulce de leche). When the mixture is a deep caramel color—it'll be unevenly dark, and lumpy-looking, but that's okay—it's ready. Use an immersion blender to smooth it out, tipping the pot to submerge the head of the blender fully. If it's lumpy or grainy, pass it through a fine-mesh sieve into a bowl before it cools. Pour into clean canning jars or other containers, let cool, cover, and put in the refrigerator. The dulce de leche will keep for at least 2 weeks.

Method 2:

2 (14-ounce/397-g) cans sweetened condensed milk

Divide the sweetened condensed milk among three half-pint (240 ml) canning jars, put the lids and rings on, and set them in the slow cooker. Add enough water to cover the jars (you'll have to fill the cooker almost to the top). Cover and cook on low for 16 to 20 hours, until the milk is a deep caramel color—lift a jar with a jar lifter or tongs with rubber bands wrapped around the ends to check. Remove the jars to the counter. The lids will likely have sealed; open them up and let the dulce de leche cool (and to break the seal—you don't want an anaerobic/sealed-canning-jar environment here, because the dulce de leche is not acidic). Put the lids back on and put in the refrigerator. The dulce de leche will keep for at least 1 month.

257

Mulled Cider or Wine

Makes about ½ gallon (2 L) cider OR *3¼ cups (750 ml) wine*

This is easily doubled for a party-appropriate batch, with some caveats: For a gallon (4 L) of cider, you'll need to use a 6-quart (6.5-L) or larger slow cooker. And because it'll take longer for the greater quantity of liquid to come to a simmer, you'll need to either (a) start up the cooker earlier in the day and cook on high for 6 to 8 hours, or (b) preheat the cider or wine in a nonreactive pot on the stovetop, bringing it to just below a simmer before pouring it into the cooker and cooking on high for about 4 hours.

The recipe is also quite customizable. I sometimes add a couple of pieces of star anise and ½ teaspoon black peppercorns for a little more kick. A knot of lemongrass or a small piece of vanilla bean would be nice additions to either the cider or the wine. And ¼ cup (60 ml) Cointreau, added just before serving, would not be unwelcome in the mulled wine.

½ gallon (2 L) apple cider or 1 (750-ml) bottle red wine

⅓ cup (75 g) packed dark brown sugar, or more to taste

½ navel orange, sliced into rounds

½ lemon, sliced into rounds

2 coins peeled fresh ginger (optional)

3 cinnamon sticks, plus more for serving, if you'd like

2 teaspoons whole cloves

2 teaspoons whole allspice berries

1 teaspoon green cardamom pods

½ nutmeg

Put the cider or wine in the slow cooker and stir in the brown sugar. Add the orange and lemon slices, and the ginger, if using. Put the cinnamon, cloves, allspice, cardamom, and nutmeg in a muslin or cheesecloth bag, pound the bag with a mortar or a heavy pot to coarsely crush the spices inside, and drop the bag into the cooker. Cover and cook on high for 4 to 6 hours.

Taste and stir in more brown sugar, if needed. Ladle into mugs (avoiding the bag and the citrus slices) and serve hot from the cooker on the low or keep-warm setting. If you'd like, add a cinnamon stick stirrer to each mug.

Rosemary Roasted Garlic

Whole heads of garlic

Olive oil

Salt

Fresh rosemary sprigs

Cut the heads of garlic almost in half horizontally, keeping the heads mostly intact. Set them in the center of a large piece of aluminum foil and drizzle generously inside and out with oil and sprinkle with salt. Tuck a rosemary sprig or two in with the garlic and fold the edges of the foil together to make a packet. Put in the slow cooker. Cover and cook on low for 3 to 4 hours, until the garlic is very soft.

Unwrap, squeeze the garlic cloves into a small airtight container, cover with more oil, if you'd like, and refrigerate, covered, for up to 1 week or freeze for up to 6 months.

ACKNOWLEDGMENTS

Thanks first to Michael Sand and my editor, Holly Dolce, for their enthusiasm for this project and their confidence in my work. I'm also grateful to their colleagues at Abrams, especially Sarah Massey, Mary O'Mara, and the book's designer, Deb Wood. Special thanks to Jane Bobko, my copyeditor, and Leda Scheintaub and Regina Castillo, my proofreaders: I know from good copyediting and proofreading, and their work was absolutely stellar.

Warmest thanks go to my agent, Leslie Stoker, who must be the most patient and helpful representative a writer could hope for. It's because of Leslie and her work that I have started referring to myself, when asked, as "a cookbook author [period]" rather than "a sort of freelancer, I guess [question mark]."

Once again, I'm indebted to my friend Rinne Allen, the photographer whose photographs are probably the reason you picked up this book in the first place. Thanks to Rinne and her husband, Lee, for making the photo shoot in Athens not just possible but a pleasure (except for those few painful hours after I lopped off a large part of my thumb, which wasn't anyone's fault but my own). Our team in steamy Georgia, Kristin Karch, Jessie Genoway, and pinch-hitting pro food stylist Tami Hardeman, deserve much of the credit for how great these photographs look. I'd also like to thank Susan Hable for loaning us her heirloom griddle (pictured on page 73), which has become for me something of an obsession.

I'd like to express my sincere gratitude to all my friends who contributed advice, recipe suggestions and feedback, and professional-level testing and tasting services: Marisa Bulzone, Krystina Castella, Suzanne Furlong, Mary Jessica Hammes, Stacy Hester and Haley Slagle, Kathy Mitchell, Jess Shoemaker, Eric Wagoner, and Jenny Wares.

To Leda Scheintaub, I offer my special thanks for her array of efforts on behalf of this book: She tested a boatload of the recipes and provided invaluable advice throughout the process; she convinced her husband, Nash Patel, to loan his amazing goat curry recipe to the project (my slow cooker adaptation of it is on page 236); and she proofread the first-pass page layouts. I'm so lucky to have her as a friend and sounding board.

Finally, thank you to my parents, Dave and Diana, who tested, tasted, and suggested a huge proportion of the recipes here—their influence is on every page. And, as always, I thank my very best friends and loves, Derek and Thalia, for eating stew after stew after stew for the last year or so—and usually enjoying it.

Main Dishes with Easy *Morning* Prep

Main Dishes with Easy *Evening* Finish

Index of Accompaniments

Salads

Toppings, sauces, and other accompaniments

INDEX

EDITOR: Holly Dolce
DESIGNER: Deb Wood
PRODUCTION MANAGER: Rebecca Westall

LIBRARY OF CONGRESS CONTROL NUMBER:
2016961376

ISBN: 978-1-4197-2667-5

Printed and bound in the United States
10 9 8 7 6 5 4 3 2 1

Abrams books are available at special discounts
when purchased in quantity for premiums and
promotions as well as fundraising or educational use.
Special editions can also be created to specification.
For details, contact specialsales@abramsbooks.com
or the address below.

ABRAMS The Art of Books
115 West 18th Street, New York, NY 10011
abramsbooks.com